Automobiles of America

Fifth Edition, revised

by

American Automobile Manufacturers Association, Inc.

Cars & Parts Magazine
911 Vandemark Road • Sidney, Ohio • 1996

President's Message

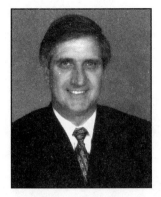

Andrew H. Card, Jr.

America reached two important milestones in 1996 – the centennial of the American automobile industry and the 40th anniversary of our National Highway System. America's car companies have given us personal mobility – I often think of the automobile as the "freedom machine." Our highway system brought us closer together as a nation and made every corner of our magnificent country accessible to each of us. Together, the automobile and the highway have enriched our lives, raised our standard of living and shaped our society like nothing else in our history.

So it is appropriate in this year of milestones the American Automobile Manufacturers Association (AAMA) issues a revised, updated edition of this book, *Automobiles of America.* This book, too, has a long history, first published 60 years ago in 1936 under the title, *A Chronicle of the American Automobile Industry.* Since that time it has been revised and updated periodically, the last time in 1974.

Our association has been instrumental in the publication of this book since the outset. The first edition of this book was based in part on a chronology of the automobile industry published by William Leslie Powlison, the librarian for the Automobile Manufacturers Association, a forerunner of today's AAMA. Over the years, AAMA researchers and writers have been responsible for updating and expanding the book.

It is just one of the many contributions to America's automobile industry made by AAMA and its predecessors, which trace their roots back to the year 1900 and the infancy of the industry it serves.

Automobiles of America is more than the story of one industry or one product. It is a story about the machines and the entrepreneurs and engineers who changed our world. I hope you enjoy it.

Andrew H. Card, Jr.

First edition © 1961, 1962

Second revised edition © 1968

Third edition, revised © 1970

Fourth revised edition © 1974

Fifth revised edition © 1996 by

American Automobile Manufacturers Association, Inc.

1401 H Street N.W.

Suite 900

Washington, D.C. 20005

Published by Cars & Parts Magazine

Sidney, Ohio 45365

Library of Congress Catalog Card No. 71-121919

ISBN 1-880524-21-X (paperback)

Printed and bound in the United States of America

Contents

Contents

Foreword

Since the beginning of automobile production in this country 100 years ago, the "horseless carriage" has utterly and irrevocably changed the way we live our lives. At the beginning of the 20th century, only a handful of cars traversed the few established roads of this country. As the century draws to a close, millions of cars zip along the ribbons of asphalt and concrete that crisscross the United States.

Although the auto traces its earliest development to Europe, the American industry "chugged" to life with the first production run of single-cylinder motor cars built in 1896 by the Duryea brothers. Within 10 years, the automobile had gained a substantial foothold in this country. When Henry Ford applied the techniques of mass production to his Model T automobile, motoring came within the grasp of the general public instead of just the wealthy. By 1915, there was no turning back — America loved the automobile.

As the auto gained acceptance and the industry flourished, literally hundreds of manufacturers took a stab at producing this exciting new device. Many amounted to little more than backyard operations, and most fell by the wayside as rapidly as they appeared. Eventually the industry came to be dominated by two giants — Ford and Billy Durant's conglomerate of companies known as General Motors. During the '20s, a new giant emerged in the form of Chrysler Corporation. This company, along with the former two, came to be known collectively as the "Big Three." Their combined power and resources, along with the Great Depression of the '30s, eventually served to bring an end to most of the "independent" auto companies. Once-proud names such as Marmon, Pierce-Arrow, Hupmobile, Graham and many others, faded into obscurity.

The automobile matured during these early decades, evolving from the motorized buggies of the early days to the sleek Art Deco designs of the '30s. Improvements such as self starting, balloon tires and hydraulic brakes, made the automobile easier to operate and more reliable, further strengthening its position in our society. Thanks largely to GM's Harley Earl, styling emerged as a potent force in selling automobiles, and form became nearly as important as function.

The dividing point in 20th century history, World War II, also served as a dividing point in the history of the auto. The monumental struggle saw civilian car production end abruptly, as the manufacturers converted their plants into the "Arsenal of Democracy."

After the war, the auto went through a radical change in form over the next 10 years. The development of the powerful, lightweight overhead valve V-8 engine gave the automobile unprecedented performance. Longer, lower and wider bodies brought a different look to cars from those produced before the war. After several years of increasingly bold designs during the '50s, more conservative styles took hold in the '60s.

That turbulent decade saw the production of some of the last truly uninhibited automobiles, as high performance muscle cars took a high profile stance in the auto culture during the late '60s and early '70s. But as the '70s began, the abundance of cars in use became a source of concern for many who felt the pollution created by those autos was doing major damage to the air we breathed. Additionally, many felt the automobile could be much safer. As the '70s progressed, the government mandated that cars be safer, create less pollution and become more fuel efficient. These concerns, and not the whims of the stylists, dictated the form of the American automobile.

The past 15 years have seen the American industry challenged by imported cars, especially from Japan. Yet Detroit has fought back and regained much of the ground lost during the '70s. With advancements in auto technology, many of today's four-cylinder economy cars offer performance nearly equal to many of the vaunted muscle cars of the past. Debate still rages over what the future of the internal combustion engine and the car should be, but the citizens of this country aren't likely to give up their cars any time soon.

As we close the door on the first 100 years of the American auto industry, this book serves as an overview of the rise of that industry. It is divided into four sections: "Milestones" begins just prior to the Duryeas' production run in 1896 and covers the significant events of each of the first 100 years of automobile production; "Pioneers" presents brief biographical sketches of some of the most prominent figures in the industry over the years; "Roll Call" provides a listing of many of the manufacturers, well known and obscure, who have endeavored to build automobiles; and "Highlights" presents a wealth of statistics about the automobile.

The first 100 years of the auto in America have been an exciting roller coaster ride. If the developments of the past few years are any indication, the next 100 years should prove equally interesting.

Acknowledgements

Automobiles of America represents the work and skill of many individuals and the facts and information from several out-of-print publications. In addition, collections of source material at both the American Automobile Manufacturers Association and the Detroit Public Library have aided immeasurably with their newspaper clippings, trade journals, catalogs, and books. Statistical data, too, reflect the valuable collection at AAMA.

Historic automotive photographs from the AAMA archives provided most of the illustrations; the following also contributed and are gratefully recognized:

> Bureau of Public Roads
>
> Detroit Public Library
>
> Henry Ford Museum
>
> Library of Congress
>
> R.E. Olds Company
>
> Smithsonian Institution
>
> Cars & Parts Magazine

Too many persons bear a close relationship to the book to permit individual acknowledgement. To those who have contributed of their time and knowledge we all owe a debt, for they have helped to tell a gallant story which deserves our understanding. It is not just an industry that is reflected in these pages, but a way of economic thinking and of life.

AAMA

Milestones

Along the ancient roadways of the world, stone markers indicated distance traveled and tracked the progress of the traveler. While modern America is transported more efficiently and guided by more elaborate road markers, the "milestone" still serves as the mark of progress. To reach its present state of highway transportation efficiency, the nation had to pass many such milestones. On the following pages are listed many of the important milestones of automotive history in America.

1893

1893 – America's first workable gasoline-engine vehicle. Designed by Charles E. Duryea, built and driven by J. Frank Duryea.

• America's first successful gasoline-engine motor vehicle was in operation on Sept. 21 in Springfield, Mass. Using the designs of Charles E. Duryea, his brother J. Frank Duryea built a single-cylinder horseless carriage called the Buggyaut. The Duryea vehicle was the first American-made car to have an electric ignition and a spray carburetor, both of which J. Frank Duryea designed and built.

• A national good roads movement sparked by cycling enthusiasts prompted establishment of the U.S. Office of Road Inquiry under the Department of Agriculture. This office later became the Bureau of Public Roads, under the Department of Commerce. The founding statute signed by President Benjamin Harrison read in part: "To enable the Secretary of Agriculture to make inquiries in regard to the systems of road management throughout the United States, to make investiga-

tions in regard to the best methods of road-making, and to enable him to assist the agricultural college and experiment stations in disseminating information on this subject, ten thousand dollars."

• The first brick surface on a rural road in the U.S. was laid on the Wooster Pike near Cleveland, Ohio. The four miles of brick pavement were completed in the fall of 1893 near route 71 of the Interstate Highway System.

1894 – Elwood Haynes in his first car. It was powered by a single cylinder engine built by Clark Sintz of Grand Rapids, Mich.

1894

• A car conceived by Elwood G. Haynes of Kokomo, Ind., was constructed by Elmer and Edgar Apperson, assisted by Jonathan Dixon Maxwell. Powered by a one-cylinder engine, the 820-pound Haynes car operated on Pumpkinvine Pike in Kokomo on July 4th, at a speed of eight miles per hour.

• Edward Joel Pennington probably operated one of his cars this year — there were several in existence by 1895.

1895

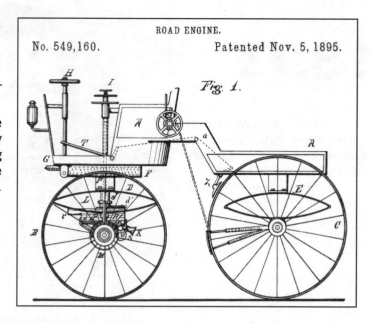

ROAD ENGINE.

No. 549,160.   Patented Nov. 5, 1895.

Fig. 1.

1895 – The patent granted to George B. Selden was regarded for many years as a master document, covering all the essential features of the gasoline automobile.

• In September the first American company established to make gasoline cars was the Duryea Motor Wagon Company, organized by Charles E. and J. Frank Duryea.

• The U.S. Patent Office granted George Baldwin Selden the patent he had applied for in 1879. The Selden Patent covered the essential features of the modern gasoline automobile. Features of special significance were: an internal combustion engine of the two-cycle type developed by George B. Brayton using liquid hydrocarbon fuel with a power shaft running faster than the road wheels, and a clutch or disconnecting device between the engine and the propelling wheels.

• Hiram Percy Maxim started a motor carriage department for Pope Manufacturing Co., bicycle makers of Hartford, Conn.

• The first U.S. motor vehicle race in which any contestants finished was sponsored by the Chicago Times-Herald and run over a snow-drifted course in Chicago on Thanksgiving Day, Nov. 28. It was won by J. Frank Duryea in a Duryea Motor Wagon at an average speed of 7 1/2 miles per hour (considering delays for repairs) over the 55 mile course. Of the six starters, only two completed the run. Second

place was won by a Mueller-Benz, driven across the finish line by Charles Brady King of Detroit, an umpire, who took over the tiller when driver Oscar Mueller collapsed from exposure an hour before the end of the race. The first Times-Herald contest had been scheduled to run on Nov. 1, but was postponed to allow entrants more time to prepare their vehicles. For those present and ready to compete the judges allowed a consolation race on Nov. 2 which was actually the first U.S. motor vehicle

race. Four vehicles started, but breakdowns and accidents put all the vehicles out of the contest.

• Public interest in horseless carriages heightened late in the year. The first American automotive trade journals started publication: "The Horseless Age," edited by E.P. Ingersoll of New York, and "The Motocycle," edited by E.E. Goff of Chicago. In addition, the nation's first automotive association, the American Motor League, was organized in Chicago.

1895 – The Duryea entry, winner of America's first motor vehicle race. J. Frank Duryea at the tiller, with Arthur W. White, umpire, of Toronto, as passenger.

1896

• J. Frank Duryea, as chief engineer of the Duryea Motor Wagon company, produced a third car. From these plans 13 cars were built that year — the first time that more than one car was made from the same design in the United States.

• George H. Morill, Jr., of Norwood, Mass., bought one of the 13 Duryea Motor Wagons, and thus became the first known purchaser of an American gasoline car.

• Charles Brady King drove the first car on the streets of Detroit, March 6. The car was powered with a four-cylinder, four-cycle, water-cooled engine that King designed and built.

• Barnum & Bailey Circus announced an exhibition of the Duryea Motor Wagon as a parade feature on April 2.

• Hiram Percy Maxim of the Pope Manufacturing Co., in Hartford, Conn., built an electric motor carriage.

• On Memorial Day, J. Frank Duryea won the Cosmopolitan Race (New York City to Irvington-on-the-Hudson and return).

• Henry Ford successfully operated his two-cylinder, four horsepower, "Quadricycle" in Detroit on June 4.

• The French word, "automobile," first began to appear in published references to motor vehicles in the United States.

• America's first motor vehicle track races were run at Narragansett Park, R.I., on Sept. 7.

1896 – Henry Ford and his experimental "Quadricycle."

1896 – The first gasoline powered car on the streets of Detroit. Charles B. King at the tiller, Oliver E. Barthel as passenger.

Seven vehicles were entered, two electrics and five Duryeas, but two of the Duryeas were disqualified. All five heats, one mile each, were won by a Riker Electric Stanhope. Average for the first mile was 26.8 miles per hour. Second prize went to a Morris and Salom Electrobat. The race was so dull that spectators demanded, "Get a horse!" This was probably the origin of the famous phrase.

• Alexander Winton of Cleveland produced an experimental two-seater motor carriage in September.

• During the same month, Ransom Eli Olds drove a one-cylinder, six horsepower car on the streets of Lansing, Mich. He had been experimenting with steam-powered

1896 — Alexander Winton and five companions in his first experimental car.

vehicles since 1886.

• Two Duryea cars participated in the Emancipation Day run from London to Brighton on Nov. 14.

This event celebrated repeal of England's "red flag" laws, and marked the first appearance of American motor vehicles in Europe.

1896 — America's first track race for motor vehicles — September at Narragansett Park, Cranston, R.I.

1897

• The first automotive press preview and open house in the United States was held at the Pope Manufacturing Co. Journalists were invited to see the Pope plant and try out the firm's automobiles.

• A Winton car was driven a mile in one minute and 48 seconds in Cleveland (on Memorial Day), and from Cleveland to New York in 10 days (July 28-Aug. 7).

• Olds Motor Vehicle Company was organized on Aug. 21 — the first automobile company in Michigan. Studebaker Brothers, carriage-makers since 1852, began experimenting with motor vehicles.

• Louis S. Clarke and William Morgan of Pittsburgh, Pa., organized Pittsburgh Motor Vehicle Co. on Oct. 21.

• Gilbert Loomis, a mechanic from

1897 – The Stanley twins in their famous Stanley Steamer.

Westfield, Mass., who built his own one-cylinder car, took out automobile insurance. The premium was $7.50 for $1,000 worth of liability insurance on a policy used for horse-drawn vehicle liability.

• Pope Manufacturing Co., Hartford, Conn., began marketing Columbia Mark III Electric Phaetons.

1897 – Hiram Percy Maxim and Bert Holcomb in a Mark VIII Pope-Columbia.

1898

• William E. Metzger of Detroit established the first independent automotive dealership.

• The earliest known franchised dealership for U.S. cars was opened by H.O. Koller in Reading, Pa., to sell Winton motor vehicles.

• Electric cab service was initiated in New York City.

• Haynes was the first U.S. motor vehicle manufacturer to use aluminum alloy.

• John Wilkinson built his first four-cylinder, valve-in-head, air-cooled motor, from which Franklin engines later evolved.

1899

1899 – The Mobile Steamer had center steering because it was felt the car could be controlled more easily.

• Experiments in collecting mail with motor vehicles were conducted in Buffalo, Cleveland and Washington by the U.S. Post Office Department.

• The Automobile Club of America was organized.

• The U.S. Army purchased its first electric vehicles for general transportation assignments.

• Alexander Winton drove one of his cars from Cleveland to New York in 47 hours and 37 minutes driving time.

• R.E. Olds organized his second company, the Olds Motor Works, and moved operations from Lansing to Detroit.

• A Haynes-Apperson car was delivered from the factory in Kokomo, Ind., to Brooklyn in 21 days.

• Freelan O. Stanley, driving a

Stanley steamer built by himself and his twin brother, Francis E., climbed Mt. Washington, N.H., in August.

• Rollin White adopted the flash boiler, developed in Europe, for experiments with steam cars.

• A.L. Dyke of St. Louis, Mo., established the first automobile parts and supply business in the United States.

• Mrs. John Howell Phillips of Chicago was the first woman known in the United States to receive a driver's license.

• American Motor Company, New York City, opened a garage with "competent mechanics always on hand to make repairs when necessary."

• Pittsburgh Motor Vehicle Company became the Autocar Company on Aug. 28.

• Percy Owen opened the first

automobile salesroom in New York City at 120 Broadway, on Nov. 1. The firm sold Winton cars.

• James Ward Packard completed and ran his first car in Warren, Ohio, on Nov. 6. With his brother, Warren D., and George L. Weiss, of Cleveland as partners, he formed the New York and Ohio Co. to build the Packard car.

• Back Bay Cycle & Motor Company of Boston, opened a stable for "renting, sales, storage and repair of motor vehicles."

• The Stanley Brothers sold their steam car rights to Mobile and Locomobile.

• "Motor Age" magazine published its first issue in September.

• International Harvester developed an experimental motor buggy.

1900

• The First National Automobile Show was held Nov. 3-10 in New York City's Madison Square Garden under the sponsorship of the Automobile Club of America. An estimated 48,000 visitors saw displays by 40 automobile and 11 parts and accessory exhibitors. There were about 300 types of vehicles exhibited, with prices ranging from $280 to $4,000. The exhibits were valued at $565,000. The Mobile Company of America built a 200-foot ramp extending 53 feet in height to the Garden roof for demonstrating the hill climbing ability and good brakes of the steamers.

• President McKinley was the first U.S. President to ride in an automobile.

• New York City acquired a motor-driven ambulance.

• The Saturday Evening Post carried its first automobile advertising.

• The publication "Automobile Topics" made its appearance.

• Gasoline engines were located under a hood for the first time in

1900 — First National Automobile Show at New York's old Madison Square Garden featured test drives on obstacle courses.

the United States by several American automobile manufacturers.

• John Brisben Walker drove his steam car to the top of Pikes Peak.

• Special kerosene lamps for automobiles were offered by the R.E. Dietz Co., New York City, featuring a 20 candlepower reflected clear white flame capable of casting a 200-foot beam. One of the primary advantages of the Dietz lamp was that it produced a steady light even over rough roads.

• A gasoline car defeated electric and steam cars for the first time in a free-for-all race at Washington Park race track in Chicago.

• Engineer's certificates were issued by New York City as drivers' licenses. Harold T. Birnie was the

first to receive one of these driving permits on May 15.

• Electric Vehicle Company, owner of the Selden Patent, brought suit against automobile manufacturers not licensed by the firm.

• Carl Breer at the age of 17 built his first motor vehicle. (Later Breer was one of the engineers for the first Chrysler car.)

• The National Association of Automobile Manufacturers was organized.

• Rambler, designed by Thomas Jeffery, was shown with steering on the left side and a front mounted engine.

• Several automobile manufacturers started to use governors and float-free carburetors.

1900 — New York to Philadelphia Highway.

1901

• Two events occurred early in the year that destined the gasoline engine to win out over steam and electric. Near Beaumont, Tex., Spindletop, the fabulous gusher, came in Jan. 10. The price of crude petroleum dropped below five cents a barrel. Nearly two months later the second event favoring the gasoline engine was a fire that destroyed the Detroit factory of the Olds Motor Works. The only thing saved was an experimental curved-dash roadster. In order to get back in business after the disaster, the firm had no choice but to use that one car as a model and to sub-contract orders for parts and sub-assemblies to small shops in the Detroit area. Most of the operators of these shops thus became automobile manufacturers, and, in consequence, Detroit came to be known as "Motor City."

• The New York-to-Buffalo endurance run demonstrated the possibility of long-distance automobile touring. As a result, automobile Blue Books with route directions were started. The Automobile Club of America launched a program to place roadside touring signs from New York to Boston.

• Packard invented an automatic spark advance.

• Autocar introduced drive shaft for automobiles.

• Connecticut passed laws regulating speed and the registrations of motor vehicles.

• The steering wheel had virtually ousted the tiller or lever steering system.

• R.E. Olds built 425 curved-dash Oldsmobiles.

• David Dunbar Buick, inventor and manufacturer of bathroom plumbing, organized Buick Auto-Vim & Power Company, Detroit.

1901 — George N. Pierce in a Pierce Motorette, forerunner of the Pierce-Arrow.

• First Jones speedometers were used on Oldsmobiles.

• New York State's licenses for motor vehicles added nearly a thousand dollars to the state treasury in the first year.

• A total of 88 exhibitors displayed their products at the Second National Automobile Show, Nov. 2-9, in Madison Square Garden. The 1901 show displayed cars that marked the end of the horseless carriage, with the almost universal introduction of the French body type, the tonneau, which was fastened into the car behind the driver's seat and carried two passengers in a pair of seats resembling cut-down barrels.

• There was a tendency toward multiple cylinders in the cars exhibited at the show. Water cooling was almost universal among the show cars, and detachable tires became more popular. Improvements were also noted in ignition systems, with the magneto generator coming into more general use.

• Roy Dikeman Chapin drove an Oldsmobile from Detroit to New York, covering the distance in 7 1/2 days, at an average of 14 miles per hour.

• A gasoline storage facility for direct service to automobiles became available at an automobile storage and repair station in New York City. The bulk gasoline tank was outside the building as a safety precaution, and connected to the basement by pipe from which gasoline could be dispensed by a self-measuring device, thus eliminating all handling and pouring of the inflammable fluid.

1902

1902 — The curved-dash Oldsmobile.

- The popularity of the tonneau body type continued to increase, not only for gasoline cars, but for steam and electric vehicles as well.

- The American Automobile Association was organized in Chicago, March 4.

- Studebaker began to make electric runabouts and trucks.

- Owing to accidents, motor cars were excluded from the parks of Omaha.

- Thomas B. Jeffery Company introduced the Rambler car and built 1,500 cars during the year.

- A 60-day guarantee on new automobiles was adopted by the National Association of Automobile Manufacturers (112 members).

- An ordinance was passed in Chicago permitting drivers to wear spectacles, but not pince-nez eyeglasses.

- Louis S. Clarke, of Autocar Co., designed porcelain spark plug insulation and patented the double reduction principle in the rear axle construction.

- The Motor Mart was established in New York City to buy and sell used cars.

- T.H. Shevlin was arrested in Minneapolis for speeding in excess of 10 miles an hour and fined $10.

- Jonathan Dixon Maxwell joined Charles Brady King to manufacture the Silent Northern, which introduced an integral engine and transmission assembly, three-point suspension of this power unit, and running boards. Maxwell also designed a siphon cooling system which Benjamin and Frank Briscoe manufactured.

- Oldsmobile production passed the 2,000 mark for the year.

- Cadillac Automobile Company was formed; the first car was completed Oct. 17.

- Ohio Automobile Company, successor to the New York and Ohio Co., changed its name to Packard Motor Car Company on Oct. 13.

- J. Stevens Arms & Tool Company began manufacture of a two-cylinder car called the Stevens-Duryea, designed by J. Frank Duryea.

- The Locomobile became the first American gasoline car with a four-cylinder, water-cooled, front-mounted engine, designed by A.L. Riker.

- Electric Vehicle Company was given the right by court decision to make and use Sterling Elliott's steering knuckle. Elliott's principle of steering is still employed on motor vehicles. The principle enables both front wheels to turn instead of the axle, when the steering device is moved.

1903

- Sponsorship of the Third National Automobile Show was shared by the Automobile Club of America and the National Association of Automobile Manufacturers. Cars displayed at the Jan. 17-24 show had several features not seen at the earlier Paris auto show, such as mechanical valves (Rambler and Oldsmobile), compensating carburetors, square "bonnets" and honeycomb radiators. The French style tonneau bodies with a pair of rear seats and closed cars with a "glass front" were feature attractions at the 1903 show.

- Cadillac made its first appearance at the 1903 show with a 6.5 horsepower, water-cooled, one-cylinder runabout.

1903 — The first transcontinental automobile trip was completed by Dr. H. Nelson Jackson and his chauffeur, Sewall K. Crocker, in this two-cylinder Winton. They drove from San Francisco to New York City in 63 days.

1903 continued

1903 — Overland, forerunner of the Willys line.

• Ford Motor Co. was organized June 16.

• The Ford Motor Company was incorporated. Henry Ford who, as chief engineer of the Detroit Automobile Company had made several successful racing cars, was named vice president and chief engineer. Original shareholders included John and Horace Dodge, who took stock in exchange for tooling their machine shop to build motors; Albert Strelow, who accepted stock as payment for his carpenter shop which Ford wanted as an assembly plant; Alex Y. Malcolmson, a coal dealer who invested $7,000; Charles J. Woodall and James Couzens, Malcolmson's employees; John S. Gray, banker and candy manufacturer; John W. Anderson and Horace H. Rackham, attorneys; Vernon Fry, real estate salesman; and Charles H. Bennett, inventor and manufacturer of windmills and air rifles.

• More than 100 American companies were producing cars.

• E.R. Thomas substituted steel for wood body panels.

• B.A. Gramm introduced the power takeoff for farm use.

• A pressed steel frame was introduced by Peerless Motor.

• The first transcontinental automobile trips were made during the summer of 1903. First to make the long drive was Dr. H. Nelson Jackson of Burlington, Vt., and his chauffeur Sewall K. Crocker. The

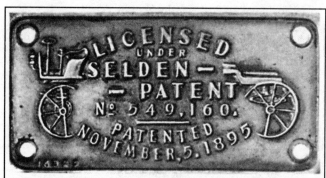

1903 — The Selden Patent Plate. Until 1911, almost every manufacturer of gasoline-propelled vehicles had to pay royalties to holders of this patent through the Association of Licensed Automobile Manufacturers.

pair drove a used Winton car, leaving San Francisco on May 23 and arriving in New York on July 26. The second cross-country automobile traveler was Tom Fetch who, starting June 20, drove a single-cylinder Packard ("Old Pacific") from San Francisco to New York in 53 days. L.L. Whitman and E.T. Hammond made the third San Francisco to New York trip in an Oldsmobile (July 6-Sept. 17).

• Packard moved to Detroit and into the world's first reinforced concrete factory building, designed by Albert Kahn.

• "MoToR" magazine began its career.

• The Association of Licensed Automobile Manufacturers was organized. It included the Electric Vehicle Co., the Winton Company, and eight other manufacturers; George H. Day was appointed manager.

• The Buick Motor Company was organized with a loan of $1,500 in cash and $2,000 in materials, advanced by Benjamin Briscoe, Jr., and Frank Briscoe. The new firm began making cars with valve-in-head engines.

• Peerless adopted pressed steel frame construction — one of the major technical improvements during the year. Three other manufacturers used the frame construction shortly afterward.

• Ford was sued as an infringer of the Selden patent.

• White Steamers made perfect scores in the 650-mile reliability trials held by the Automobile Club of Great Britain and Ireland.

• General adoptions this year: T-head cylinders, sliding gear transmissions, mechanically-operated intake valves, and shock absorbers.

• Berner Eli ("Barney") Oldfield, former cycle racer, began to achieve fame as the driver of Henry Ford's racer, "999." His chief competitors were Wridgeway, in a Peerless; Fosdick, in a Winton; Carl Fisher, in a Mohawk; Walter C. Baker, in the "Torpedo Kid;" and Charles Schmidt, in a Packard.

• The Brownlow-Latimer Federal Good Roads Bill, first of its kind to be introduced in Congress, received strong support from the automotive industry and automobile clubs across the nation. The bill died in committee.

1903 — Barney Oldfield at the tiller of Ford's "999" racer.

1904

• The Fourth National Automobile Show, held Jan. 16-23, was larger than any of its predecessors, with 185 exhibitors, including 87 automobile exhibits. A "convertible" of sorts made its appearance at this show; a touring car, to which could be attached a glass-sided, solid top, called "California top" for use in inclement weather was also shown.

• Automatic lubrication was another

1904 — Out for a spin in a 1904 Waverly Electric, Model 21, made by Pope Motor Car Co., Indianapolis, Ind.

1904 — A 1,258-mile motor tour from New York to St. Louis was the forerunner of the famous Glidden Tours.

1904 continued

feature found on some cars, including the Autocar. Some models featured a fan to cool the water pipes used in the engine cooling system. Standard quick-demountable rims appeared on many new cars.

• Studebaker sold its first gasoline motor vehicle.

• R.E. Olds sold his interest in the Olds Motor Works and organized the Reo Motor Car Company.

• The Detroit Y.M.C.A. established a school for automobile mechanics.

• Carl Graham Fisher and James A. Allison organized the Prest-O-Lite company to perfect a safe method of using acetylene gas for automobile headlights.

• A disastrous fire at the Cadillac plant delayed production and forced the company to return dealer deposits on 1,500 cars.

• Curved windshields were used for the first time.

• Mechanical improvements and innovations included sleeve-valve engine and gas headlights.

• W.K. Vanderbilt Jr. drove a mile

1904 — The First Vanderbilt Cup Race was held on Long Island.

in 39 seconds, beating Henry Ford's record of 39 2/5 seconds made on the ice.

• Pope-Hartford was criticized by competitors for including lamps as standard equipment.

• The Fischer car was equipped with an air brake system for the rear wheels and drive sprockets. An auxiliary engine powered the air compressor.

• The National Association of Retail Automobile Dealers was formed.

• Ford Motor Company opened its first branch (on Jefferson Avenue, Detroit).

• One of the earliest cars in the United States to attempt an auto-

matic transmission was the Sturtevant. The car featured a centrifugal clutch which had low and high speed ranges. The Sturtevant also featured an air brake system.

• A motor tour of 1,258 miles was organized to drive from New York to the Louisiana Purchase Exposition in St. Louis. Of the 71 cars that started, only 59 reached St. Louis. Col. Augustus Post, general chairman of the pilgrimage, gave the signal to start the 17-day motor trip on July 25. One of the tourists, Charles Glidden, impressed with the tour, later proposed what became the famous Glidden Tours.

• The first Vanderbilt Cup Race was held Oct. 8 on Long Island.

1905

• The trend toward large gasoline cars was noticeable at the Fifth National Automobile Show at Madison Square Garden — 177 were gasoline cars, 4 steam cars and 31 electrics, including 9 electric trucks. Only one car (Waltham Buckboard) had wire spokes — all others had artillery type wheels with wood or steel

1905 — Motor car provided new mobility, brought the country close to city folks.

1905 — Two Oldsmobiles, "Old Scout" and "Old Steady," completed a transcontinental race from New York to Portland in 44 days.

spokes. The French tonneau with a rear door had been replaced by longer bodies with side doors. Comfort and ease in riding were stressed in the new models; speed was secondary.

• Cape or folding tops were introduced by several manufacturers, and some replaced the canopy tops.

• The first Glidden tour of 870 miles was routed from New York to the White Mountains and return. Percy Pierce with a Pierce-Arrow won the award.

• Pierce-Arrow had a cast aluminum body.

• The Society of Automobile Engineers was founded with Andrew L. Riker serving as the first president.

• Cars were sold on the installment plan.

• The American Motor Car Manufacturers Association was organized.

• Two Oldsmobiles completed a transcontinental race from New York to Portland, Ore., in 44 days.

• The Ariel car offered a motor air cooled in winter and water cooled in summer.

• Leland & Faulconer Manufacturing Company was merged with Cadillac Automobile Company, and the name was changed to the Cadillac Motor Car Company.

• Mechanical developments included power tire pumps, ignition

locks, Goodyear universal rims to take either clincher or straight side tires, Weed tire chains and Gabriel tubular exhaust horns.

• H.L. Bowden made a mile in 34 1/5 seconds.

• The Holsman Motor Buggy offered 48-inch wheels; the Stearns boasted a 119-inch wheelbase.

• A bill was introduced in the 59th Congress to regulate the operation of automobiles and other motor vehicles by the states. This, the first attempt by the Federal government to regulate motor vehicles, died in committee.

• The Diamond T Company was organized by C.A. Tilt.

1905 — Lined up in front of the Mt. Washington Hotel in New Hampshire are 36 of the cars, including four non-contestants, in the first Glidden Tour. The tour covered 870 miles from New York City to Bretton Woods, N.H., and return.

1906

• Cars displayed at the Sixth National Automobile Show indicated that manufacturers were striving to develop better and stronger materials — chrome-nickel steel, phosphor bronze and high carbon steel were prominent. The Marmon cast aluminum body was an example of attempts to build lighter cars.

• A Stanley Steamer, with Fred Marriott driving, ran a mile in 28 1/5 seconds, averaging 127.66 mph, at Ormond Beach, Fla., Jan. 27.

• Buick included a storage battery as standard equipment.

• Six-cylinder cars were the talk of the country. National, Stevens-Duryea, Ford, Franklin and Pierce-Arrow offered sixes.

• Motor vehicles aided in relief operations following the San Francisco earthquake and fire. Walter C. White organized a caravan of White trucks in Los Angeles to carry help and supplies to the victims of the stricken city.

• Prest-O tire tanks were introduced for tire inflation; each tank had the capacity to inflate 25 tires of 34 x 4 size up to 80 pounds pressure.

• In addition to the craze for six-cylinder cars, a wide variety of engines was offered by some manufacturers.

1906 — Fred Marriott became the first human to travel more than two miles a minute when the streamlined Stanley Steamer "Rocket" averaged 127.66 mph at Ormond-Daytona Beach, Fla. on Jan. 27.

1906 — Motor vehicles were used extensively in relief and rescue operations following the earthquake and fire that destroyed much of San Francisco.

1906 — The date "1877" on the car represents the year in which the invention was conceived. Patent Office rules permitted the inventor to assert a date of invention two years prior to the date of his patent application — in Selden's case, 1879.

• Reo had its first four-cylinder car; Olds introduced a two-cycle engine; Maxwell built a 12-cylinder racer; and Adams-Farwell offered three- and five-cylinder rotary engines, an innovation which later influenced rotary aviation engines.

• Front bumpers appeared on some cars, but not as standard equipment.

• L.L. Whitman drove a Franklin from New York to San Francisco in 15 days, 2 hours, 15 minutes.

• Backed by Edwin Ross Thomas, Buffalo manufacturer, Roy D. Chapin, Howard E. Coffin, Frederick O. Bezner and James J. Brady, former Olds employees, organized the E.R. Thomas-Detroit Company.

• Automobile plants in Detroit produced 550 to 600 cars a week. Packard alone built an average of six cars a day.

• Mechanical improvements included magneto ignition, storage batteries as standard factory equipment and front bumpers.

• The year saw 21,614 automobiles produced.

• Oldsmobile introduced a 2-cycle engine.

1907

• Technical advances noted by the press at the Seventh National Automobile Show, Jan. 12-19, were the prevalence of selective transmissions, a gain in six-cylinder engines, larger brakes (some equipped with camel's hair cloth covering on the friction surfaces), improved body finishes (up to 30 coats of paint), and twin carburetors (on the Stearns, Columbia and Matheson).

• International Harvester Company built its first automotive vehicle in January, 1907, in Chicago.

• Oakland Motor Car Company was organized by Edward M. Murphy, buggy builder, of Pontiac, Mich., to make a two-cylinder car designed by Alanson P. Brush. Nineteen years later Oakland would introduce a companion car, the Pontiac, which would survive the parent.

• Gasoline economy runs were much in vogue; one of the most popular was conducted in Chicago.

• Henry Ford purchased 60 acres of land in Highland Park, Mich., and started construction of a new factory.

• Hewitt introduced a V-8 touring car, the first U.S. production touring car with an eight-cylinder engine. It had a displacement of 452 cu. in. Other bodies were also available.

• A Reo crossed and re-crossed the continent, negotiating such climbs as Mt. Hood and Raton Range.

• The Association of Licensed Automobile Manufacturers presented a formula for figuring horsepower; the formula was adopted by many states as a basis for taxation.

• Oldsmobile employed nickel plating for trim parts that had hitherto been brass.

• Humps were purposely built into streets at Glencoe, Ill., to discourage speeding.

• Buick adopted a four-cylinder engine with a sliding-gear transmission, and won the Dead Horse Hill Climb at Worcester, Mass.

• A Franklin was driven 1,060 miles from New York to Chicago in 39 hours, 36 minutes.

• A bill was introduced in Congress providing for regulation of speed, identification and registration of motor vehicles engaged in interstate travel. Supported by motor vehicle manufacturers and automobile clubs, it died before it reached the floor of the House of Representatives.

• Engine timing gears were enclosed in many cars. Mud aprons were becoming more general under the engine.

• Despite the business depression, both Packard and Ford made profits of more than a million dollars.

1907 — An air-cooled Franklin light runabout crosses a stream that flows over an early road.

1908

• Wheelbases on most of the new models were longer, and manufacturers moved the rear seats toward the center of the car to provide more comfort. The four-cylinder vertical engine was almost standard at the Eighth National Automobile Show. Most of the cars exhibited offered sliding gear transmissions. Other mechanical improvements included the increased accessibility

1908 — One of the first 800 Ford Model T's.

1908 — French de Dion

of parts, bigger and better brakes, better enclosed clutches, and easier controls.

• General Motors Company was chartered Sept. 16, 1908, in New Jersey by William Crapo Durant, with William Eaton as first vice-president.

• Cadillac became the first American car manufacturer to win the Dewar Trophy, awarded by the Royal Automobile Club of Great Britain for the greatest contribution to advancement of the industry. Cadillac was honored for inter-

changeability of parts. Three Cadillacs were completely disassembled, the parts of the cars mixed and then the cars were reassembled from the mixed parts. The cars were then run at top speed for 500 miles to demonstrate that the parts were truly interchangeable.

• The Model T Ford made its first appearance on Oct. 1.

• A four-cylinder, 70-horsepower Thomas Flyer won the New York-to-Paris Race, against a field of five other cars, all from Europe. The

race began in Times Square on Feb. 12, headed westward across the United States, Asia and Europe, and ended 169 days later in Paris, France. Overcoming many obstacles, and at times fabricating new parts for the car, the crew of the Thomas Flyer drove a total of 13,341 miles in 88 days with an average of 151 miles per day.

• J.M. Murdock of Johnstown, Pa., was the first motorist to drive his family across the United States. They left Los Angeles on April 24 and arrived in New York on May 26.

- The Columbia Mark XLVI used a gasoline engine to drive an electric generator. From this generator, separate electric motors propelled the wheels. The aim of this "gasolect" car was to provide a smooth flow of power by eliminating the conventional gear shift transmission.

- Buick, Oldsmobile and Oakland became units of General Motors.

- C. Harold Wills developed the use of vanadium steel for Ford.

- Pierce-Arrow won fourth successive victory in the Glidden Tour.

1908 — A Thomas taxi cab in Central Park. The meter was an innovation.

- Approximately 60,000 persons were employed in the industry which produced 50,000 cars during the year.

- Ford developed a detachable cylinder head.

- The average price of motor cars was $1,926.

- John North Willys was made president and general manager of Overland, which became Willys-Overland.

- Fred J. and Charles T. Fisher organized Fisher Body Company.

- Autocar discontinued passenger car production to concentrate on 1 1/2-ton trucks of 97 in. wheelbase, with engines under the seat.

1908 — Packard

- Otto Zachow and William Besserdich, of Clintonville, Wis., developed the first successful four-wheel drive motor vehicle.

- Innovations: Stewart magnetic speedometers; Charles Y. Knight's invention of sleeve-valve engines; left-hand steering; silent timing chains; motor-driven horns; baked enamel finishes; helical gears.

- The Commercial Car Manufacturers Association was formed, with G.M. Weeks as president and Walter Wardrop as manager.

1909

• At the Ninth National Automobile Show, more emphasis was placed on pleasing the public than on booking orders from dealers. Four-cylinder cars accounted for 71 percent of the gasoline automobiles, 27 percent were six-cylinder, and only two single-cylinder models were displayed. Air self-starters were found on several of the cars exhibited. Another new feature was a steering wheel with the underside corrugated so the driver's hand would not slip.

• The Indianapolis Speedway was organized.

• Mechanical improvements included multiple disc clutches and transmissions in unit with the motors.

• First rural mile of concrete pavement in the United States opened July 4 in Wayne County, Mich. The pavement was constructed on Woodward Avenue (now U.S. 10) between Six Mile and Seven Mile Roads at a cost of $13,534.59.

• Louis Chevrolet, famous racer, began work on a six-cylinder passenger car of his own design in his Detroit shop.

• The Selden Patent was sustained as valid and infringed upon by Ford.

• Mrs. John R. Ramsey became the first woman to drive across the United States. She left New York in a Maxwell car with three women companions on June 9 and arrived in San Francisco 53 days later.

• W.S. Seaman & Company (later

1909 — Mrs. John R. Ramsey and three companions in a Maxwell touring car were the first women to drive an automobile across the United States.

1909 — Hudson

Seaman Body Corp.) built its first automobile bodies in Milwaukee.

• Carl Graham Fisher and his associates completed the first Indianapolis Speedway. After the first races on Aug. 19, the track was paved with brick for a two-day meet in December.

• The Hudson Motor Car Company was organized.

• Cadillac was one of many companies that became part of General Motors during 1909. General Motors paid its first preferred stock dividend.

• The White Company built a gasoline engine car to replace the famous White Steamer.

• The 1909 Glidden Tour from Detroit to Denver and back to Kansas City covered 2,636 miles — the longest Glidden Tour up to that time.

• Fabric tops, often called "one-man tops," appeared on the market.

• The year was marked by an acceleration of earlier trends in engineering, production techniques and uses of materials: magnetos showed a steady gain; cellular radiators were gradually displacing tubular ones; high-tension ignition systems were used on the majority of cars instead of the make-and-break system; selective gearsets had a 10-to-1 lead over the progressive type. The fashion was to cast cylinders in pairs, but the block casting was getting under way in small models; and there was a large increase in the use of chrome nickel steel and vanadium steel.

• At the end of the year there were 290 different makes of automobiles produced at 145 cities in 24 states. Detroit had 25 different car makes and a total of 45 makes were produced in Michigan. Chicago had the second highest number with 14 different brands, then Indianapolis with 12 and Cleveland with 10. Indiana rated second among states with 44 and Ohio third with 39 makes.

1910

• A new type of automobile body, the torpedo, made its first appearance in the United States at the 10th National Automobile Show. This new body resembled a bathtub on wheels. The dashboard and its instruments were brought up closer to the driver, by means of a cowl, and the sides were extended upward, in some cases almost to shoulder height. Previously, motorists and their passengers had perched on cars, high and exposed; now they could sit in them, low and sheltered.

• The year witnessed a trend toward standardization, many car makers changing transmission, motor starting or some other detail to bring their cars in line with the rest of the field. Clutches, however, still showed great variety — and little efficiency. Haynes used a contracting band; E-M-F had a leather faced cone with cork insert; Knox, Thomas and Stevens-Duryea featured a multiple-disc clutch.

• Several important marketing changes took place. The Owen car, designed by Ralph Owen, offered as standard equipment: top, windshield, electric horn, electric-acetylene headlamps, electric-oil side lamps and an electric tail lamp.

• Another make, the Overland, announced its model "38" as a completely equipped car at $1,000

1910 — The Owen offered a top, windshield, electric horn, headlamps and a tail lamp as standard equipment.

and was the first car in this class to carry as standard equipment at list price a top, windshield, lamps and magneto.

• Peerless adopted electric lighting.

• A four-cylinder Reo won the silver cup in the James Gordon Bennett reliability contest.

• The production of cars reached a new high at 181,000 units for the calendar year.

• The Owen had an electric horn.

• Benjamin Briscoe started the $16,000,000 United States Motor Car Corporation by combining and affiliating 130 separate companies with the firm. Some of these included Columbia Motor Car Company (successor to the Electric Vehicle Company that controlled the Selden patent), Brush Runabout Company, Alden Sampson Company, Dayton Motor Car Company and Maxwell-Briscoe Motor Company. (Over-expansion

and lack of working capital forced United States Motor Car Company into receivership in September 1912.)

• Four Wheel Drive Auto Company, Clintonville, Wis., began manufacture of four-wheel drive vehicles.

• Racing at Indianapolis Speedway this year featured a three-day series ending May 31, a three-day meet ending July 4, and two days of racing on Sept. 3 and 4.

• Automobile production started at the Ford Motor Company, Highland Park plant.

• Patents were issued on the Knight valve principle which was the forerunner of the Knight engine to be introduced in the United States in 1911.

• Central Oil Co. built what may have been the first drive-in gasoline station with an island, in Detroit.

1910 — Motorists had their problems — poor roads, flat tires and almost no protection from the weather.

1911

- The four-door car became popular at the 1911 National Automobile Show — nearly every manufacturer exhibited a model.

- The hazards of starting engines by hand-cranking were reflected in the devices offered during the year as possible solutions to the problem. An Amplex had a compressed-air starter; also available for nearly all cars was the Geiszler Starting device, an apparatus that was supposed to start the engine with an electric charge.

- The Selden Patent, previously sustained in the U.S. District Court, was declared "valid but not infringed" by Ford and other manufacturers, in the U.S. Court of Appeals. (The payment of royalties that disrupted the early industry had come to an end.)

- Diamond T Motor Car Company discontinued making passenger cars to concentrate on trucks.

- Hudson offered a "simplified chassis" (including a new four-cylinder monoblock engine with cross-shaft in front carrying magneto and water pump) and multiple disc clutch.

- Edward N. Hines originated painted center lines on highways in Wayne County (Detroit), Mich.

- Chevrolet Motor Company of Michigan was organized on Nov. 3, and production began with the aid of W.C. Durant.

- The first 500-mile Indianapolis Speedway Race was won by Ray Harroun in a six-cylinder Marmon "Wasp," which introduced the first use of a rearview mirror in the United States. Time: 6 hours, 42 minutes, 8 seconds.

- For the first time, securities of automotive companies were listed on the New York Stock Exchange. General Motors became the first automobile stock to be listed.

- The Studebaker Corporation was recapitalized, and manufacture of electric vehicles was discontinued to allow concentration on gasoline cars.

- Knight sleeve-valve engines were introduced on the American market by Stearns, Stoddard-Dayton, and Columbia.

1912

- The 12th National Automobile Show was sponsored by the new Automobile Board of Trade, formed to succeed the A.L.A.M. which disbanded in 1911.

- The self-starter was the vogue at the 1912 show. There were 13 types of acetylene starters on display, six compressed air, seven electric, 14 mechanical, two gasoline and one — the Winton — exhaust gas.

- Stewart Motor Corporation was formed to make cars and trucks.

- Cadillac adopted an electric starter developed by Charles F. Kettering of the Dayton Engineering Laboratories Company (Delco), along with a generator-battery lighting system.

- Engine temperature indicator, the Boyce Moto-Meter, was introduced.

- The all-steel body developed by Edward Gowen Budd (an open car model) was offered by Oakland and Hupmobile.

- Chicago adopted an ordinance limiting horn use.

- Electric car makers organized and held separate shows.

- Traffic lines made their appearance on the streets of Redlands, Calif.

- The Lincoln Highway was suggested.

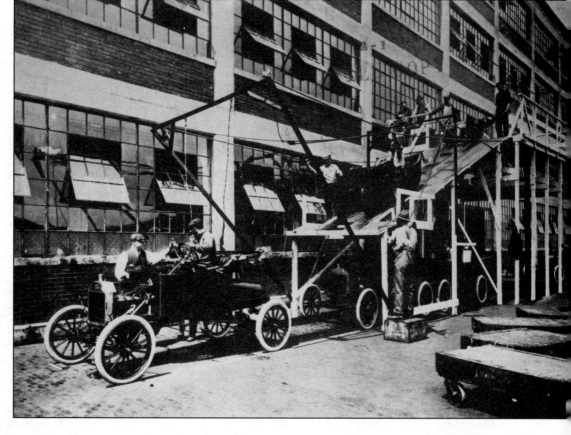

1913 — The Model T's popularity led the way to mass production. This overhead body drop at the Ford Highland Park, Mich. plant was one of the features which speeded output.

1913

• A single ticket at the 13th National Automobile Show was good for the double showings in both Madison Square Garden and Grand Central Palace. The popular priced cars were on display at the Palace and the high-priced and high-powered cars were at the Garden. A general trend toward sloping fronts and hoods was noticed at the 1913 show, along with strides toward smoother lines and longer curves. Designers went back to colonial days and Louis XIV coaches for the popular coupes, which flared out at the top.

• Dealers, worried about used car sales, asked the National Association of Automobile Manufacturers to investigate.

• The National Automobile Chamber of Commerce was organized (predecessor of the American Automobile Manufacturers Association) through a merger of the Automobile Board of Trade and the National Association of Automobile Manufacturers.

• A standard 90-day warranty for passenger cars and commercial vehicles was recommended to its members by the NACC.

• Chevrolet operations were moved to Flint and merged with the Little Motor Car Company.

• Installment payment plans were used in automobile financing.

• Cadillac won the Dewar Trophy for the second time. The award was given for the development of the electric starter.

• Wire wheels were offered as standard equipment on several production cars.

• The Bendix drive for electric starters was shown for the first time.

• Ford production attained a rate of a thousand cars a day.

• Kissel Kar introduced a new wrap-around windshield on several of its 1913 models, though it wasn't called by that name.

• The National Association of Automobile Advertising Men was organized.

• Packard used forced feed lubrication and worm bevel gears.

• Carl Graham Fisher, who was promoting an ocean-to-ocean highway, turned his pledges over to the Lincoln Highway Association.

• Pierce-Arrow put headlamps on the fender mudguards.

• Spaulding touring cars were equipped with folding backs on front seats in order to convert into beds. Electric reading lamps and air mattresses were included.

• Gulf Oil Company was the first U.S. petroleum firm to distribute free road maps.

• There were 1,258,062 motor vehicles in the United States.

• High price of gasoline (22 to 25 cents a gallon) affected design of cars.

1914

• A novelty of the 1914 show was the display of cyclecars. There were five such showings of these tiny one- and two-passenger vehicles. One cyclecar, the Argo, was priced at $295. The first cyclecars had appeared in 1913, and had been dismissed as "toys" and "a silly fad" by most motorists and vehicle manufacturers. After their formal debut at the National Automobile Show, the market for them expanded enormously. The craze was, however, short-lived; few of the little "economy" vehicles remained on the market after 1915.

• During the show week Henry Ford announced a $5 minimum daily wage (including a profit-sharing plan) for all non-salary employees over 22 years of age, and an eight-hour day.

• Chevrolet discontinued its six-cylinder model, and began making four-cylinder cars.

• Cadillac developed and introduced a V-8 high-speed automobile engine.

• The Rambler's name was changed to Jeffery.

1914 — First stop sign used to control traffic was in Detroit.

• Horace and John Dodge started production of the Dodge automobile.

• Alfred Reeves became general manager of the National Automobile Chamber of Commerce.

• Hand brake at driver's left was introduced by Packard.

• Maxwell offered an adjustable driver's seat.

• A Detroit ordinance prohibited gasoline pumps at curbs.

• The first stop sign to control traffic was installed in Detroit.

• Electric traffic lights were installed in Cleveland, Ohio, in August.

• Henry Ford announced plans to rebate between $40 to $60 to each purchaser of a new Ford Model T providing the Ford Motor Company sold more than 300,000 cars from August 1914 to August 1915.

• The traffic department of the National Automobile Chamber of Commerce suggested dimensions of automobile box cars to railroad companies. The NACC also drafted a road-building code, setting forth the views of the automobile manufacturers on highway conditions.

• The Society of Automobile Engineers organized several research committees to study gas-electric vehicles, kerosene carburetors, greases, engine characteristics, governors, and non-electric continuous torque transmission.

• Buick changed to a six-cylinder engine.

• Spiral bevel gear was adopted by Packard engineers.

1915

• The outstanding feature of the 1915 National Automobile Show was the eight-cylinder engine. Cadillac, King, Briggs-Detroiter and Remington all offered such engines. Cadillac introduced a V-8 several months before.

• Another auto show attraction was the "sociable" body offered by Packard, Winton, Kline and Kissell, with the corridor or salon body with

1915 — This Saxon, priced $395, illustrates the trend to light cars in this period.

an aisle between the two front seats allowing passengers to move freely between front and back seats. Another novel car was the Gadabout roadster with a wicker body. The National had another original seating arrangement — four armchairs that could be moved on casters in any direction.

• There were no cyclecars exhibited at the 1915 show, thus signaling the end of the short-lived fad.

• Briscoe and Owen offered convertible roadsters on which the top, when down, was completely concealed at the rear of the body.

• For the 1916 model year, Packard added a 12-cylinder model, the "Twin Six," America's first, and the first automobile engine with aluminum pistons.

• Franklin put the spare tire in the trunk of its roadster model.

• Ford produced its one-millionth car since the company's inception.

• General Motors declared its first dividend ($50 a share) on common stock.

• Demountable rims replaced the clincher types.

1915 — The Briscoe featured a "cyclops-eye" headlight.

• Cadillac offered tilt-beam headlamps.

• Oldsmobile offered a top and windshield as standard equipment.

• World War I began to create material shortages.

• During this year a great wave of five-cent jitneys arose in various cities that had been hit by transit strikes.

• Automobiles were admitted to Yellowstone National Park on Aug. 1 over a carefully prepared one-way route.

• Ford Motor Company refunded $50 to those who purchased Model T's between August 1914 and August 1915. Checks were distributed Aug. 15.

• Prism lenses for headlights made their first appearance.

• There were approximately 450 automotive and auto parts manufacturers in the United States by the end of 1915.

• A Hudson broke a 24-hour record for speed.

• Motor vehicles manufactured totaled 892,618.

• Aluminum alloy pistons appeared for stock cars.

• Cross licensing agreements pertaining to patents became effective in the auto industry.

1916

• New models displayed at the 16th National Automobile Show generally featured lower prices and more powerful engines. Most of the cars were under $1,250, including many six-cylinder models. Five manufacturers — Enger, Haynes, National, Packard and Pathfinder — exhibited 12-cylinder models.

• New design features noted at the 1916 show included the slanted windshields, and double-cowl bodies, in which "tonneau cowls" separated front and back seats.

Increased use of wire wheels was also noted.

• Studebaker displayed a gold chassis reportedly worth $25,000 at the 1916 National Automobile Show. The most unusual car exhibited, however, was the light-weight Marmon 34, with aluminum body and fenders, aluminum engine castings and other aluminum parts. The seven-passenger touring car, with a wheelbase of 136 inches, weighed only 3,540 pounds.

• Charles W. Nash left General Motors to take over the Thomas B. Jeffery Company and form Nash Motors Company.

• The number of makes offering V-8 engines grew to 18 models. They included: Abbott, Apperson, Briscoe, Cadillac, Cole, Daniels, Hollier, Jackson, King, Monarch, Oakland, Oldsmobile, Peerless, Pilot, Ross, Scripps-Booth, Standard and Stearns-Knight.

• The Fordson Tractor was announced by Ford Motor Company.

• Ford bought a factory site on the banks of the Rouge River in Dearborn, Mich.

• The National Automobile Chamber of Commerce passed a resolution branding the advertisement of deferred payments as "unethical."

1916 –
Passage
of the
Federal
Aid Road
Act was
the
begin-
ning of a
nation-
wide
system
of
inter-
state
highways.

1916 continued

• United Motors Corporation was formed with Alfred P. Sloan, Jr., as president.

• Hand-operated windshield wipers, stop lights, and rearview mirrors appeared as standard equipment on several cars.

• Prices of gasoline and automobiles advanced during the year, and economy tests of stock cars

became so numerous that the Society of Automobile Engineers published requirements for such tests if they were to be recognized.

• The Federal Aid Road Act, signed by President Woodrow Wilson on July 11, was the first Federal law aimed at the establishment of a nation-wide system of interstate highways. The act provided for the construction of "rural public roads" and defined them as "any public road over

which the United States mails now are or may hereafter be transported." Federal contributions would not exceed 50 percent of the total cost of each project, and the matching portion would be furnished by the states. The act also put more emphasis upon the organization of a state highway department before a state could receive Federal highway aid.

• Slanting windshields became a feature.

1917

• All car and truck manufacturers offered full co-operation to the government as the United States entered World War I.

• Many automotive companies participated in the development and production of Liberty aircraft engines, designed by Jesse G. Vincent and E.J. Hall.

• The first Nash appeared, with a six-cylinder valve-in-head engine.

• Henry M. Leland, former president of Cadillac, formed the Lincoln Motor Company.

• Chevrolet offered a V-8 model.

• Studebaker developed and adopted an internal manifold hot-spot to vaporize the fuel mixture more efficiently.

• The Society of Automobile Engineers became the Society of Automotive Engineers (S.A.E.).

• Paige introduced a coupe with a rumble seat and a V-type windshield.

• Hudson Motor Car Company organized the Essex Motor Car Company to manufacture a light car.

• Several closed cars exhibited at the 1917 National Automobile Show were equipped with heaters.

• John North Willys and Col. Charles Clifton represented the

automotive industry on the National Industrial Conference Board.

• Frederick Furber developed a built-in radiator shutter which was introduced by Columbia.

• By the end of the year various boards for organizing the motor industry were formed to bring about the standardization of design for war production. The result of large war contracts was seen in a considerable number of mergers and an extraordinary number of capital stock increases.

• Passenger car production was curtailed while automobile plants produced Army trucks, tanks, gun carriages, Eagle boats, Liberty motors and tractors.

1918

1918 — The first Nash-designed car had a six-cylinder overhead valve engine.

• The country was in the midst of war when the 18th National Automobile Show was held at New York's Grand Central Palace. There were fuel shortages of coal and petroleum, due mainly to the nation's almost total dependence for transportation on war-burdened railroads and talk of the possibility that motor vehicle production would be curtailed, or even stopped altogether. As far as official Washington was concerned, motor vehicles were dispensable luxuries, and the wartime excise levies taxed them as if they were tobacco, whiskey, furs, perfume or jewelry.

• Factories were turned over to war work, men drafted into the army, and women took their places at benches, machine tools, and even in repair shops. The industry's war production included shells, helmets, caissons, aircraft engines, tractors, tanks, naval craft, anti-aircraft guns, gun carriages, artillery recoil mechanisms, in addition to military vehicles.

• Dealers began to stock tractors as essential merchandise.

• Because of the war, accessory and automobile manufacturers offered many new devices for prolonging the life of cars, and introduced carburetors designed to use low-grade fuels and even kerosene.

• There were heatless days and gasless Sundays to conserve fuel; everything was done to check the use of motor cars unless vehicle travel was necessary. Motorless Sundays ended Oct. 13.

• Designers borrowed from the armored cars and other military vehicles that were produced at the time. Four cars — Paige, Oldsmobile, McFarlan and Anderson — had steel wheels that resembled military wheels. Straight lines, higher hoods and the steel wheels gave many of the new models a war-like appearance.

• Closed cars (which were 10 percent of production) had more glass area in 1918, giving more visibility. More attention was given to the driver's seat of closed cars for those owners who wanted to do their own driving, their chauffeurs having become part of the war effort.

• The first unit of highway construction authorized under the Federal Aid Road Act of 1916 was completed Jan. 30, from Richmond to the Alameda County line in California. The 2.55 mile road was built at a cost of $53,938.85, of which Federal aid totaled $24,244.56.

• Four-wheel hydraulic brakes were developed by Malcolm Loughead of California. Along with E.A. Featherstone, D.O. Scott and Otto C. Lang, Loughead (Lockheed) formed a company to promote the patents which were used later (in 1920) on production automobiles.

• Passenger car production, already curtailed by plant facility shortages, was given a government steel allocation to balance inventories for building 50 percent of the cars produced during the previous year. After the armistice in November, the percentage was increased to 75 percent.

• White discontinued passenger car production to concentrate on trucks.

• Chevrolet became part of General Motors.

• The National Automobile Dealers Association was organized in Washington in response to a call from F.W.A. Vesper to combat a threat to take all men out of the dealer shops.

• As the year closed, the price situation puzzled all car makers. The fact was that cheaper materials were expected, but prices did not drop. The troubles of readjustment were at hand.

1919

1919 — Essex helped boost the popularity of the economical closed car.

• Few new ideas were exhibited at the 19th National Automobile show; there was too little time after the armistice to work on new models. Some manufacturers, however, did bring out changes in design and detail, particularly better brakes, wiring, and suspension. The war had taught ways of improving these three parts. A low-priced, four cylinder Essex, made by Hudson, was the only new car at the Show. A white Daniels sport touring car displayed a golf bag attachment over the running board for the eager golfer who liked to be ready when he passed a country club.

• The flat rate system of repair was tried out.

• Ford produced 750,000 cars, more than one-third of the industry's total output.

• General Motors Acceptance Corporation was formed.

• Henry Ford bought out minority stockholders, and Edsel Bryant Ford became president of Ford Motor Company.

• Front and rear bumpers were offered as standard equipment on the Westcott touring car.

• The world's first three-color traffic control light was installed in Detroit, and Detroit police pioneered in offering safety instruction in school classrooms.

• Car makers were swamped with orders by May, but were unable to fill them because of parts and material shortages.

• Strikes, rising wages, and a shortage of automobiles were major problems confronting the automotive industry in July as dealers were clamoring for new models.

• General Motors bought an interest in Fisher Body Company, and Nash bought an interest in the Seaman Body Corporation.

• Indirect lighting of instruments on the dash appeared on some cars. Approximately 90 percent of all passenger cars made during the year were open models, i.e., touring cars and roadsters.

• Ralph De Palma set a world's speed record of 149.8 miles an hour in a Packard 905.

• One of the innovations offered during the year was a back-up lamp which was turned on automatically when the car was reversed. This was combined with the tail-lamp on the Wills-St. Claire.

1919 — A Hupmobile touring car at Yosemite Falls, Calif.

1920

1920 — Bullet-shaped headlamps were one of the features on the Kissel. The hood ventilator cooled the engine in the summer and permitted fumes to escape.

• The first post-war National Automobile Show sponsored by the National Automobile Chamber of Commerce was held Jan. 3 through Jan. 10. Closed cars continued to gain over open cars (119 closed models in 1920 compared with 79 in the previous show). The marked change in the cars displayed was the increase in the number of owner-driven, as opposed to chauffeur-driven cars. Convertible cars had almost disappeared — only two were displayed at the show. (At that time, the term "convertible" meant a touring car or roadster — which could be purchased, for about $500, a "California top" — a solid-roofed structure with glazed windows — which could be stored in a stable or garage in summer, but would replace the folding fabric top in autumn.)

• Sloping windshields were evident everywhere. Also, heaters were standard equipment. Wire wheels were more numerous than wooden artillery wheels.

• Buick and McFarlan offered solid metal wheels on passenger cars.

• A compass and camera were offered as standard equipment on the Templar touring roadster. Flower vases were part of the standard equipment on the sedan model.

• General Motors Research Corporation was organized under the direction of C.F. Kettering.

• Duesenberg appeared; it was the first U.S. car with a straight-eight engine and first licensee to use hydraulic four-wheel brakes developed by Malcolm Loughead in 1918.

• Packard introduced the Lanchester vibration dampener.

• William C. Durant again lost control of General Motors, and Pierre S. duPont was named president.

• In May the manager of the Kansas City Federal Reserve Bank declined to discount any paper from member banks based on passenger car stocks. This action caused great concern within the automotive industry, for it meant a tightening of credit.

• In August, a bankers' committee took over the Maxwell plant.

• A nation-wide program of highway research on a large scale was launched. As a result of problems in highway construction and maintenance, the Highway Research Board of the National Research Council was organized. Tests on experimental roads were conducted at Arlington, Va., Pittsburg, Calif., and near Springfield, Ill.

• By October, completion of Federal-aid highway projects totaled 191 miles.

• Alemite chassis lubrication was introduced.

• Studebaker discontinued carriage making to concentrate on motor vehicles.

1921

• Most popular body type at the 21st National Automobile Show was the open touring car, seating five, six, or seven passengers. Glass windshield wings made their eastern debut — the first seen at a New York show, although they had been popular for years in Southern California.

• The post-war depression brought a drastic curtailment of sales.

• Studebaker developed nickel-molybdenum steel for commercial use.

• Ford weathered a financial crisis with the help of dealers. Ford car production passed the five million mark, or 55.45 percent of the industry's total output.

• Hudson offered a coach, the Essex, priced at only $300 more than a touring car.

• Fred M. Zeder, Owen R. Skelton and Carl Breer incorporated as consulting automotive engineers to begin design of cars with new concepts. Later the Chrysler was one of their cars.

• W.C. Durant retired from General Motors directorate and organized Durant Motors, Inc.

• Nickel plating appeared on radiators and lamps.

• Cadillac offered thermostatic control of carburetion.

• On March 4, Warren G. Harding became the first U.S. President to ride in an automobile to his inauguration. The car was a Packard Twin-Six.

• Cadillac moved into a new factory on Clark Avenue, Detroit, Mich.

• Detroit police experimented with synchronized traffic signal lights and raised-platform safety zones.

• The General Motors Building in Detroit was opened and became the home of many departments of the corporation.

• Herbert Hoover, Secretary of Commerce, asked the National Automobile Chamber of Commerce to appoint a committee to promote automotive business in the U.S. and abroad. J. Walter Drake was made chairman, and, later that year, the Automotive Division of the Bureau of Foreign and Domestic Commerce in the Department of Commerce was organized, with Gordon Lee as the manager.

• On Dec. 9, Dr. Thomas Midgley, Jr., and associates proved effectiveness of tetraethyl lead in gasoline to eliminate knock.

• The Essex coach led the landslide toward closed cars.

• Hudson introduced an adjustable front seat.

• The Federal highway system got under way.

• Nash Motors bought LaFayette Motors Corp.

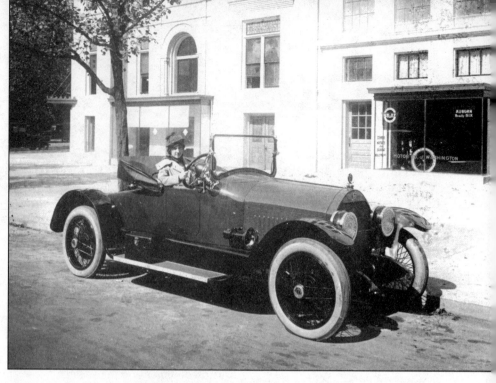

1921 — The famous Stutz Bearcat.

1921 — A distinctive feature of the Willys-Knight was the sleeve-valve engine that reportedly "improved with use."

1921 — Dort touring car.

1922 — The Peerless, one of the heavy cars of the '20s.

• A new body style at the 1922 National Automobile Show was the roadster-coupe, primarily a business car, which consisted of a roadster body with a permanent top.

• Balloon tires and air cleaners were introduced on 1923 model passenger cars.

• Ford bought Lincoln Motor Company at a receiver's sale and began production of higher-priced cars.

• Durant bought Locomobile and Mason.

• The earliest known electrically interlocked traffic signal system was installed in Houston, Texas.

• Charles M. Schwab gained control of Stutz.

• Elwood Haynes received the John Scott medal for metallurgical achievement in stainless steel, stellite, and chrome iron.

• Several cars introduced a gasoline gauge on the instrument panel.

• An Oldsmobile set a record of 67 miles an hour, traveling 1,000 miles in 15 hours.

• Automobile insurance policies were revised to cover the actual value rather than the purchase price of a car. Declining automobile prices led many insurance firms to believe motorists were deliberately destroying their cars to collect claims covering their depreciation on their automobiles.

• In October Ford Motor Company astonished the automotive industry with a $50 reduction on all models.

• Rickenbacker Motor Co. was launched.

• The air cleaner was introduced on the Rickenbacker.

1923

• Most popular body styles at the 23rd National Automobile Show were the five-passenger closed car and the permanent-top phaeton. The four-door phaetons featured windows that lowered or could be removed for storage within the car.

• Optimistic predictions over a peak production year proved correct. It was an all-time high record that stood until 1925. A total of 4,034,012 motor vehicles was sold by the manufacturers.

1923 — The Rickenbacker bore the "hat-in-the-ring" insigne of the famous flying ace.

• Introduced June 1922 as a 1923 Model, Dodge offered steel closed bodies, in which sheet steel replaced wood everywhere except on the roof, which was an insert constructed of wood bows and slats covered by waterproof fabric.

• Packard introduced the first mass-produced straight-eight L-head engines.

• Springfield Body Corporation offered a factory-installed radio as optional equipment.

• Zeder, Skelton, Breer Engineering Company joined Walter Chrysler, then board chairman of Maxwell-Chalmers Corp., to develop a new car to carry the Chrysler name.

• Four-wheel brakes, foot-controlled headlamp dimmer switches and power-operated windshield wipers were adopted by several manufacturers as standard equipment.

• "Ethyl" gasoline was first put on the market Feb. 2, in Dayton, Ohio, by General Motors Research Corporation.

1923 — The Star, Durant's bid for the light-car field, offered the first production station wagon.

• Ford Motor Company announced a weekly purchase plan under which a customer was issued a coupon book and made at least $5 weekly payments to the local dealer. When the total price of the car had been paid, the dealer delivered the car. The lowest price Model T was the runabout, selling at $265. (At the end of two years, more than 300,000 Ford cars were sold under the plan.)

• With transmission gears locked in high, E.G. "Cannon Ball" Baker drove an Oldsmobile from New York to Los Angeles in 12 1/2 days. The car was equipped with large gasoline tanks, and refueling enroute was accomplished by raising the rear wheels off the ground in order to keep the engine running.

• Ford production exceeded two million cars during the year.

• Alfred P. Sloan, Jr., became president of General Motors.

• The Chrysler 6 was introduced featuring hydraulic brakes and oil filters.

1924

• Not one electric, not one steamer, made the four-acre display at the 258th Field Artillery Armory in New York, the first 100 percent gasoline National Automobile Show. Top mechanical attractions at the 24th national show were the increased number of cars featuring four-wheel brakes and balloon tires as standard equipment.

• Six-cylinder vehicles were the most prized, a sensation being the Essex Coach priced under $1,000. Also of interest was the baked-enamel finish on low-priced cars.

1924 — Flint Six touring car sported disc wheels and front bumper.

• The Chrysler light six, introduced by Maxwell-Chalmers Corp., featured a high-compression engine (4.5-to-1), seven-bearing crankshaft, four-wheel hydraulic brakes and a replaceable cartridge oil filter.

• In addition to Packard and Duesenberg, straight-eight engines were offered by Auburn, Hupmobile, Jordan, Rickenbacker and several engine manufacturers.

• General Motors Proving Ground at Milford, Mich., was completed.

• Ethyl Corporation was organized by General Motors and Standard Oil (New Jersey).

• The Winton Company discontinued manufacture of automobiles. Later, the firm was reorganized to produce Diesel engines.

• Major Award Trophy was presented to the White Motor Company by the U.S.S.R. for reliability and endurance.

1924 — Cars let families combine city living with country pleasures. A Model T Ford.

• Ford Motor Company produced its 10-millionth car.

• There was now one automobile for every seven persons in the United States.

• Two-filament bulbs, permitting use of direct and diverted light, appeared in headlights of some cars.

• Hudson announced its price on a coach which was $5 more than an open car.

• Ford began manufacturing accessories for Ford cars.

• Adoption of S.A.E. standards saved automobile manufacturers an estimated $124 for each car produced.

1925 — Wills Sainte Claire had balloon tires.

1925

• The most discussed mechanical aspect of new cars at the 25th National Automobile Show was the continued trend toward straight-eight engines. Balloon tires created the need for easier steering systems which were offered in 1925 models.

• Other car features widely discussed were rumble seats, one-piece windshields, mohair upholstery and crank-type window lifts. Synthetic quick-drying pyroxylin finishes that could be sprayed on and baked gave the industry a wide range of colors in high-gloss finishes.

• Accessories available to the automotive consumer included: balloon tire jacks, stop signals, locking radiator caps, trunk racks, all-weather enclosures for touring cars, mirrors, ash-trays, cigar lighters and heat indicators.

• For the first time, more closed than open models were sold.

• General Motors acquired control of the Yellow Truck and Coach Manufacturing Company.

• Oldsmobile introduced chromium plating in place of nickel plating.

• A.C.F. acquired Fageol Motors Company of Ohio and moved operations to Detroit.

• Maxwell-Chalmers was reorganized as Chrysler Corporation.

• Ford production exceeded 9,000 units a day.

• Fisher Body acquired Fleetwood, a custom body-building company.

• More than 150 electric railway

systems were now operating motor buses.

• Chrysler offered rubber engine mounts.

• The 25-millionth U.S. motor vehicle was produced.

• A national chain of drive-it-yourself stations was established.

• "Automotive Daily News" began publication (later the name changed to "Automotive News").

• Uniform markings for Federal-aid highways were adopted. Even numbers were assigned to east-west roads, odd numbers to roads running north-south.

1926

• Narrower steel roof support posts gave the '26 models better vision.

• "Shock-proof" windshield glass was offered by Stutz and Rickenbacker. The Stutz windshield had wire running horizontally through the glass at intervals, while Rickenbacker's windshield was a sandwich of transparent celluloid between two sheets of glass.

• Engineering features included heavier crankshafts, shorter strokes and faster engines.

• The new Rickenbacker sport sedan was a low car with no running boards and a fender-mounted spare tire. The radiator, wire wheels, lamps and other exterior trim were brass finished, while the bumpers (shaped to resemble airplane propellers) were brass-bound mahogany. Gold plating was used on the interior hardware.

• Edward "Ned" Jordan, president of the Jordan Motor Car Company, established a new trend in automobile advertising by shifting empha-

Somewhere West of Laramie

SOMEWHERE west of Laramie there's a broncho-busting, steer-roping girl who knows what I'm talking about. She can tell what a sassy pony, that's a cross between greased lightning and the place where it hits, can do with eleven hundred pounds of steel and action when he's going high, wide and handsome.

The truth is—the Playboy was built for her.

Built for the lass whose face is brown with the sun when the day is done of revel and romp and race.

She loves the cross of the wild and the tame.

There's a savor of links about that car—of laughter and lilt and light—a hint of old loves—and saddle and quirt. It's a brawny thing—yet a graceful thing for the sweep o' the Avenue.

Step into the Playboy when the hour grows dull with things gone dead and stale.

Then start for the land of real living with the spirit of the lass who rides, lean and rangy, into the red horizon of a Wyoming twilight.

JORDAN
JORDAN MOTOR CAR COMPANY, Inc., Cleveland, Ohio

sis from technical details to the pleasures of driving. His ads, with eye-catching headlines such as "Somewhere West of Laramie," became famous.

• A few models had small glass "eyes" at the rear of the headlamps to enable the driver to see if his lights were on.

• Three companion cars were introduced at the National Automobile Show. Ajax, a Nash-built six-cylinder car, and Moon's Diana had been on the road a few

1926 — A new style of automobile advertising was pioneered by the Jordan Motor Car Company.

months earlier, but the show was their first "public" appearance. Pontiac, made by Oakland (General Motors), was first displayed at the industry-sponsored show.

• Packard offered hypoid gears which permitted the propeller shaft to be lower, thus making it possible to lower the body line.

• Ford announced plans to discontinue manufacture of the Model T.

• General Motors bought Fisher Body Corporation.

• Ford inaugurated the five-day work week.

• All outstanding Nash preferred stock was retired.

• Chandler offered a one-shot lubrication system.

• Hot water car heaters were introduced in the United States.

• Reo introduced the Flying Cloud models.

1927

• A definite trend toward the small car was apparent at the 27th National Automobile Show. In addition to the new Erskine, made by Studebaker, other small cars included the Little Marmon, in several models and styles; the Whippet and Whippet Six, made by Willys; and the Jordan Little Playboy. Four-wheel brakes were standard equipment on virtually all the cars at the show. Air cleaners, gasoline filters, crankcase ventilators, oil filters, windshield wipers, balloon tires and rear-view mirrors were all becoming common.

• The Packard and Little Marmon were equipped with hypoid rear axles, devised in response to demands for lower cars.

• Cadillac introduced the LaSalle V-8.

• The Fageol brothers organized the Twin Coach Company.

• Carl Breer began the study of aerodynamics in relation to automobile body design, which led to the "Airflow" design and mono-coque type of body and chassis construction.

• Graham-Paige Motors Corporation succeeded Paige-Detroit Motor Car Company.

• Studebaker celebrated its Diamond Jubilee.

• General Motors stockholders received $134,836,081 in dividends.

• Nash announced that employees owned $20,000,000 worth of stock.

• An electric drive with no gear shift was developed by E.M. Frazer.

• Packard built a 500-acre proving ground with a two and one half-mile concrete oval test track at Utica, Mich.

• Ford produced the last (mass-produced) Model T on May 31. A total of 15,007,033 Model T's were assembled by the company since it was introduced in 1908. After a six-month changeover period, Ford introduced the Model A.

• Chrysler shareholders received $10,000,000 in dividends.

• Lockheed (Malcolm Loughead) introduced an internal expanding hydraulic brake system.

• Chevrolet outsold Ford for the first time.

• Dr. Graham Edgar devised the octane scale for gasoline.

1927 — Ford introduced the famous Model A.

1928 — Reo's Flying Cloud sport coupe with a rumble seat was typical of a popular body style of the later 1920's.

1928

• Lower prices and an increase in the number of eight-cylinder cars were two predominant features of the new models in the 28th National Automobile Show. Higher compression ratios, combined with better fuel, brought about a higher horsepower average for the industry.

• Cadillac introduced a synchro-mesh transmission, and safety plate glass in all windows.

1928 continued

• Chrysler entered the low-priced field with the Plymouth, and offered the DeSoto as another new line of cars.

• Most Graham-Paige models featured a four-speed transmission.

• Chrysler purchased Dodge Brothers, Inc., July 30.

• Studebaker acquired control of Pierce-Arrow.

• Ford offered shatter-proof glass as standard equipment.

• Coast-to-coast bus service began.

• Chandler offered Westinghouse vacuum brakes that reduced pedal pressure by two-thirds.

• Buick celebrated its silver anniversary.

• The publication "Fleet Owner" made its appearance.

1929

• Public interest in new automobiles reached such heights that most Manhattan hotel lobbies were packed with displays of cars during the 1929 National Automobile Show. A number of redesigned models were first displayed at the show. Auburn had one streamlined aluminum model that resembled an airplane cabin; Franklin's le Pirate model concealed the running boards under the doors.

• Hupmobile acquired two Chandler-Cleveland plants in Cleveland.

• More than 80,000 De Sotos were sold during the first year of production.

1929 — The Viking with a V-8 engine was Oldsmobile's companion car.

• Cord offered front-wheel drive.

• Radios were offered as optional equipment on some automobiles.

• Chrysler adopted a down-draft carburetor for better fuel distribution and increased efficiency.

• Nash offered an eight-cylinder engine for the first time in its 1930 model.

• Ford raised its wage scale to $7-a-day minimum.

• Companion cars were offered by two major manufacturers.

• Oldsmobile introduced the Viking, a V-8; Buick offered the Marquette.

• Motor vehicle production broke all records in 1929. Output totaled 5,337,087 units (the greatest until 1949).

• Almost 90 percent of all American cars sold in 1929 were closed models (sedans, coaches, coupes, etc.), whereas almost 90 percent sold in 1919 had been open models.

• Chevrolet reverted to six-cylinder engines instead of four's.

1929 — The Marquette model 30 was introduced by Buick.

1930

1930 — Austin Bantam had a 75-inch wheel base and was powered by a 14.8 horsepower four-cylinder engine.

• Confusion was apparent on prices of new models at the 30th National Automobile Show. Four makes had a higher price tag, while five other lines reduced prices.

• Cadillac offered V-16 and V-12 engines. The new V-16 engine, rated at 185 horsepower, had a complete fuel system for each bank of cylinders, and a power brake operated by the manifold vacuum.

• Graham-Paige offered rubber-cushioned chassis springs and aluminum pistons with Invar struts for reduced weight and added strength.

• The National Automobile Chamber of Commerce launched a plan which would withdraw 360,000 antiquated motor vehicles from use.

• American Austin Car Company was organized in 1929 to build the 1930 Austin Bantam.

• Studebaker developed a carburetor intake silencer.

• Cadillac, Chrysler, Dodge, LaSalle, Marmon and Roosevelt cars were wired for radio installation.

• Plymouth franchises were given to all Chrysler, De Soto and Dodge dealers.

• Pontiac developed tin plated pistons and pressed steel axle housing.

• Police cars were being equipped with radios.

• Cadillac offered automatic hydraulic tappet clearance adjusters.

1930 — Cord featured a front-wheel-drive.

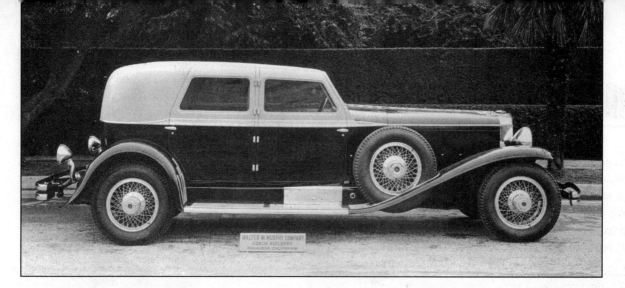

1931

1931 — An unlimited number of custom-built body designs were available on the standard straight-eight Duesenberg chassis.

• With all business still in decline, the 31st National Automobile Show reflected the automobile manufacturers' dilemma quite clearly: whether to risk vast sums on completely new models, or reduce drastically the prices of existing models. Most of the makers had the larger, more powerful, more luxurious cars that the public had signified it most wanted until the chill of the Great Depression had set in. They now offered these big cars at reduced prices.

• During National Auto Show week, the National Automobile Chamber of Commerce passed a resolution favoring the grouping of new model announcements in November and December. This plan had a twofold aim: it was hoped that buying would be stimulated in the fall and winter, rather than have it create a rush every spring. By thus changing buying habits, it was hoped that the unhappy conditions of summertime rush and wintertime decline in factory work might be changed for the better.

• The Oakland line of cars was discontinued in favor of its companion car, the Pontiac, which offered eight- and six-cylinder models.

• Plymouth offered "floating power" rubber engine mountings designed to give the engine an independent axis.

• Buick adopted an eight-cylinder engine.

• Free-wheeling was available on Auburn, Chrysler, DeSoto, De Vaux, Dodge, Essex, Graham, Hudson, Hupmobile, Lincoln, Marmon, Peerless, Pierce-Arrow, Plymouth, Studebaker, Willys and Willys-Knight.

• Oldsmobile adopted a synchromesh transmission.

• Pontiac produced a radiator grille made of pressed steel.

• The 50-millionth U.S. motor vehicle was produced during the year.

• A retractable hardtop convertible was patented by B.B. Ellerbeck of Salt Lake City.

• A standard warranty for passenger cars for 90 days or 4,000 miles, and 90 days and/or 5,000 miles for commercial vehicles was recommended by the National Automobile Chamber of Commerce directors.

• Chrysler offered an eight-cylinder engine for the first time.

1931 — The dual-cowl Packard phaeton was one of the luxury cars of the period. It has been certified as a genuine "classic" car.

1932

1932 — First year for the Ford V-8.

• The year opened in the gloomy economic climate of a deepening depression. It was destined to be the poorest auto production year since 1918. In general, the new models were heavier, but the power had not been increased correspondingly. Five makes displayed 12-cylinder models. Convertibles, both phaetons and coupes with disappearing tops, were popular at the exhibition.

• Chrysler this year strove for silence with improvements to silence fans, air-intake and exhaust.

• Ford offered a new model with a V-8 engine to replace the Model A.

• Graham introduced full-skirted fenders.

• Pierce-Arrow introduced hydraulic valve-lifters.

• Buick, Cadillac, Chrysler, De Soto, Dodge and LaSalle offered vacuum-operated clutches. Nearly all other makes featured free wheeling, which could be engaged by a control on the dash of the car.

• Inside visors began to replace outside shades in an effort to decrease wind-resistance.

• Oldsmobile and Packard offered automatic chokes on their 1932 models.

• Backed by Walter C. Marmon, Col. Arthur William Sydney Herrington, military transport engineer, began production of all-wheel-drive vehicles for lumber and petroleum industries.

• Olds offered a straight 8 engine.

1933

• Aerodynamic streamlining was beginning to be noticed at the 33rd National Automobile Show. The skirted fender, V-front grille, sweeping tail lines, and slanted windshield were more prominent. Economy seemed to be important. Gasoline mileage was advertised by many manufacturers, and durability was stressed by nearly all companies.

• Power brakes became available on a number of makes.

• Valve seat inserts, independent wheel suspension, and reflex glass tail- and stop-lights were introduced.

1933 — Depression and the ravages of nature combined to drive thousands to pack their belongings on the car or in trailers and leave home for better opportunities.

• Fisher bodies offered "No-Draft Ventilation," with the front section of the side windows pivoted on the top and bottom to control the flow of air inside the car.

• Use of the accelerator pedal for starting the engine was adopted on several makes to eliminate a separate starter pedal on the floor.

1934

1934 — De Soto's Airflow.

• Two features that drew most attention at the 34th National Automobile Show were streamlining and the independent suspension of the front wheels. Streamlining was particularly stressed by the new and quite revolutionary De Soto and Chrysler "Airflow" models. Hupmobile and, to a degree, LaSalle also featured it. Nearly all cars had one of the three forms of independent front wheel suspension then shown.

• At the show, several makers had automatic de-clutching devices. A low-priced Graham had a mechanical supercharger that forced air into the carburetor. Several makes had rear fender covers, then called "pants."

• There was a noticeable trend to larger cars on the new models, even among those of lower price. Nearly all models were longer and wider and offered more room inside. Several were even wide enough to seat three persons comfortably in the front seat. Doors were made wider; on some models door openings were cut back over fenders to provide more room for entering and leaving the vehicle.

• Chevrolet produced its 10-millionth car to celebrate its 23rd anniversary.

• The name of the National Automobile Chamber of Commerce was changed to the Automobile Manufacturers Association, Inc. (AMA).

• Studebaker emerged from receivership.

• Cadillac introduced a high output generator and voltage regulator to keep the battery fully charged for extra loads.

• Reo offered a gear shift on the dash.

• Radio controls built into the instrument panel appeared on several makes.

• All General Motors cars — Cadillac, Buick, Oldsmobile, Pontiac and Chevrolet — offered the first production all-steel turret top in December for their line of 1935 models.

• A drive-in theater was opened in Camden, N.J.

1935

1935 — Chevrolet pioneered the first all-steel station wagon body; it was on a panel delivery truck chassis.

• The 35th National Automobile Show was sponsored by the Automobile Merchants Association of New York after the Automobile Manufacturers Association decided to wait until November for its show in an effort to stabilize employment.

• Ford Motor Company, which had not participated in national shows since early in the century, took part in the 1935 show.

• Hudson and Terraplane introduced a new "electric hand" fingertip control for gear shifting. The control was mounted on the steering column.

• A trend toward lower-priced cars was noticed for the 1935 model year. New models, with fewer features or less power, were announced by Chrysler, De Soto,

Graham, Hudson, Hupmobile, Packard, Pontiac and Reo — all with lower prices.

• An AMA report disclosed that motorists paid one of every eight tax dollars.

• A trend toward two-door and four-door sedans developed.

• Ford introduced the Lincoln-Zephyr as a 1936 Model.

• Nash offered a new type of "sealed-in" motor with the manifold cast inside the block.

• Approximately 3 million automobiles had radios by the end of 1935.

• Pontiac produced its one-millionth car.

• Chevrolet adopted a new type of frame without the X-member.

• The great break with tradition

1935 — The first Lincoln-Zephyr.

characterized the 36th National Automobile Show in November. Since it had been decided that a fall show would possibly help level the peaks and valleys in the industry's sales and employment, the manufacturers moved their new-model announcements ahead two months. The innovation won plaudits from the nation's leaders. President Roosevelt saluted the industry for its leadership in the "vanguard of recovery." Sales were encouragingly better than they had been at recent shows; some exhibitors jubilantly reported that they more than doubled.

• The new 1936 model cars featured hand brakes on the left of the driver to give more room in the front seat.

• Nash exhibited a car with twin travel beds.

1936

• Automobile manufacturers were optimistic that the buying spirit at the 1936 model introduction in the previous fall would carry through the year. It turned out to be the best year since 1929.

• The AMA reported that 95 percent of all cars were sold under $750 wholesale.

• The Department of Commerce announced that 54 percent of all U.S. families owned cars.

• Reo discontinued passenger car manufacturing to concentrate on a line of commercial vehicles.

• The three-millionth Buick was built.

• Hudson introduced a "radical safety control," a steel torque arm which resulted in easier steering and the elimination of "nosing

1936 — Fisher Body enhanced the safety of GM vehicles with the one-piece solid steel "Turret Top."

down" when braking. Also offered on the Hudson was a double automatic emergency braking system with a separate reserve brake system that went into use in the event the primary brakes failed.

• Sloping side windows and built-in defrosters appeared on many cars.

• Exhibits at the 37th National Automobile Show in November were of a more popular nature with less technical and mechanical detail than in past years. Emphasis was on the comfort and beauty of new models. House trailers were also displayed at the show as an accessory for touring and camping.

1937

- The Waterman Arrowbile was one of the earliest flying automobiles.

- Buick made a new-model changeover in the record time of 10 days.

- Chrysler spent $22 million in plant improvements, and built more than one million cars and trucks during the year.

- Ford offered a choice of 60 h.p. and 85 h.p. engines.

- Steering column gearshifts began to replace floor gearshifts.

- Several of the cars on display at the 38th National Automobile Show, Oct. 27 through Nov. 3, featured the storage battery in a location under the hood, making it more accessible and near other regularly serviced items.

1937 — Cord offered a supercharged front-wheel drive model.

- Chrysler offered an adjustable seat that moved not only back and forth, but up and down as well. Chrysler cars also offered safety padding on the back of the front seat.

- Windshield washers were offered by Studebaker.

- Nash Motors Company of Kenos, Wis., merged with Kelvinator Corporation of Detroit to form Nash-Kelvinator Corporation. Charles W. Nash became board chairman, and George W. Mason president.

1938

- The year saw one of the worst slumps in automotive history — production was down 40 percent. New models for 1939 and the National Automobile Show in the fall were looked upon as the necessary stimulus to bring the automotive business out of its economic low.

- Ford Motor Company introduced the 1939 model Mercury line of cars. The new make was aimed for the medium price field and equipped with a V-8 engine.

- Studebaker spent $4.5 million in tooling for the new low-priced Champion 1939 model.

- Nash introduced "conditioned air" heating and ventilation which heated and filtered fresh air from the outside, and then circulated it inside the car with a fan.

- Packard offered "Econo-drive," an overdrive transmission for its 1939 model.

- Pontiac adopted "Duflex" rear springs that were used with a smaller auxiliary leaf spring for uniform riding quality under any load. A remote gearshift control on the steering column was also introduced.

- Hudson introduced a 112-inch wheel-base model in the low-priced field.

- Several manufacturers offered coil spring rear suspension in place of leaf springs.

- Chevrolet introduced a vacuum operated gearshift for its 1939 model.

- Chrysler developed "Superfinish," a method of finishing parts with no scratches more than one-millionth of an inch deep. The company also introduced a fluid coupling for the Chrysler transmission.

- Ford spent $40 million for plant expansion.

- New car models exhibited at the 39th National Automobile Show had several interesting features, including Buick's directional signals, and Plymouth's safety signal speedometer and vacuum operated convertible top.

1939

- Automotive production milestones were reached during the year. The 75-millionth motor vehicle was made in the United States. Ford produced its 27-millionth vehicle, and the 15-millionth Chevrolet was produced.

- Hudson introduced "Airfoam" cushions and a hood lock release under the dash.

- White built 300 scout cars for the U.S. Army.

- Packard designed and built a high-speed marine engine for the U.S. Navy's famous PT boats.

- Powel Crosley Jr. introduced the Crosley, a small car.

- Nearly every manufacturer held its 1940 new car announcement until the 40th National Automobile Show in October, so the impact of the new models would be strong. The Show was held 27 days earlier than in past years to facilitate the group announcement.

- There was a wide range of colors on the 1940 models exhibited at the National Automobile Show, and the colors were made more lustrous by the use of metallic pigments. Two-tones were displayed at many exhibits. The most popular body style at the Show was the four-door, six passenger sedan, followed by the two-door sedan. There was great spectator interest in the new station wagon models displayed.

- Sealed Beam Headlamps were generally adopted for the first time by the automotive industry for the 1940 models.

- Push-button radios appeared in cars.

1939 — Powel Crosley Jr. and the new Crosley car.

1939 — Plymouth offered a convertible top operated by vacuum power.

- Lincoln-Zephyr and several models of other makes omitted running boards or enclosed them under the door.

- Automatic overdrive became available on several makes of cars.

- Several models featured an under-the-seat heater for better air circulation. Heaters and defrosters were standard equipment on many 1940 models.

- Oldsmobile offered "Hydra-Matic Drive," an automatic transmission for its 1940 model.

- Oldsmobile featured all-coil-spring suspension, four-way stabilization, and knee-action front-wheel suspension on all models.

- Pontiac began production of taxicabs.

- 1939 was the last year for rumble seats.

1940 — Oldsmobile offered Hydra-Matic automatic transmission as an option. Station wagons accounted for less than 1 percent of total motor vehicles in the country.

1940

• Col. Arthur W.S. Herrington invited a group of automotive engineers to Fort Benning, Ga., in March to witness demonstrations of a small armed vehicle designed and built by Capt. Robert G. Howie. This demonstration resulted in the development of the wartime one-quarter ton, four-wheel-drive military vehicle, the forerunner of "Jeep" vehicles made by Willys Motors, Inc.

• The war in Europe converted many U.S. automobile branch plants on the Continent to military production.

• William S. Knudsen, president of General Motors, went to Washington at the invitation of President Roosevelt to direct production for national defense.

• Packard contracted to build Rolls-Royce aircraft engines.

• Ford contracted to build Pratt & Whitney aircraft engines.

• Chevrolet produced one million cars in less than 10 working months.

• Cadillac discontinued the LaSalle.

• The 41st National Automobile Show in the Grand Central Palace Oct. 12-20 was the last of a series that had run without break from 1900. Before the event opened, AMA directors announced that all manufacturers had shelved plans for the 1941 show and new model introductions so that time and attention, as dictated by the emerging needs, could be devoted to production for national defense.

• Ford Motor Company exhibited Ford, Lincoln and Mercury cars and Ford trucks for the first time in a National Auto Show sponsored by the AMA or its predecessors.

• Interchangeable six- or eight-cylinder engines on a basic frame were offered by Oldsmobile and Pontiac. A supporting radiator frame or longer fan shroud made up the difference in shorter engines.

• Chrysler introduced a safety-rim wheel that kept the tire on the rim in the event of a blowout. Two-speed electric windshield wipers were also offered by Chrysler.

• The Automotive Committee for Air Defense was established on Oct. 30 to facilitate aircraft production.

• A nationwide plan for financing automotive repairs on an installment basis was announced.

• An air conditioning unit was offered by Packard.

1941

1941 — The Nash Ambassador offered a folding seat which formed a bed.

• Production records were set by at least three car makers. Oldsmobile made its 2-millionth unit, Plymouth made its 4-millionth unit, Dodge built its 5-millionth car and the 29-millionth Ford was produced.

• The new 1942 models had a lower, longer, broader and more massive look. Grilles were wider, bumpers heavier and running boards were either absent or concealed.

• Many makes substituted a light-weight iron alloy for pistons. Substitute materials were also used for trim and decoration.

• Nash introduced its "600" series, a pioneer of the mass produced unitized body.

• Hydra-Matic Drive was made available on all Cadillac models. Fluid Drive became available on Dodge, De Soto and Chrysler cars.

• Buick offered a dual compound carburetor that cut in a second carburetor when the throttle was depressed to floor.

• Enclosed running boards were generally adopted throughout the industry.

• Power-operated windows were introduced on the 1941 Packard.

National Defense

• Buick built a new aviation engine plant.

• Oldsmobile produced shells for the U.S. Army in a modern forge plant.

• Chrysler achieved mass production of tanks, delivered its first anti-aircraft guns and proceeded with scores of defense contracts.

• Ford began production of combat cars.

• Oldsmobile produced 100,000 cars equipped with Hydra-Matic transmission.

• Pontiac began work on Oerlikon anti-aircraft guns.

• General Motors divisions began production of machine guns.

• Studebaker took a contract to produce aircraft engines.

• American Bantam, Willys and Ford submitted designs and prototypes for a military reconnaissance car that came to be known as the Jeep. Though the Bantam was the first one produced, the Willys model was subsequently approved and it was used as the standard. The Jeep was built by Willys and Ford.

• Forces from Japan struck Pearl Harbor Dec. 7 — war against Japan was declared by the U.S. Congress on the following day.

• The Automotive Council for War Production was organized on Dec. 31 to apply the full facilities of the automotive industry to the task of production for the armed forces.

1942

1942 — Military service and rationing put many automobiles into storage for the duration of World War II.

• Front fenders were extended to the middle of the front door on General Motors cars.

• Hudson offered a combination automatic clutch with a semi-automatic transmission. The driver could select either the manual or semi-automatic shift with buttons on the dash.

• De Soto's headlamps were concealed in the front fenders. The lamp doors disappeared upward when a knob under the instrument panel was pulled; this also turned on the lights.

• All automobile companies halted production of civilian passenger cars on Feb. 9.

• Car rationing began March 2.

• On May 3, the national speed limit was set at 40 m.p.h. to conserve fuel. It was later cut to 35 m.p.h.

• Gasoline supplies were cut 50 percent in 17 eastern states on May 15.

• Also in May the Ford Willow Run Michigan Bomber Plant opened.

• By July war output of automotive companies exceeded their peacetime production rate.

• On Sept. 10 President Roosevelt ordered nation-wide gasoline rationing effective Dec. 1 to conserve fuel and rubber.

• Graham-Paige began production of amphibious tanks.

• Nash-Kelvinator produced Pratt & Whitney engines, Hamilton

Standard propellers, Sikorsky helicopters.

• Chrysler spent $40 million to increase tank production and started a huge aircraft engine plant in Chicago.

• Pontiac was the first automobile manufacturer to win the Navy "E" Award. When this award was superseded by Army-Navy "E," Chrysler Tank Arsenal was accorded the first such award in the United States.

• At the year's end the Automotive Council for War Production reported the industry's 1942 production of arms at $4,665,000,000.

1943

• The Office of Price Administration (O.P.A.) banned non-essential driving in 17 eastern states in January.

• O.P.A. disclosed that 25 million gasoline ration books had been issued.

• By June, production for war in

1,000 automotive plants had doubled in 12 months; employment total: 1,250,000.

• Henry Kaiser announced plans to manufacture automobiles after the war.

• William B. Stout developed a "flying automobile" for postwar production.

• By November employment in U.S. plants formerly manufacturing motor vehicles and bodies reached

its wartime peak and began to taper off due to demands for manpower in armed services; output of such plants was now double the rate of the best peacetime year.

• The Automotive Council for War Production reported 1,038 automotive plants voluntarily cooperating in the industry-wide effort to maintain maximum production and that value of products thus made had reached a total of $13 billion.

1943 — Military vehicles rolled along assembly lines for the duration of the war.

1944

1944 — Automotive companies produced 57 percent of the tanks delivered to U.S. and allied armed forces during World War II.

• Willys-Overland announced plans to produce a civilian version of the Jeep after the war.

• The Detroit region was shown accountable for 13.6 percent of the nation's war production.

• The basic gasoline ration was reduced to two gallons a week.

• Joseph W. Frazer, board chairman of Graham-Paige, announced plans to manufacture automobiles after the war.

• In September the Office of War Information revealed that passen-

ger cars were now being scrapped at the rate of 4,000 a day.

• The War Production Board announced formation of the Automobile Industry Advisory Committee to consider basic problems to be dealt with in eventual resumption of passenger car production.

• It was revealed that the United

States had supplied the U.S.S.R. with more than 345,000 motor vehicles.

• The Automotive Council for War Production revealed that the automotive industry produced $9 billion worth of armament in 1944, and that costs to the Government had been reduced one-third since 1941.

1945

1945 — Henry Ford II drove the first civilian postwar automobile from the assembly line on July 3.

• The Automobile Manufacturers Association statistics disclosed that 48 percent of all passenger cars now in use were more than seven years old.

• Crosley Corporation announced its intent to produce small cars powered with four-cylinder lightweight engines after the war.

• In April the War Production Board announced a program for transition to civilian motor vehicle production after V-E Day.

• V-E Day became reality on May 8 when Germany surrendered to Allied Forces.

• On May 11 the War Production Board announced that reconversion to motor vehicle production could begin July 1.

• On May 22 all restrictions on manufacture of replacement parts were lifted.

• Willow Run Plant closed on June 23 after delivering 8,685 bombers.

• Ford began production of passenger cars on July 3.

• Formation of Kaiser-Frazer Corporation was announced on July 26.

• World War II ended with the surrender of Japan on Aug. 14.

• Gasoline rationing ended the day following the Japanese surrender.

• The Automotive Council for War Production was dissolved on Oct. 15.

• Production of 1946 motor vehicles started. New models were announced by Chevrolet, Buick, Cadillac, Pontiac, Oldsmobile, Studebaker, Nash, Hudson and Packard.

• A strike began in General Motors plants on Nov. 21.

SUMMARY OF AUTOMOTIVE INDUSTRY'S WAR PRODUCTION

The automotive industry contributed more materiel to the armed services of the United States and Allies than any other single industry. In addition to all the armored cars used, it supplied 92 percent of the scout cars and carriers, 87 percent of the aircraft bombs, 85 percent of the steel helmets, 75 percent of the aircraft engines, 57 percent of the tanks, 56 percent of the carbines, 50 percent of the diesel engines, 47 percent of the machine guns, 10 percent of the completed aircraft, 10 percent of the torpedoes, 10 percent of the land mines and 3 percent of the marine mines.

By the end of the war, almost $29 billion worth of products for war had been delivered. This total was approximately 20 percent of the national output of such products.

1946

1946 —
Studebaker
pioneered a
trend in
post-war
styling.

1946 —
The
Crosley
entered
the small
car field
after
World
War II.

• Kaiser and Frazer joined the ranks of U.S. passenger car manufacturers in offering new models bearing their names.

• A corporation to build Preston Tucker's rear-engine car was organized with $40 million capitalization. Tucker leased the Chicago Dodge plant, which had formerly been used for war production, during the latter part of the year.

• Despite a coal strike that impeded automotive production, the one-millionth passenger car assembled since the end of World War II was built in August.

• A 12-day celebration in Detroit from May 29 through June 9 marked the Automotive Golden Jubilee.

• Radio telephones were used in motor vehicles.

• Disabled veterans could obtain cars equipped with special mechanical aids developed by the Society of Automotive Engineers.

• Chevrolet Division was one of the first automotive firms to advertise on network television.

• The Public Roads Administration removed all restrictions on Federal Aid highway construction not requiring structural steel.

• Price and wage controls were lifted by the Federal Government from the automotive industry on Nov. 9.

• Willys-Overland Motors, Inc., introduced a seven-passenger Jeep all-steel station wagon.

1947

1947 – Chrysler offered a Town and Country series that combined features of a station wagon and convertible.

1947 — The Kaiser was the low-priced car made by Kaiser-Frazer Corp.

1947 — A few Tucker "48" pilot models were produced for public displays around the country. The Tucker had a rear engine and a third headlamp which turned with the front wheels.

• Motor vehicle manufacturers built and purchased a number of new plants. General Motors opened a new assembly plant in Wilmington, Delaware; Studebaker bought a wartime aircraft engine plant at South Bend; and Chevrolet opened new passenger car and truck assembly plants in Flint, Mich., and Van Nuys, Calif.

• Kaiser-Frazer Corporation purchased the automotive assets of the Graham-Paige Motor Corporation.

• Sun visors outside the windshield appeared again as accessories. The trend for such visors had declined during the early '30s.

• Driver education courses were offered in many high schools.

• Packard produced its one-millionth car and offered power-operated windows and seat adjustment.

• Tucker Corporation's Torpedo (later called the "48") was unveiled in Chicago.

1948 — Styling and engineering changes in the 1949 model Ford were extensive. It was the first completely new design for Ford since the end of World War II.

1948

- Because there had not been a National Show since 1940, each automotive firm offered its new models when they were ready.

- Willys-Overland introduced a six-cylinder Jeep station wagon and a convertible called the Jeepster.

- Goodrich introduced tubeless tires.

- Under the direction of Charles F. Kettering, General Motors revealed development of a new type of high-compression engine that was designed to use high-octane fuel.

- The 100-millionth motor vehicle was produced in the United States during August.

- Oldsmobile opened a new plant especially tooled to manufacture its new high compression V-8 engines.

- Buick introduced the Dynaflow transmission, with a hydraulic torque converter.

- Kaiser-Frazer bought the Willow Run plant near Ypsilanti, Mich.

- Cadillac, Buick and Oldsmobile offered curved, two-piece wind-shields.

- Pontiac offered the Hydra-Matic automatic transmission as optional equipment.

- New motor vehicle assembly plants were opened on the East and West Coasts: General Motors at Framingham, Mass., Lincoln-Mercury at Los Angeles and Dodge Division at San Leandro, Calif.

- Great Britain, Canada and the United States signed an agreement for standardization of threads on screws, nuts and bolts. This became known as the A.B.C. thread standard.

- Oldsmobile produced its 500,000th car equipped with Hydra-Matic transmission.

- Tucker Corporation reported completion of its first assembly line model.

- More than 1,000 dual-control cars were loaned by automotive companies to high schools in the United States for training student drivers.

- Most 1949 model American-made cars were introduced to the public in the fall.

- Three new cars were offered — Playboy, Keller and Davis.

1949

1949 — Buick introduced a hardtop convertible which became a popular body style.

- General Motors' first show since 1940, "Transportation Unlimited," opened in New York.

- Kaiser-Frazer introduced three new body styles — a utility car, a taxicab and a cloth-covered hardtop sports sedan.

- Cadillac offered a high compression V-8 engine with hydraulic valve lifters.

- Bonded brakes were adopted by Chevrolet, Chrysler and Crosley.

- Oldsmobile introduced its new "88" series with a high compression V-8 engine.

- Ford Division was organized to assemble and market Ford cars and trucks.

- Dodge introduced an inexpensive three-passenger roadster, the Wayfarer — the first car of this body style since before World War II.

- Buick, Oldsmobile and Cadillac started production of their hardtop (a sedan without center pillars) models, the Riviera, Holiday and Coupe de Ville, respectively.

- Hupp Corporation announced plans to sell its Detroit plant and apply funds to expansion elsewhere.

- Government controls on automobile installment credit (Regulation W) limiting financing to 24 months ended June 30.

- De Soto introduced a nine-passenger station wagon.

- Willys-Overland introduced a new four-wheel drive all-steel station wagon as part of the Jeep series.

- Plymouth introduced the Suburban, an all-steel station wagon.

- Chrysler adopted a new method of starting the engine by using only the ignition key.

- Kurtis-Kraft, Inc., racing car manufacturer, entered the passenger car field with the announcement of a low-slung convertible sports car.

- Steel and coal strikes forced production curtailment at auto plants in the fall.

- Crosley introduced a new sports car, the Hotshot.

- Ford and Studebaker contracted with Borg-Warner for a new automatic transmission.

- Tucker Corporation was ordered by the Federal Court to return its leased Chicago plant to the War Assets Administration.

- Nearly all U.S. passenger car manufacturers offered their 1950 models in the fall. Some of the new features included Powerglide automatic transmission on the Chevrolet, Hydra-Matic on some Nash models, and hydraulically-operated valves on the Cadillac, Oldsmobile and Buick.

- As the year ended, the automotive industry broke its own 20-year-old annual record to hit an all-time high of 6,253,651 units.

- Nash-Kelvinator offered seat belts.

1949 — Cadillac introduced a high compression V-8 engine with hydraulic valve lifters. The engine was one of the first postwar designs offered to the motoring public.

1950 —
Nash
Rambler
with
100-inch
wheelbase.

1950

• Nash-Kelvinator displayed the NXI, a two-passenger experimental car, as part of a survey of public reaction to a new light car. As a result of the findings, the firm introduced the Metropolitan in 1954.

• Many of the 1950 cars had reduced prices.

• Hardtop models were offered by Buick, Cadillac Chevrolet, Chrysler, Dodge, De Soto, Oldsmobile and Pontiac.

• Crosley introduced the Super Sports model, priced to sell for less than $1,000.

• The three-millionth Oldsmobile was produced in February. In October Oldsmobile discontinued its six-cylinder engine to concentrate output on the Rocket V-8 engine.

• Oldsmobile produced its one-millionth car equipped with Hydra-Matic transmission.

• Goodrich offered puncture-sealing tubeless tires.

• Marmon-Herrington Co., Inc., bought the manufacturing rights to Ford motor coaches.

• Nash-Kelvinator introduced the Rambler series.

• Chrysler celebrated its 25th anniversary.

• Hostilities in Korea started June 25.

• Nearly all automotive companies were awarded military contracts for defense products.

• U.S. Department of Defense revealed plans for the reactivation of an Ordnance Tank-Automotive Center in Detroit to expedite mobilization of the automotive and allied industries.

• Installment credit was tightened for new and used cars to 15 months with one-third down.

• Crosley introduced a farm and road vehicle, the Farm-O-Road,

with a 10-to-1 compression ratio engine.

• Willys built a small engine for Kaiser-Frazer's Henry J car, which was displayed in September.

• Several 1951 models were introduced in the fall. Some of the new features included: V-8 engines and automatic transmissions on Studebaker models; one-piece curved windshields; plastic-insulated ignition system to guard against moisture on the Nash; tinted non-glare glass on the Buick; automatic transmission on Ford (Fordomatic) and Mercury (Merc-O-Matic); crash pads on the Kaiser; and an all-steel station wagon for Chrysler (Town and Country).

• Chevrolet produced its 25-millionth vehicle in December.

• As the year ended, material shortages resulting from the military buildup caused temporary shutdowns in automotive assembly plants.

1951

• Civilian use of nickel, zinc and tin was ordered cut by the Federal government. Automotive companies used new methods and materials in producing car components as a result of the government cutback.

• By the first part of the year most automotive companies had already received, or were in the process of negotiating, military contracts for the Korean conflict.

• The National Production Authority halted the shipment of spare tires in new automobiles. Later in the year this ban was lifted.

• Several new models were added this year. Ford offered a hardtop model — the Victoria, Lincoln introduced the customized Capri, Plymouth offered the Belvedere hardtop, Kaiser offered four new utility models, Nash added the two-passenger Nash Healey sports car (built by the Donald Healey Co. of

1951 — Increased emphasis was placed on all-steel station wagons by nearly all manufacturers, including Willys.

England), a hardtop model was added to the Nash Rambler series, Packard added the Mayfair hardtop model to its line of cars and Oldsmobile introduced the Super 88.

• Buick displayed its XP 300 experimental car with a 300 horsepower V-8 supercharged engine. General Motors exhibited the Le Sabre experimental convertible, and Chrysler displayed its K-310 experimental car.

• General Motors added 1,000 acres to its Milford Proving Ground to facilitate testing military vehicles.

• Ford offered an in-line six-cylinder engine with overhead valves.

• Continental Motors acquired rights to nine gas turbine engines developed by Societe Turbomeca in France.

• Power steering was offered by Chrysler and Buick.

• Oldsmobile offered a watch mounted in the hub of the steering wheel as an option.

• Automobile installment credit was extended to 18 months with one-third down payment.

• The Internal Revenue Act of 1951 increased automotive excise taxes from 5 to 8 percent on trucks, 7 to 10 percent on passenger cars and 5 to 8 percent on automotive parts and accessories.

• Kaiser-Frazer suspended production of the Frazer car at the end of 1951.

• Sears, Roebuck and Company introduced the new 1952 model Kaiser-Frazer-made Allstate passenger car. The car was displayed in 19 cities in the South and Southwest a week before Christmas.

• Michigan State College (later, University) established a driver-training professorship.

1951 — Oldsmobile introduced the Super 88 series which featured a new body design combined with a high compression V-8 engine.

• The 100-millionth passenger car built in the United States was assembled in December.

1952

1952 — Sears, Roebuck and Co. offered the Allstate. The car, a version of the Henry J made by Kaiser-Frazer, was available with four- or six-cylinder engine.

• The year marked important milestones for two automotive companies. Studebaker, which began as a wagon-maker, celebrated the 100th anniversary of the company's founding, and Cadillac marked its golden anniversary.

• Some innovations offered on 1952 models included: Oldsmobile's automatic headlamp dimmer; a suspended brake pedal under the dashboard and ball joint front wheel suspension on the Lincoln; suspended clutch and brake pedals on the Ford; dual range Hydra-Matic on the Pontiac; 12-volt electrical system on the Chrysler Crown Imperial; four-way seat adjustment on the Packard; automatic overdrive on the Plymouth; and a V-8 engine on the De Soto.

• The last nine miles were opened on New Jersey's 118-mile turnpike in January.

• General Tire and Rubber bought Crosley Motors in July; production of the Crosley car stopped during the same month.

• Dodge and Fisher Body used plastic dies to produce steel stampings for automotive components.

• Automotive companies continued to produce military goods for the Korean conflict. In addition to military motor vehicles and tanks, they built aircraft engines, jet and piston type; electronic aircraft gun sights; diesel marine engines; aircraft; and a number of miscellaneous components for weapons.

• Hudson introduced a new low-priced car in September, the Jet.

• University of Michigan formed a Transportation Institute within the College of Engineering to encourage better understanding of the need for more efficient transportation.

• Willys-Overland Motors added the Aero Ace and Aero Lark to its Aero series of passenger cars.

• Dearborn Motors Corporation paid $9,250,000 to Harry Ferguson, Inc., in settlement of a judgment which ended the Ford-Ferguson tractor patents litigation.

• Lincoln-Mercury Division of Ford Motor Company moved into its new assembly plant at Wayne, Michigan, a Detroit suburb, for production of the division's two cars.

• The U.S. Chamber of Commerce estimated that private automobiles carried about 85 percent of the nation's combined local and long distance traffic.

• Chrysler Corporation started construction on its 3,800-acre proving ground at Chelsea, Michigan.

1953

• Three significant milestones in the automotive industry were passed during the year. Buick and Ford Motor Company celebrated their golden anniversaries; and Plymouth celebrated its 25th year.

• Kaiser-Frazer changed its name to Kaiser Motors Corporation. In April, Kaiser purchased Willys-Overland Motors, Inc.

• White Motor Co. purchased Autocar Company and announced plans for a $2 million Autocar plant at Exton, Pa.

• General Motors dedicated its new

2,280-acre Desert Proving Ground near Phoenix, Ariz.

• Six experimental cars were displayed by U.S. auto makers during 1953. Buick had the Wildcat; Lincoln-Mercury displayed its fiberglas body XL-500; Packard unveiled the Balboa; Hudson introduced the Italia; Dodge exhibited the hand-

1953 — Dodge offered a V-8 engine. It was the first year in U.S. automotive history that more eight- than six-cylinder engines were produced.

1953 continued

built Firearrow; and De Soto showed a four-passenger sports car, the Adventurer.

• Motor vehicles were used in an atomic bomb test in Nevada during March to determine the effects for civilian defense data.

• General Motors purchased the outstanding stock in the Euclid Road Machinery Company.

• Ford Motor Company purchased a 177-acre site at Mahwah, N.J., for a Ford Division assembly plant.

• Chevrolet announced plans to add 160,000 square feet to its Cleveland plant.

• Chrysler Corporation purchased the automotive plants and machinery of the Briggs Manufacturing Company.

• The Korean truce agreement was signed at Panmunjom, July 26.

• A multi-million-dollar fire destroyed the General Motors transmission plant in Livonia, Mich., on August 12, cutting off production of Hydra-Matic transmissions. Until other facilities could be arranged, Cadillac and Oldsmobile used Dynaflow transmissions and Pontiac adapted Powerglide units as optional equipment. Hydra-Matic production operations were shifted to another plant until General Motors purchased the Willow Run assembly plant from Kaiser Motors for automatic transmission output.

• Radio Corporation of America (RCA) announced the development of safety electronic steering and braking controls which would stop or change the course of a car when an obstacle was in the path of the vehicle.

• Production started on Chevrolet's plastic laminated Fiberglas body sports car, the Corvette.

• An American Automobile Association study showed that the average motorist drove 10,000 miles a year and paid about $908 for car maintenance and operation.

• Features offered in 1953 included: air conditioning on a number of makes; automatic transmissions on nearly all cars as optional equipment, and standard equipment in more expensive models; 12-volt electrical system, to replace six-volt systems; warning lights to replace oil pressure and generator gauges in several makes; and tinted, Plexiglas roofs on some hardtop models.

• With the popularity of V-8 engines, the number of eight-cylinder engines exceeded the six-cylinder power plants in new passenger cars for the first time.

• Buick offered the Skylark deluxe convertible in the $5,000 price bracket. It was built to commemorate Buick's 50th anniversary.

1954

1954 — Buick offered the Century series. Power windows and power front seat were standard equipment on the convertible.

• Several long-established automotive companies merged. Nash-Kelvinator Corporation and Hudson Motor Car Company combined into American Motors Corporation; Studebaker Corporation and Packard Motor Car Company formed Studebaker-Packard Corporation.

• Nearly all automotive companies announced major expansion programs. Research facilities and assembly plants received the largest share of capital expenditures. General Motors announced it would spend more than $1 billion in two years; Chrysler worked out a 100-year loan of $250 million with Prudential Insurance Company of America for expansion and modernizations; and Ford invested millions in property and construction for future needs.

• The Automotive History collection of the Detroit Public Library was opened to the public in February. Some of the acquisitions of automobilia in the collection included: Charles B. King Collection, Andrew Lee Dyke Collection and the Nicholas Lazarnick Picture Collection. The Automobile Manufacturers Association and others donated funds for the purchase of many important acquisitions in the Automotive History Collection.

• Eight experimental cars were introduced during the year — Dodge's Granada; Packard's Fiberglas sports model, the Panther; a gas turbine-powered XP-21 Firebird by General Motors; the Belmont and Explorer by Plymouth; Lincoln-Mercury's Monterey XM-800; the FX-Atmos dream car by Ford; and De Soto's Adventurer II.

• Packard adopted tubeless tires as standard equipment in June. By the end of the year, all other U.S. manufacturers offered tubeless tires as original equipment.

• The first section of New York State's $962 million Thruway system opened June 24.

• A gas turbine engine developed by Chrysler Corporation was installed in a regular production Plymouth passenger car and successfully road tested. The test demonstrated the solution to two major problems in gas turbine engineering — high fuel consumption and exhaust heat — which had previously blocked passenger car application of gas turbine power.

• Ford introduced the two-passenger Thunderbird in October.

• All automotive manufacturing in American Motors was moved to Kenosha, Wis.

• Ford Motor Company purchased 4,000 acres of land near Romeo, Mich., for development of a multi-million-dollar proving ground. Chrysler dedicated its new Engineering Proving Ground near Chelsea, Mich.

• Kaiser Motors Corporation transferred Willys body operations from Detroit to Toledo, Ohio.

• Improved sealed-beam headlamps, developed cooperatively through engineering committees of the Automobile Manufacturers Association and lamp manufacturers, were demonstrated. The new headlamps were on all new U.S. passenger cars by the middle of 1955.

• West Virginia's new 88-mile turnpike was opened on Nov. 8.

• A 22-mile section of the Northern Ohio Turnpike opened to the public on Dec. 1, linking Youngstown with the Pennsylvania Turnpike.

• Louis Matter of San Diego, Calif., and two friends completed the first non-stop motor trip from Anchorage, Alaska, to Mexico City, Mexico, a distance of 6,391 miles.

• General Motors Corporation produced its 50-millionth car, a 1955 Chevrolet.

• President Dwight D. Eisenhower authorized the creation of a permanent President's Action Committee for Highway Safety.

• New features offered by car makers on 1955 models included panoramic wraparound windshields; safety padding on dash boards; cowl ventilator air intakes at the bottom of the windshield; automatic transmission selector lever on the dash of Chrysler Corporation cars; dual headlamps and curved glass side windows on the Cadillac El Camino; V-8 engines for Plymouth and Chevrolet; overhead valves for all Ford car and truck engines; and push button control for lubrication of chassis and suspension on the Mercury and the Lincoln.

1955 —
Continental
Mark II.

1955

• The automotive industry broke all records in motor vehicle production during 1955. Output totaled 9,204,049 units, including 7,950,377 passenger cars, 1,249,576 trucks and 4,096 motor coaches.

• Ford Motor Company announced plans to build a glass manufacturing plant at Nashville, Tenn., and moved assembly operations from Edgewater to Mahwah, N.J.; Chrysler Corporation bought Universal Products Company, makers of automotive drive shafts and their components; Plymouth opened its new V-8 engine plant in Detroit; Chrysler announced plans to construct a large stamping plant at Twinsburg, Ohio; and General Motors automotive divisions added to their plant facilities.

• Newcomers to the automotive field were Tri-Car, Inc., with a three-wheeled plastic body model selling for about $1,000, and Dual Motors Corporation of Detroit with a limited production sports car, the Firebomb, with a Ghia-built body from Italy on a U.S.-produced chassis.

• Kaiser and Willys announced plans to drop passenger car production to concentrate on Jeep vehicles.

• Kaiser Motors Corporation was reorganized as Kaiser Industries Corporation, with Willys Motors,

Inc., a wholly owned subsidiary.

• The U.S. Department of Commerce announced plans to conduct a road test near Ottawa, Illinois, to determine the durability of several methods of highway construction. Cooperating with funds, personnel and equipment were: Bureau of Public Roads, American Association of State Highway Officials, Department of Defense, Automobile Manufacturers Association, petroleum industry and other allied fields.

• Improved sealed-beam headlamps were installed in all new passenger cars by July.

• Ohio's 241-mile turnpike was opened from the Pennsylvania Turnpike to west of Montpelier, Ohio, on Oct. 1.

• Safety door latches to help prevent doors from being forced open in collisions were made standard equipment on nearly all makes. Vehicle manufacturers also increased emphasis on seat belts.

• Michigan was the first state to require a course in driver education before licenses could be issued to youths under 18.

• Four-door hardtop models, offered by several manufacturers, became the vogue in body style.

• Experimental vehicles displayed during the year were: Chevrolet's Biscayne, the Strato-Star by Pontiac, Oldsmobile's Delta, the Wildcat III from Buick, Cadillac's Eldorado

Brougham, the V-6 powered LaSalle II by General Motors, Chrysler Corporation's Flight Sweep I and II along with the Falcon, Ford's plastic Mystere, General Motors' Firebird II gas turbine car, Ford's Futura – a $250,000 laboratory on wheels- and the Universelle truck by General Motors Coach and Truck.

• Ford Motor Company's Continental Mark II was introduced at most Lincoln dealerships in October as a 1956 model.

• Studebaker entered the sports car field with the 1956 model Hawk in November.

• American Motors offered a V-8 engine in the Ambassador line; Packard introduced a V-8 along with torsion bar suspension; and Chevrolet added the Nomad model at the top of its station wagon line.

• The American Automobile Association stopped its sanctioning of automobile races.

• Cadillac offered a trunk lid lock control operated from the driver's seat.

• A push-button, automatic-transmission selector replaced lever controls on the steering columns of 1956 model Chrysler, Imperial, De Soto, Dodge, Plymouth and Packard cars. A record player was also optional on Chrysler Corporation cars. Packard offered electrically-controlled door-latches and a non-slip differential.

1956

1956 — A 41,000-mile national network of super highways was started under a $32.4 billion interstate highway program.

• Ford Motor Company stock was offered to the public for the first time; more than 10 million shares owned by the Ford Foundation were offered at $64.50 per share. At the first public stockholders' meeting in May, Ford officials announced a $592 million expansion program for 1956.

• A new Dual Headlighting System for motor vehicles was announced by the Automobile Manufacturers Association. Scheduled for introduction by the automotive industry for the 1958 models, the system comprised four 5 3/4-inch sealed-beam headlamps instead of two 7-inch units. This enabled the high and low beams to be aimed separately.

• Armco Steel Company purchased the grounds and buildings of the American Bantam Company; the remaining assets were bought by Pressed Metals of America, Inc.

• Dual Motors Corp. changed the name of its car from Firebomb to Dual-Ghia.

• General Motors displayed a free-piston engine which burned any type of fuel — from high octane gasoline to whale oil, peanut oil and other vegetable fats.

• Ford Motor Company joined the Automobile Manufacturers Association, Inc.

• A 41,000 mile interstate highway system was approved as a result of the Highway Act of 1956. The law committed the federal government to meet 90 percent of the cost, with states and localities supplying the remainder. The highway program was set up on a "pay-as-you-go" basis with the establishment of a Highway Trust Fund supported by highway use taxes to finance the federal share. Federal gasoline and diesel oil taxes were increased one cent on July 1 when the Highway Act became effective.

• Production of the Packard car in Detroit stopped at the end of the 1956 model year; all operations were transferred to Studebaker-Packard Corporation's plants in South Bend, Ind.

• The 156-mile Northern Indiana Toll road was opened Sept. 18. It crossed the state from Gary, at the west edge of Indiana, to the western terminal of the Ohio Turnpike, completing a toll system and enabling motorists to drive from the Chicago area to New York City on super-highways.

• Chrysler Corporation's gas turbine powered experimental Plymouth was driven from New York to Los Angeles.

• American Motors Corporation developed a 62-horsepower V-4 air-cooled engine that weighed 200 pounds.

• The 42nd National Automobile Show, first since 1940, was held in New York's new Coliseum. More than 300,000 square feet of exhibition space on three floors were filled with 1957 car and truck models, and a musical revue was presented on a huge stage. All American passenger cars were displayed along with 11 truck and bus exhibits. It was the first time a National Automobile Show was televised — an estimated 21,600,600 people, in 115 communities across the nation, saw the hour-long network show. The speaker at the industry's traditional banquet was Vice President Richard M. Nixon, who delivered the first major foreign policy address ever made by a vice president of the United States.

• New features on the 1957 models displayed at the National Auto Show included: torsion bar suspension on Chrysler Corporation cars; optional fuel injection on the Rambler, Pontiac and Chevrolet; dual headlamps on some makes; rear facing seats in nine-passenger Plymouth station wagons; 14-inch wheels on three-quarters of the 1957 makes; curved side window glass on the Imperial; retractable rear window controlled from the dash on the Mercury; the Turbo-glide automatic transmission (three turbines and planetary gears with a hill retarder) on the Chevrolet; a metal top retractable convertible introduced by Ford; six-way power seats offered by several manufacturers; electric door locks offered by several luxury lines; a speedometer buzzer which sounded when a preset speed was reached; and a non-slip differential offered by several manufacturers.

1957

1957 — Rambler station wagons featured a roof travel rack.

1957 — Ford introduced a retractable hardtop convertible.

• Historic and production milestones for the year included Oldsmobile's 60th anniversary, Pontiac's golden anniversary (founded as the Oakland Motor Car Company), the Automotive Safety Foundation's 20th anniversary, Plymouth's 10-millionth car, and the three-millionth Mercury.

• The Bureau of Public Roads approved 85 miles of the Kansas State Turnpike for inclusion in the Interstate Highway System.

• White Motor Company purchased the assets of Reo Motors, Inc., of Lansing, Mich., a Pioneer automotive firm.

• A station wagon body was offered on the Packard Clipper — the first of this style for Packard since 1950.

• Studebaker offered a low-priced economy model with minimum trim details, the Scotsman.

• The board of directors of the Automobile Manufacturers Association, Inc., at its annual June meeting adopted a resolution to exclude speed and racing from automotive advertising and publicity.

• Ford production of its two-passenger Thunderbird stopped to prepare for a four-passenger model.

• Nash and Hudson names were dropped by American Motors Corporation with the end of the 1957 model. The firm announced its 1958 cars would be part of the Rambler line.

• The five-mile Mackinac Bridge, linking the two Michigan peninsulas, opened in November. Before the bridge was built motorists used state-operated ferry boats to cross the Straits of Mackinac.

• Chevrolet and General Motors Truck and Coach Division displayed an experimental turbine-powered truck, the Turbo-Titan.

• Ford Motor Company developed an aluminum experimental military vehicle with unitized construction.

• One new car make and a number of features were offered for the 1958 model year. The Dual Headlamp System (four lamps) was adopted by nearly all makes. Ford Motor Company introduced the Edsel, which had self-adjusting brakes, push button automatic transmission in the center of the steering wheel, a floating drum-type speedometer and a single air conditioner and heater control. The

Lincoln and Continental had unit body construction; an exterior side mirror with adjustment controls inside the car was available on the Lincoln-Continental and Cadillac; and air suspension was optional equipment on the Ford, Mercury and all General Motors cars. An off-center rear spring mounting to reduce diving when braking was offered by Studebaker-Packard. Paper air cleaners were used on a number of makes. Aluminum brake drums with cooling fins were offered on the Buick; a double compound windshield extended into the roof line on all Chrysler Corporation cars; and rear coil springs were offered on more than half of the models. Body dip method of prime painting to reduce rust was used on the Rambler, Lincoln and Continental. A removable transistor radio on some General Motors cars was optional equipment, and a device designed to hold a car at a preselected speed for long open country trips was available on Chrysler, Imperial and Cadillac. Hardtop models were added to the Studebaker's President and Commander series; and Chevrolet added the luxury Impala series to its line of cars.

1957 — Plymouth had a low silhouette and featured a torsion bar front suspension system.

1958

• Four automotive milestones were noted during the year. Ford Motor Company produced its 50-millionth motor vehicle; Chrysler Corporation assembled its 25-millionth motor vehicle; General Motors Corporation celebrated its 50th anniversary of incorporation; and Ford Division commemorated the 50th anniversary of the Model T by reassembling a 1909 Model T at the Mahwah, N.J., plant.

• Connecticut's 129-mile turnpike opened to traffic in January, extending from Greenwich to Killingly on the Rhode Island state line.

• Additions to the 1958 models included: Mercury's Medalist economy model; American Motor's 100-inch wheelbase Rambler American; and new four-passenger Thunderbird by Ford with unitized body, in hardtop and convertible body styles.

• An additional $1.8 billion was authorized in April to speed up con-struction on the Interstate Highway System.

• Four-Wheel-Drive Auto Company was bought by Paradynamics, Inc., of St. Louis, Mo.

• Ford Motor Company merged three of its car divisions into the Mercury-Edsel-Lincoln (M-E-L) Division.

• Studebaker-Packard Corporation announced cessation of the Packard automobile and concentration on a car with a new smaller wheelbase, the Lark.

• Chrysler Corporation purchased 25 percent of the stock of Simca, a French automotive firm.

• Plans for a $17,000 hand-made car to be called the Argonaut were announced by Argonaut Motor Machine Corp. of Cleveland, Ohio.

• A seven-year study by the University of Michigan to design a secondary school test for prospective students of automotive mechanics was launched by the Automobile Manufacturers Association, Inc. The study was planned to aid in selection and

1958 — The Thunderbird was restyled with a rear seat and unitized body construction.

1958 — Chevrolet added the Impala series which featured sculptural styling.

1958 continued

guidance and thus to relieve the shortage of competent mechanics.

• Goodyear Tire and Rubber Company introduced a double-chambered captive-air safety tire to avoid complete blow-outs.

• At least three full size or scaled-down operating models of antique automobiles were offered for sale.

• General Motors engineers demonstrated a car equipped to steer itself over a special road with wire buried in the road surface. Later in the year the firm displayed the Firebird III experimental car with a single-stick control system which eliminated the steering wheel, brake pedal and accelerator pedal. The car also had a separate power plant for accessories.

• Ford Motor Company displayed a three-foot model of a Glideair vehicle which traveled on a thin cushion of air instead of wheels. A scooter version was also displayed.

• The Automobile Information Disclosure Act, more commonly known as "the price label law," was passed during the summer to be effective Oct. 1. The new law required every automobile manufacturer to affix a label to the windshield or side window containing the following information: make, model and serial number, final assembly point, name and address of the dealer receiving the car, method of transport from the final assembly point to place of delivery, suggested retail price of the car, factory installed optional accessories, and transportation and delivery charges.

• Checker Motors Corporation announced plans to produce the Superba passenger car.

• Highlights and features offered in the fall for the 1959 model year included: swivel front seats as optional equipment on Chrysler Corporation cars; side view mirror controls inside the car on several makes; on Chrysler cars an electronic control which changed the rear view mirror to non-glaring

automatically when a headlamp beam hit its surface. Oldsmobile offered a flanged brake drum for faster cooling; the Lark compact car was introduced by Studebaker-Packard; the Galaxie luxury series was added to the Ford line; a town car and limousine were offered in the Continental line; new body finishes that retained a luster for a greater period without waxing became standard on most passenger cars; a trunk lid catch electrically released inside the car by the driver was offered by Ford Motor Company; individually adjustable separate reclining seats were available on the Rambler; Buick renamed its line of cars — Electra (luxury), Invicta (medium) and LeSabre (lowest priced); a seat lock to prevent the back of the right front seat from suddenly moving forward was offered by Buick; and metals on tail pipe and muffler components were plated and made heavier.

1959

1959 —
The Imperial
Southhampton
hardtop had
a stainless
steel roof.

• During this year Pontiac Motor Division of General Motors produced its seven-millionth motor vehicle.

• Five experimental vehicles were displayed in 1959: De Soto had a scale model of the Cella I which featured an electrochemical system that converted liquid fuel into electrical energy to power the car; Cadillac showed its Cyclone experimental car equipped with a radar device to warn the driver of objects in the car's path; Ford Motor Company demonstrated the Levacar which floated on a cushion of air above the ground and was propelled by small jets of compressed air; Curtiss-Wright Corporation announced the development of its Air-Car, a 300-horsepower vehicle designed to travel on a cushion of low-pressure, low velocity air at a height of six to 12 inches; and Chevrolet displayed a heavy duty Turbo-Titan II dream truck equipped with an experimental gas turbine engine.

• Three firms announced plans to manufacture electric vehicles — Nic-L-Silver Battery Company of Santa Ana, Calif.; Stinson Aircraft and Tool Engineering Corporation of San Diego, Calif.; and Cleveland Vehicle Company of Cleveland, Ohio.

• National Standard Parts Association and the Motor and Equipment Wholesalers Association merged to form the Automotive Service Industries Association.

• Chrysler Corporation announced plans to produce glass at its Detroit-area McGraw plant. The firm also realigned its car sales division by forming the Plymouth-De Soto Division, Chrysler-Imperial Division and the Dodge Division (cars and trucks).

• Ford Motor Company established a credit and financing subsidiary, the Ford Motor Credit Company, with the first office in Indianapolis, Ind.

• The launching of the first mass produced Jupiter ballistic missile, made by Chrysler Corporation in Detroit, was announced by the U.S. Army.

• A caravan of 16 motor vehicles with 39 men, women and children, known as the '59ers, drove from Detroit to Alaska's Susitan Valley (90 miles north of Anchorage) to homesteads in the 49th state. Marino Sik of Detroit led the pioneers over the 4,239-mile trip in 25 days.

• Two new types of power plants were reported during the year: Curtiss-Wright Corporation and NSU Werke of West Germany announced a rotary internal combustion engine for automotive, aircraft and marine use — the engine reportedly had only a few moving parts. Williams Research Company of Walled Lake, Mich., reported the development of a low-cost, lightweight, medium horsepower gas turbine engine using a heat exchange principle.

• Willys offered the Maverick Special — a deluxe Jeep station wagon.

• Plans for the 43rd National Automobile Show to be held in Detroit's new Cobo Hall in October of 1960 were announced by the Automobile Manufacturers Association, Inc.

• Federal tax on gasoline was increased from three to four cents a gallon to keep the Interstate Highway System on a "pay-as-you-go" basis.

• A new seven-inch headlamp, with the approximate low beam advantages of the Dual Headlamp System, was offered for vehicles using two, instead of four, headlamps. It was developed by lamp and motor vehicle manufacturers through a committee of the Automobile Manufacturers Association.

• Four new makes were offered to the motoring public for 1960. Dodge Division introduced the

1959 continued

Dart; Chevrolet offered a light aluminum air-cooled rear engine car — the Corvair; Ford introduced the Falcon economy line; and Plymouth offered its new Valiant.

• Highlighted features offered on the 1960 models included: a convertible and four-door station wagon added to the Studebaker Lark series; electroluminescent dash lighting to reduce eye strain in night driving on Chrysler Corporation cars; an alternator and rectifier a.c. generating system on the Valiant; unit body construction for Plymouth, De Soto, Dodge, Chrysler, Valiant, Corvair and Falcon; folding rear seat for luggage space on the Corvair; vacuum operated remote trunk lock control inside the car on the Oldsmobile; and vacuum safety door locks on most Chrysler cars. Also offered were: torsion bar suspension on Chevrolet trucks; a dual chambered water pump for even distribution on both cylinder banks on the V-8 Pontiac; an automatic control to turn on headlamps when driving at dusk on the Buick; an air cooled torque converter transmission on the Falcon; and an adjustable mirror on the Buick to reflect the instrument panel for different heights of drivers. Other features were: a side-hinged rear station wagon door on the Rambler; self-adjusting brakes on the Cadillac; an automatic vacuum parking brake release when the transmission is put into drive position on the Cadillac; a sliding sunroof on Thunderbird hardtop models; an anti-theft ignition switch with three blade terminals in Ford Motor Company cars; non-round steering wheels by Chrysler; and a four-light emergency flashing system on Chrysler cars.

• Ford Motor Company discontinued the Edsel line in November.

• A device designed to eliminate substantial portions of smog-producing hydro-carbon emissions from automobiles would be offered on 1961 American cars produced for sale in California, the Automobile Manufacturers Association, Inc., announced on Nov. 30. The device reduced vapors from the engine crankcase by diverting them through the intake manifold.

1960

1960 — National Auto Show, for the first time in Detroit, drew 1,403,872 visitors.

• Five new smaller, or compact, automobiles were introduced during the year, bringing to 10 the total of American makes in this class. Lincoln-Mercury offered the Comet (1960 model) in March. The other four makes were 1961 models introduced in the fall — Buick's Special (aluminum V-8 engine), Oldsmobile's F-85 (aluminum V-8 engine), Pontiac's Tempest (front-mounted four-cylinder engine or a V-8 as optional equipment, and a trans-axle in the rear), and Dodge's new Lancer.

• Eight automotive companies expanded their operations. American Motors added to its Kenosha and Milwaukee, Wis., plants. Ford Motor Company purchased Sherman Products (manufacturers of Ford tractor accessories) and announced plans for a glass research and development center in Lincoln Park, Mich. Chrysler Corporation dedicated a new assembly plant near St. Louis, Mo. General Motors expanded its facilities at Warren and at Willow Run, Mich., and at Tarrytown, N.Y. Mack Trucks, Inc., announced plans to build a new plant at Hagerstown, Md.. Studebaker-

Packard Corporation acquired three firms. White Motor Company bought Oliver Corporation's farm equipment manufacturing business.

• Several announcements in the experimental field were reported: General Motors offered the "electric fence" which would warn the driver if the vehicle was near the pavement edge, and a nuclear-powered combat vehicle for the Defense Department; Chevrolet displayed the XP-700 Corvette experimental car, and Plymouth exhibited the NXR experimental sports car; Ford announced a new process for making open hearth steel that would cut production time in half.

• Glen Pray of Tulsa, Okla., purchased the assets of the Auburn, Cord and Duesenberg auto plant at Auburn, Indiana, and announced plans to produce parts for the three cars.

• Several all-weather radiator coolants were offered by antifreeze makers.

• Studies by the Automobile Manufacturers Association, Inc., showed windshield and window areas of 1960 cars provided 15 percent greater vision for the driver compared with 1950 models. The AMA also announced grants totaling $1,706,000 to a number of organizations to promote traffic safety and efficient use of highways.

• The U.S. Bureau of Public Roads reported that more than 9,100 miles of the 41,000-mile Interstate Highway System were completed, and that 4,700 additional miles were under construction.

• International Harvester Company reported it would produce a sport utility vehicle, the Scout. The new vehicle would have a four-cylinder engine and an integral body.

• The National Automobile Show in Detroit's new 10-acre Cobo Hall during October officially opened the 1961 model year. Sponsored by the

1960 — One feature of Detroit's Show was a carousel of cars circling the great stage.

Automobile Manufacturers Association, it was the first national show since 1956 and the first industry-sponsored show to open outside New York City. The show, with its "Wheels of Freedom" theme, set a new international record for attendance at any industrial show — nearly 1.5 million persons. More than 300 cars, trucks and motor coaches were displayed in the 300,000 square foot exhibition space. Suppliers to the automotive industry co-operated with the vehicle manufacturers to put on an "Auto Wonderland" exhibit, a 104,000 square-foot display telling how a car is made. The U.S. Post Office issued a special Wheels of Freedom commemorative four-cent stamp in conjunction with the show's opening day. President Dwight D. Eisenhower was the principal speaker at the industry's traditional banquet.

• New features on the 1961 models displayed at the National Auto Show included: an economy line of trucks and vans by Ford (Econoline) and Chevrolet Corvair; a four-door soft top convertible on the Lincoln-Continental; pre-lubrication on a number of chassis points with a special grease for 30,000 miles on Ford, Mercury and Lincoln-Continental; a life-time chassis lubrication on Cadillac; a sliding soft roof on the Lark; aluminized

mufflers and self-adjusting brakes on the Ford; ceramic-coated muffler and tail pipe on the Rambler; an aluminum six-cylinder Rambler engine; a swing-away steering wheel to assist the driver getting into or out of the Thunderbird; and two-level air conditioning to cool the top level of the car while heating the lower level for dehumidifying on the Cadillac.

• Each U.S. automobile company provided embossed pads in the floor pan so dealers could make seat belt installations more easily.

• New car warranties were extended by all manufacturers to at least 12 months or 12,000 miles, whichever came first.

• The Lincoln-Continental warranty was extended to 24 months or 24,000 miles.

• Chrysler Corporation announced it would discontinue the De Soto at the end of November.

• Two rebate plans were disclosed. Studebaker-Packard offered shareholders a refund of $100 for buying a Studebaker car or truck during a three-month period. American Motors Corporation offered U.S. savings bonds as rebates to purchasers of its cars during a four-month period, providing the firm's car sales rose 10 percent above the same period in the previous year.

1961

1961 —
Restyled
Falcon
featured a
convex-
shaped
aluminum
grille.

1961 — The extra space
in the passenger
compartment and trunk
introduced a pleasant
luxury to the Dodge
Lancer.

• Chevrolet Motor Division produced its 44-millionth vehicle.

• Five experimental vehicles were exhibited during the year. Chrysler Corporation displayed its Turboflite and X7, both powered by a gas turbine engine. Ford Motor Company exhibited the two-wheeled gyroscope-controlled Gyron. Dodge Division's Fleetwing went on display in New York. Ford Motor Company unveiled a scale model of a 200-passenger Levacar, called the Aerolus. The vehicle moved on a film of air a fraction of an inch above special rail surfaces.

• New mid-year models introduced by the industry included: Cadillac Division's Town Sedan in the Calais series; Oldsmobile Division's Starfire sports convertible, a three-seat station wagon in the F-85 series, the F-85 Cutlass and F-85 economy club coupe; Chrysler Corporation's Enforcer, a new

model especially equipped for police work, and the Hylander in the Newport series; American Motors' Custom 400 Series in the Rambler American, Classic and Ambassador V-8 lines; Ford Division's Futura in the Falcon line; Dodge Division's 770 Lancer sports coupe; and Buick Division's Skylark, a top-of-the-line model in the Special series.

• New models offered in the fall for the 1962 model year included: Chevrolet's new Chevy II series; Mercury's Meteor series; Pontiac's Gran Prix series and LeMans in the Tempest series; Studebaker-Packard's Gran Turismo in the Hawk series; and Chrysler's 300-H, a high performance sports-type car.

• Numerous product innovations were introduced with the 1962 models. Dual-brake systems became standard equipment on all 1962 American Motors and Cadillac

models. American Motors announced it would offer factory-installed seat belts on all Ramblers for both front and rear seats. American Motors also introduced the E-stick automatic clutch transmission on its Rambler American series. The driver shifts gears manually, but the clutch is automatically engaged and disengaged.

• Ford Motor Company introduced a clutch interlock for manual transmissions that prevented shifting into low or reverse by mistake.

• Single-leaf rear-spring suspension systems were offered on the Chevy II. Dodge Dart, Phoenix, and Pioneer models adopted dual tail lights as standard equipment. Ford Motor Company offered an engine coolant said to be good for 30,000 miles or two years of driving.

• The Detroit Diesel Engine Division of General Motors

unveiled a group of 12 engines which could run on a complete range of fuels from gasoline to diesel fuel. In addition, the division developed conversion kits which could change present diesel engines into multi-fuel engines.

• Ford Motor Company purchased the Philco Corporation and two Electric Autolite company plants. Studebaker-Packard purchased Chemical Compounds, Inc., makers of STP, a motor-oil additive, and bought Curtiss-Wright Corporation's South Bend plant.

American Motors opened a new engineering and research unit in Kenosha, Wisconsin. Chrysler Corporation combined the marketing operations of its Chrysler-Imperial Division and Plymouth Division into a single Chrysler-Plymouth Division. Oldsmobile Division dedicated a new engineering center.

• Most major tire producers developed two-ply tires as a replacement for four-ply tires on compact cars. Goodyear Tire and Rubber Company announced production of

Budene, a new synthetic rubber expected to nearly double the life of tires.

• Chrysler Corporation engineers drove a turbine-powered Dodge Dart from New York to Los Angeles for an engineering evaluation run.

• Secretary of Commerce Luther H. Hodges announced the official start of the National Driver Register Service. The service cross-indexed data on motorists in 43 states whose licenses have been revoked on charges of drunken driving or highway-death cases.

1962

1962 — The Studebaker Gran Turismo incorporated a low silhouette, flat roof line and long tapering hood.

• General Motors produced its 75-millionth car, a Bonneville convertible, made by Pontiac Division. Ford Motor Company became the first automobile manufacturer to reach the 30 million mark in production of V-8 engines.

• Shelby American, Inc., a Los Angeles-based firm, began producing a high-performance sports car called the Cobra. The car was powered by a Ford V-8 engine, the chassis and aluminum body were made in England.

• Studebaker dropped the Packard name from its corporate title.

• Amber lights for front turn signals were adopted by the entire industry after a recommendation by the Automobile Manufacturers Association Board of Directors. Extensive visibility tests proved that amber signals are seen more readily against glaring reflections than white signals.

• Fourteen mid-year makes were introduced: Buick's new sports models, the Wildcat hardtop and the Skylark convertible; Checker Motors Corporation's new station wagon, the Aerobus, available in 9- or 12-passenger models; Chevrolet's Corvair Monza convertible and Monza Spyder; Dodge's Custom 880; Ford's Galaxy 500XL,

Fairlane Sports Coupe and Falcon Sports Futura; Lincoln-Mercury's Villager, a compact station wagon; Oldsmobile's Jetfire sports coupe, the first American production car equipped with a fluid injected turbo-charged V-8 engine; Plymouth's Sports Fury; and Studebaker's new sports coupe, the Avanti.

• New models introduced in the fall included: Buick's Riviera; Checker's station wagon, the Texan; Chrysler's two-door hardtop model, the 300-J; and Studebaker's new Lark Standard series, aimed at the fleet buyer.

1962 — Simulated wood paneling distinguished the styling of the Mercury Comet Villager.

1962 continued

• The tire and rubber industry announced several new developments. A new tire cord made of polyester fiber that combined the best features of nylon and rayon was developed by Goodyear Tire and Rubber Company. A tire introduced by the General Tire and Rubber Company was claimed to last 50,000 miles or more. A new chemical bonding agent that solved the problem of ply and tread separation was introduced by U.S. Rubber.

• Numerous new features and product innovations were introduced on new model cars. Studebaker's 1963s featured front-wheel disc brakes as an option, and as standard equipment on the Avanti. Self-adjusting brakes were installed on most 1963 models. All models were provided with seat-belt anchors for the front seat. Pontiac offered a fully transistorized ignition system as an option on its 1963 models.

• The industry started nationwide installation of positive crankcase ventilating systems on all 1963 model cars and light trucks.

• Developments in the gas turbine-engine field continued. To test consumer acceptance, Chrysler Corporation started building 50 turbine-powered passenger cars for distribution to selected motorists in the latter part of 1963. Ford Motor Company tested an experimental turbine-engine in a 1955 Thunderbird.

• New experimental cars exhibited during the year included: Ford's Cougar 406, a sports model featuring electrically operated gull-wing doors; Chevrolet's Cerv-I; Pontiac's Monte Carlo, a two-passenger luxury model featuring magnesium wheels; and American Motors' Metropolitan Royal Runabout.

• Continental Motors produced a new multi-fuel engine for the Army, called the Hypercycle LDS-427-2.

• The 44th National Automobile Show was visited by 1,147,742 persons during its nine-day run in Detroit's Cobo Hall.

• A scaled-down version of the famed Cord 810, the Sportsman, was announced by Glenn Pray of Oklahoma for limited production.

• The International Rectifier Company unveiled a solar energy-propelled Baker electric (1912 vintage) car. The vehicle was outfitted with a roof deck composed of 10,640 individual solar cells.

• American Motors opened an Eastern Division Parts Warehouse in Philadelphia and announced a major expansion program at its Kelvinator plant in Grand Rapids, Mich. Ford Motor Company completed a major expansion program at its Metuchen, N.J., plant. General Motors erected new buildings or additions at its plant in Warren, Mich., at its Saginaw Steering Gear Division Plant and at its Cadillac Division Detroit plant. Chrysler Corporation purchased a plant in Warren, Mich., for the construction of mobile airport lounges. Studebaker Corporation acquired Paxton Products, Inc., a maker of superchargers for automobiles and other vehicles, and also purchased the Franklin Manufacturing Company, a Minneapolis manufacturer of refrigerators and other appliances.

1963

1963 — An engineering and consumer evaluation program was launched by Chrysler Corporation with its specially designed turbine car.

• Studebaker halted production of automobiles in the United States on December 20. While continuing to sell cars in the U.S. market, the company moved its primary base of automotive manufacturing to Hamilton, Ontario.

• The Marmon-Herrington Company, after 31 years in operation, announced it would leave the automotive business.

• Kaiser Jeep Corporation, formerly Willys Motors, Inc., moved its headquarters from Toledo, Ohio, to Oakland, Calif. The Automotive Division of the corporation maintained its executive offices and operations in Toledo.

• Two production milestones were established during the year. Ford Motor Company produced its 60-millionth vehicle, and Chevrolet Division produced its 50-millionth vehicle.

• New 1963 models introduced included: Chrysler's new luxury model, the New Yorker Salon; Lincoln-Mercury's Comet Sportster and the Marauder in its regular series; and Studebaker's Super-Lark and Super-Hawk.

• Checker Motor Corporation revealed technical details of a new Town Custom limousine scheduled for limited production.

• Five new 1964 models were introduced in the fall of the year. Chevrolet brought out a new line of cars called the Chevelle.

Oldsmobile introduced its new Jetstar 88 series and a new sports-type car, the Jetstar I. Studebaker unveiled its new model, the Challenger. Lincoln-Mercury added the Caliente series to its Comet Line.

• Lincoln-Mercury dropped its Meteor line at the end of the 1963 model run.

• Experimental vehicles with internal combustion engines and turbine power plants were exhibited during the year. Chrysler Corporation introduced a new turbine engine in a specially styled Chrysler turbine

1963 — The highly stylized Buick Riviera was introduced in the fall of 1962 as a two-door hardtop.

1963 continued

car. Ford Motor Company began testing a 300-HP turbine engine in an experimental truck. Pontiac introduced the X-400. Oldsmobile exhibited the J-TR, a four-passenger convertible. Plymouth unveiled its experimental convertible, the Satellite. The Monza GT and Monza SS were exhibited by Chevrolet. Ford Motor Company unveiled the Allegro, Cougar II and Mustang II.

• Lincoln-Mercury introduced the Super Cyclone, Mercury Montego and Super Marauder.

• Major construction completed at existing plant sites during the year included: General Motors' expansion and modernization of its Tarrytown, N.Y., Chevrolet and Fisher Body assembly plants; Ford Motor Company's expansion of its assembly facilities at the Rouge plant in Dearborn, Mich.; and completion of a new final assembly line at American Motors' Kenosha, Wis., assembly plant.

• Studebaker Corporation, following a policy of making running rather than annual model changes, began installing seat belts during March. Front seat belts were installed as standard equipment on all other cars beginning with the 1964 model run. Other innovations developed during the year included: the all new design of the Corvette Sting Ray featured electrically operated headlamps that rotated into position at the flick of a switch; Cadillac Motor Division offered Twilight Sentinel, an option that automatically turned headlights on at dusk or off at dawn when the ignition switch is on.

• Goodyear Tire and Rubber Company introduced a premium safety tire featuring an inner "spare" on which a motorist could continue to drive for 100 miles or more after the outer shell blew.

1964

1964 – The Ford Mustang featured a long hood and short deck with its sports car styling.

• Four automotive milestones were passed during the year. General Motors Corporation, with its five divisions, produced more than four million vehicles in the 1964 model year, the first time any manufacturer had done so. For the first time new car registrations went over the eight million mark. Dodge Division celebrated its 50th year in the automotive industry. Studebaker Corporation stopped producing engines with the close down of its South Bend, Indiana, plant. The company began using engines produced by General Motors.

• Four new sports-type cars appeared during mid-1964. Ford introduced the Mustang, Chrysler-Plymouth unveiled the Barracuda and American Motors brought out the Marlin. Also, Pontiac launched the modern high performance era with the GTO, an optional package on the Tempest.

• New models introduced in the fall for the 1965 model run included: Chrysler-Plymouth's 300-L; Dodge's new intermediate Coronet series, and the Dodge Monaco, a top of the line two-door hardtop; Ford's LTD in the Galaxie series; and Buick's Gran Sports models of the Skylark and Riviera series.

• Fritz Duesenberg, son of one of the brothers who produced Duesenbergs in the 1920s and 1930s, announced that a new firm had been founded in Indianapolis to build modern luxury cars patterned after the famous old Duesenberg.

• The selector pattern of automatic transmissions was standardized as Park-Reverse-Neutral-Drive-Low. Manufacturers began switching to anti-glare suede paint for dashboards. They also offered disc brakes on many 1965 models. Ford applied paint primer by a new process called electrocoating on '64 Thunderbirds and Lincolns.

• American Motors, Ford and General Motors adopted a two-year or 24,000-mile warranty, whichever came first, on all parts except tires. Chrysler Corporation offered a five-year or 50,000-mile warranty on the engine, transmission, driveline and rear axle.

• New plants and expansion programs completed by manufacturers included: General Motors' Fremont, California, assembly plant; Cadillac Division's expansion program at its Detroit facilities, including the dedication of a new engineering center; Ford Motor Company's expansion and conversion of its Nashville, Tenn., factory to the manufacturing of float glass, and the completion of its new steel making facilities at its Rouge plant in Dearborn, Michigan; and American Motor's new engine and axle plant in Kenosha, Wis.

• New experimental vehicles exhibited during the year included: Lincoln-Mercury's Park Lane 400, featuring electric blanket-type heating elements installed in the seats; General Motors' Firebird IV, Runabout and GM-X; Chevrolet's Toronado and Chevy II Super Nova. Other vehicles shown included: Buick's Silver Arrow; American Motors' Rambler Tarpon; Dodge's Charger II; and Ford's experimental station wagon, the Aurora.

• Chrysler Corporation continued its public testing program of its turbine car.

1964 — The fast-back styling of the Plymouth Barracuda included a smooth contour line made by the roof, rear window and rear deck.

1965

• Passenger car and commercial vehicle production in 1965 established all-time records. Automobile production totaled 9,335,277 units, almost 1.4 million above the previous peak established in 1955. Truck and bus production climbed to 1,802,603 units, more than 240,000 vehicles above the previous high established in 1964.

• The United States and Canada agreed to eliminate tariffs on new motor vehicles and original parts for production of new vehicles. The agreement was known as the Automotive Products Trade Act of 1965.

• The U.S. motor vehicle industry granted $10 million to the University of Michigan to establish a highway research institute and to aid in its support for the first five years. The grant was described by university officials as the largest corporate gift ever received by a university for any purpose.

• Chevrolet Division of General Motors became the first producer in the industry to build more than three million cars and trucks in a single year.

• A program to establish a nationwide communications network to aid motorists in distress was announced by the Automobile Manufacturers Association. The system known as HELP for Highway Emergency Locating Plan, called for the use of Citizens Band two-way radio equipment in private passenger cars. Motorists in need of aid would make their needs known on CB Channel Nine where the message could be picked up by a round-the-clock monitoring station within the 10-to-20-mile range of the equipment.

• Experimental vehicles displayed during the year included: American Motors' St. Maritz and the Tahiti; Plymouth's XP-Vip; Lincoln-Mercury's Mercury Astron, Comet Escapade, Comet Cyclone Sportster and Lincoln Continental Coronation Coupe; Dodge's Charger II; Ford's Bordinet Cobra, Mercer Cobra, GT Mark I and the Black Pearl; and Chevrolet's Mako-Shark II and Concours.

• Rear seat belts became standard equipment on all 1966 models. Pontiac introduced an overhead camshaft six-cylinder engine standard on all Tempest, Tempest Custom and LeMans models for

1965 — Fender skirts and stainless steel on the lower body were two styling highlights of the 1965 Pontiac Bonneville.

1965 — Dodge's new intermediate Coronet line of cars included the Coronet 440 four-door sedan.

1965 continued

1966. All Ford station wagons featured a dual tailgate that opened either as a tailgate for loading cargo or sideways as a conventional passenger car door.

• American Motors Corporation dropped the "Rambler" prefix on its Ambassador line.

• The Avanti II, a car similar in design to the Avanti formerly made by Studebaker Corporation, was introduced in August. Made by the Avanti Motor Corporation, South Bend, Ind., the new Avanti had a Fiberglas body and was powered by a Chevrolet engine.

• The Cord Automobile Company of Oklahoma began production of the scaled-down model of the classic Cord of the 1930's called the Sportsman.

• Chevrolet Division introduced the Sportsvan, a vehicle built with a commercial chassis but including passenger car equipment.

• Oldsmobile Division introduced its 1966 Toronado, the first car with front-wheel drive to be built in the United States since 1937. Other new models offered during the fall included: Chrysler-Plymouth Division's Town and Country Station Wagon in the Chrysler Newport series and the Plymouth VIP in the Fury line; American Motors' three new top of the line models, the DPL in the Ambassador line, Rebel in the Classic line and the Rogue in the American line; Ford Motor Company introduced the Bronco, a four-wheeled drive sport utility vehicle, and added the Fairlane 500/XL and Fairlane GT as new models to its existing line; Chevrolet Division introduced the 1965 1/2 Caprice, a top of the line

model in its Impala series; Lincoln-Mercury Division added the Capri to its Mercury Comet series; Dodge Division introduced its new sports fastback, the Charger; and Shelby American, Inc., introduced the Shelby GT 350, a modified high performance version of the Ford Mustang Fastback.

• Chrysler Corporation announced that it had purchased the Lone Star Boat Company of Plano, Texas.

• Major construction of manufacturing facilities completed in 1965 included: Ford Motor Company's Woodhaven, Mich., stamping plant; and Chrysler Corporation's Belvidere, Ill., assembly plant and its stamping plant in Sterling Township, Mich. General Motors dedicated its new training center in Detroit.

1966

1966 — The Vixen, an American Motors experimental car, featured a landau-type roof with canted vents in the rear.

1966 — The distinctive Oldsmobile Toronado featured front-wheel drive.

• After 64 years as an automobile manufacturer, Studebaker Corporation in Canada terminated car production in March. The first Studebaker, an electric vehicle, was built in 1902. The corporation ended production in the United States in December 1963.

• The National Traffic and Motor Vehicle Safety Act was enacted to provide and coordinate a national safety program and establish safety standards for motor vehicles. The Highway Safety Act sought to establish a coordinated national highway safety program through financial assistance to the states to accelerate highway-traffic safety programs. The Department of Transportation was formed to ensure that the general welfare and the economic growth and stability of the nation would benefit from policies that would ensure fast, safe, efficient and convenient transportation at the lowest cost consistent with other national objectives.

• New interest in electric vehicles was aroused as two major motor-vehicle manufacturers outlined their research and testing programs for electric cars. General Motors demonstrated two electric vehicles, a fuel-cell van called the Electrovan and battery-powered Corvair, the Electrovair II. Ford Motor Company announced the development of a new sealed sodium-sulphur battery for electric vehicles designed to last the life of the vehicle.

• Collapsible steering columns were installed on all General Motors, Chrysler Corporation and American Motors cars. Ford Motor Company offered a newly designed energy-absorbing steering wheel featuring a padded hub. Oldsmobile Division offered as an option an engine pre-heater designed to keep carburetor inlet temperatures at about 100 degrees, allowing easier cold-weather starting. Optional on 400- and 425-cubic-inch V-8 Oldsmobile engines was an ultra-high-voltage capacitor system. The new system fired fouled plugs to boost their life nearly four times and eliminated engine ignition tuneup for at least 24,000 miles. General Motors, Ford and American Motors followed Chrysler Corporation in adopting the five-year or 50,000-mile warranty on the engine, transmission, driveline and rear axle. Chrysler extended its total car warranty to 24 months or 24,000 miles. All 1967 cars had underbodies made of corrosion-resistant galvanized steel for added antirust protection.

1966 continued

• Two new sports-type cars were introduced during the fall of the year as 1967 models. Lincoln-Mercury Division brought out its Cougar, and Chevrolet Division introduced its Camaro. Other new models offered included Chevrolet's Concours, an addition to the Chevelle series; Dodge's two additions to its Coronet series, the Coronet SE and R/T; Kaiser JEEP Corporation's Super Wagoneer, a luxury station wagon available in 2-

or 4-wheel drive; Lincoln-Mercury's new series, the Mercury Marquis and Mercury Brougham; Cadillac's five-passenger Fleetwood Eldorado; and the Shelby GT 500 by Shelby American, Inc.

• Production of the Sportsman, a smaller model of the Classic Cord, terminated in July. Less than 100 of the vehicles had been built when the company was placed in receivership.

• Five idea cars were exhibited during the year to test consumer reaction. American Motors displayed Cavalier, Vixen, AMX and AMX II, and Pontiac introduced its Banshee.

• New facilities completed during the year included: the Huber Avenue Foundry in Detroit; General Motors' new Chevrolet and Fisher Body assembly plants at Lordstown, Ohio, and its Central Foundry Division's new iron foundry at Defiance, Ohio; Ford Motor Company's automotive safety research center in Dearborn, Mich.; and American Motors completion of a major expansion program at its proving ground near Burlington, Wis.

1967

1967 — The five-passenger Fleetwood Eldorado combined front-wheel drive, variable ratio power steering and automatic level control for luxury driving.

• By the beginning of 1967, 57 percent of the proposed 41,000 mile National System of Interstate and Defense Highways had been opened to traffic. The year was marked by continuing attention to such problems as safety, exhaust emission, mechanic training and car thefts. Designs for cars produced in 1968 were announced; manufacturers incorporated over 600 new features into their various models during the year.

• Research on electric vehicles reached new levels with the U.S. Department of Commerce holding

a seminar on the subject; eight papers on electrically-powered cars were presented at the annual Society of Automotive Engineers meeting. Ford announced that in conjunction with Ford of Britain it had produced the Comuta, a passenger car driven by electricity. Ford joined with Mobil Oil in a $7 million project to develop emission-free, gas powered vehicles. General Motors showed Electrovair II at the New York International Auto Show and undertook a joint project with the University of Pennsylvania to explore the feasibility of a fleet of small, limited-emission vehicles.

Westinghouse unveiled the Markette, a two-passenger electric.

• Dual braking systems were made available on all 1967 U.S.-produced cars.

• Seven additional states enacted periodic motor vehicle inspection laws, bringing to 26 the number with such laws.

• Mid-year model introductions included: Pontiac Firebird; Buick GS350; new sports models for the Jeepster Commando series; the Opel Rallye Kadett, a German-made car sold by Buick dealers; a new,

1967 — Chevrolet's answer to the popular Ford Mustang was a sporty car called Camaro.

nine passenger, suburban-type station wagon by General Motors Corporation.

• The Pontiac Firebird came with a deflated spare tire as standard equipment, along with a charge of Freon gas for inflation.

• Under the terms of the United States-Canada Import-Export Free Trade Agreement effected in 1965, 1,162,953 vehicles were exported and imported from the United States and Canada during the three years ending in 1967.

• To curb thefts (557,000 reported in 1966), General Motors equipped cars with buzzers that sounded when drivers left their cars while the keys were still in the ignition. Chrysler placed an ignition switch connector in vehicles, making access to the rear of the switch more difficult.

• Medium blue was the most popular color with car buyers in 1967; white was their second choice.

• Ford established an Industrial and Chemical Products Division and formed two subsidiaries, Ford of Europe, Inc., and Ford, Philippines, Inc.

• A.J. Foyt in a Ford-powered Coyote Special won the Indianapolis "500" at a record average speed of 151.207 m.p.h.

• General Motors received a federal grant to study ways to perfect a method whereby motorists can find their destination without maps or road signs. The goal was to develop equipment into which a driver could dial his destination at the start of a trip. A device would then pick up the code of the roadside landmarks and transmit instructions to the driver.

• The Cadillac Eldorado – a 1967 model – featured front-wheel drive.

• Lincoln Continental offered dual chamber tires as original equipment. If the outer chamber of the tire went flat, the inner chamber permitted driving until repairs could be made.

• Reflective racing stripes along the rocker panels and reflective painted wheels were presented as options for some Ford cars.

• Almost four out of every 10 cars (38 percent) produced in 1967 had air conditioning units.

• General Motors built its 100-millionth vehicle, a Chevrolet Caprice; Ford its 70-millionth, a Galaxie.

• The Classic, a 1931 Ford "A" replica, and a replica of the Auburn Speedster were placed on the market.

• The 1968 autos continued a growing trend toward specialty sports-type cars with a wide range of personal and sports models on all price levels. Plymouth introduced the Road Runner, a new intermediate model; the Javelin was a new American Motors Corporation offering; Ford showed a fastback series called the Torino; and Mercury named a newly styled intermediate series the Montego.

• All makes had exhaust emission control systems as standard equipment. A few lines offered pneumatic load levellers to help maintain normal rear end standing or riding height regardless of load distribution. Disc brakes were more common. A few of the many new safety features on the '68s included seat belts for all passengers, side marker lights, non-reflective windshield surfaces, padded interiors and front seat backs, and no spinner hubs.

• The 1968 Fords came with a "controlled crush" front end to manage the energy and lessen impact on occupants in case of head-on collisions and new squeeze-type door handles recessed within arm rests.

• Concealed windshield wipers were standard on most General Motors cars and ventless side windows on some. A special safety seat for children was offered on General Motors models.

• Pontiac's energy-absorbing bumper and an electrical charging system that used integrated microcircuits were innovations.

• Lincoln offered a new option: a transistorized automatic headlight dimmer.

• Chrysler and Dodge wagons could be bought with a washer-wiper for the tailgate window.

• Oldsmobile featured a horn ring partially imbedded in the inside diameter of the steering wheel.

• A buzzer in American Motors Corporation cars warned the driver when the lights were left on.

1968

• New car registrations in 1968 totaled 9,403,862 units, smashing a record set in 1965. Figures for 1968 showed that for the first time highway travel in the U.S. exceeded one trillion vehicle miles.

• Autolite's "Lead Wedge," traveling at a speed of 138.862 m.p.h., set the first official United States Auto Club speed record for battery-powered vehicles.

• Many Formula I racing cars started using air foils, a high-mounted horizontal wing installed at the rear of the car to provide additional down thrust.

• Warranties on '69 models were set at 12 months/12,000 miles for the full car, five years/50,000 miles on the drive train components. Coverage was restricted to first and second owners.

• Mercury and Chrysler adopted a wood-like paneling applique on some hardtops and convertibles.

• A new official United States presidential limousine, a glass-roofed Lincoln Continental, was put into service.

• Two new mid-year models, American Motors' fastback two-seat AMX sports coupe and the Lincoln Continental Mark III, were placed on the market.

• General Motors dedicated a new safety laboratory and a 67-acre vehicle dynamics test area at its Milford Proving Grounds.

• Checker Motors Corporation offered diesel-powered models on taxicabs and passenger cars, becom-

1968 — Shoulder harnesses were required equipment on all cars sold after Jan. 1, 1968.

1968 — The sporty fastback Cyclone, introduced by Mercury, included energy-absorbing steering columns and steering wheels as safety features.

ing the only U.S. manufacturer with such an option.

• The Amitron, an electric compact powered by lithium-nickel fluoride batteries, was shown. The vehicle was developed by American Motors Corporation in conjunction with Gulton Industries.

• Rowan Controller Corporation presented an electric car at the New York International Auto Show. Chevrolet's Astra II and Ford Mach II, both mid-engine prototype cars, were exhibited at the same show.

• Ford expanded its training program for mechanics, graduating 1,200 in 1968, compared with 840 in 1967. General Motors instituted Project Transition to help men soon

to be separated from the armed forces to learn automotive repair skills.

• Experimental activity during 1968 included General Motors and Chrysler built cars with fluidic controls in which air was used instead of mechanical or electrical devices to activate various accessories; Lincoln-Mercury and Plymouth experimented with a periscope-like device to aid rear and side vision; automotive safety engineers experimented with gas bags that would inflate instantly in case of an accident to cushion the occupants of the car.

• Pontiac introduced the "Mini-Pump," an emergency air pump to inflate tires, driven by the car's engine.

• Chrysler Corporation's 20th annual Trouble Shooting Contest was held on the front stretch of the Indianapolis Speedway. More than 200 teenagers competed to detect and correct "bugs" planted in 1968 Plymouths.

• Michigan International Speedway held its first race. It was estimated that paid attendance at all auto race events in the United States would exceed 60 million in 1968.

• A 12-cent postage stamp commemorating the 105th birthday of Henry Ford was issued.

• The highest price — $45,000 — ever paid at public auction for an antique car was brought by a 1913 Mercer Raceabout. This eclipsed the previous high of $31,000, paid in 1967 for a 1913 Stanley Mountain Wagon.

• Several new models were included in the 1969 line-up of new cars: the Pontiac Grand Prix "J," a hard-

top coupe boasting the longest hood in the industry, and the Mercury Marauder, a sports-type hardtop.

• Among the new features were: a skid-control braking system actuated by a miniature computer as an option on the Ford Thunderbird and the Lincoln Continental; safety door beams to protect passengers against side impacts on most General Motors cars; and special energy absorbing frames with an S-shaped front section to reduce forces on occupants in front end collisions on the large Ford models and Mercurys.

• Other developments on the '69s: Pontiac Grand Prix, radio antenna imbedded in the windshield; a sealed cooling system on the Cadillac; and Chevrolet's Liquid Tire Chain, a device to spray blended resins on tires to give increased traction on ice or snow.

• The Chevrolet Corvette came with headlamp washers. Chrysler's station wagons featured air spoilers

on their roofs to help keep the rear windows clear.

• American Motors Corporation adopted translucent battery cases for see-through fluid level checking and made Fiberglas, bias-belted tires standard on the AMX line. Locking steering columns appeared on General Motors cars as an anti-theft measure.

• The U.S. motor vehicle industry reached a historic milestone in January 1968 when the 250-millionth vehicle was produced.

• GM premiered the energy-absorbing steering column to reduce chest injuries to drivers in frontal crashes.

• The first Federal Vehicle Safety Standards took effect Jan 1.

1969

• Nearly 106 million drivers' licenses were in force at the beginning of 1969, representing a 12 million increase over a 5-year period.

1969 — The Ford Maverick, with a 103-inch wheelbase and a suggested retail price of $1,995, challenged the U.S. imported car market.

• Plans for United States-built compacts and sub-compacts were readied as final tabulations of new car sales for 1968 revealed that imports had claimed nearly one million sales for the year. The Ford Maverick, a small 103-inch wheelbase model priced to sell under $2,000, was a new compact offering; American Motors followed with a 179-inch over-all length economy compact called the Hornet.

• Mid-year introductions brought these new models to the market: American Motors Corporation's SC/Rambler, a custom-built car in the high performance category; a four-wheel-drive utility vehicle called the Blazer by Chevrolet; a new high performance Pontiac Firebird with an air foil spanning the rear deck; a new Mercury performance model, the Cyclone Spoiler; International's restyled

compact recreational vehicle, the Aristocrat, with a convertible top in a vinyl-coated fabric; and the Dodge Charger Daytona, featuring concealed headlights, rear stabilizer and a 375 h.p. engine.

• Mobil Oil announced the discontinuance of its annual Economy Run.

• Pontiac's 13-millionth car was produced.

• General Motors fitted their vehicles with "tell-tale" odometers designed to provide visual evidence if someone turns back mileage readings. Five experimental special purpose vehicles for limited urban use were demonstrated as part of the General Motors "Progress of Power" show: two were gasoline powered, one electric, another gasoline-electric and the fifth was a hybrid gasoline-electric with front-wheel drive.

• In mid-year car makers switched to bias-belted tires on about two-thirds of new car production. Remaining cars were fitted with bias-belted tires at the beginning of the 1970 model year.

• A U.S. Senate staff report prepared for the Commerce Committee urged the government to start developing steam powered cars to help combat air pollution.

• The Post Office Department awarded a contract to Electric Fuel Propulsion, Inc., of Ferndale, Mich., to build four experimental electric vehicles for test and evaluation.

• The government issued advance notice of a proposed rule that would require the installation of inflatable air bags in the dashboard of vehicles for passenger protection. Some of the safety features incorporated into the 1970 autos were bigger and brighter turn signals, lighting systems with four front lamps operating at night, side impact door beams, concealed headlights that open in three seconds and bias-belted tires. The Tire Industry Safety Council was formed by U.S. tire manufacturers in response to growing public interest in tires and tire safety.

• American Motors Corporation launched a major expansion program to increase its styling, engineering research and planning facilities in Detroit by more than 50 percent.

• A copy of the Stutz Bearcat would be produced, it was announced by the Stutz Motor Car Co. of America.

• The federal Truth in Lending Law went into effect, requiring auto dealers selling on installment plans to state the cost, terms and conditions of credit in a uniform way so that prospective purchasers could compare credit terms.

• Aerocar III, a flying automobile produced by Aerocar, Inc., in Longview, Wash., was shown.

• Representatives of the major independent auto service associations agreed to form a National Certification Board to certify automotive mechanics and paint and body workers. Ford expanded by 10-fold its Project Transition training program, which prepared soldiers nearing the end of their military service to become auto mechanics, after a successful pilot project.

• Ford changed to a simplified, 12-month warranty with its 1970 models. The warranty had no limitation on mileage or number of owners. It also eliminated all requirements for validation of maintenance.

• All the car makers presented auto theft protection in their cars in the form of steering column locks.

• A move toward body-on-frame construction, as opposed to unitized body construction, was followed by some manufacturers. Other trends in the 1970 models were seen in such features as concealed radio antennas and windshield wipers, increased use of plastic grilles, front seat back locks that automatically unlatch when a door is opened, tamper-proof odometers, electronic skid control brake systems, electrically heated rear glass defrosters, and disc brakes as standard equipment on more models than before.

• General Motors offered, as an option on many cars, a fingertip wiper control system whereby wipers and washers could be operated from the turn signal lever. Cadillac offered a new luxury option for production cars — an electrically operated sunroof. Pontiac installed plastic gas tanks on some of its station wagons. The Monte Carlo, a prestige-type specialty car from Chevrolet, came with a hood that measured six feet from grille to windshield wiper, the longest hood in Chevrolet history.

• Mercurys featured a Freon-filled shock absorber, and some Ford Motor Company cars adopted a ventilation system which brought fresh air in through the cowl area and out through the door pillar.

• Chrysler offered a headlamp delay system on Plymouth, Dodge and Chrysler, which gave the driver the choice of leaving headlights on for approximately 90 seconds after turning off the headlight and ignition switch. Plymouth Barracudas and Dodge Challengers had a new roll-over structure set under the roof panel as a safety feature.

• American Motors cars displayed a new type windshield with a chemically treated inner pane which granulated into tiny blunt-edged particles upon impact, reducing the possibility of facial lacerations. The inner pane also stretched on impact to provide a cushioning effect. Some AMC cars offered an optional low fuel warning light.

• Hood scoops, air spoilers in the rear, and racing stripes continued to identify many of the performance cars which offered a large array of special equipment for the auto enthusiast.

• U.S. car makers produced a total of 351 models for 1970.

1970

1970 - AMC introduced the Gremlin, which was the first American-built sub-compact car since the Crosley in 1939.

1970 - After a lengthy delay, Chevrolet introduced the restyled second-generation Camaro as a 1970 1/2 model.

• GM's pony cars came in for a major redesign, as the Pontiac Firebird and Chevy Camaro got all-new bodies for the 1970 model year. Because of production delays, the new Firebird and Camaro were introduced in February as 1970 1/2 models. A slightly revised 1970 Corvette debuted at the same time. The biggest mechanical change for the 'Vette was the replacement of the 427-cid V-8 with a larger 454 V-8.

• American Motors entered the sub-compact market in April with the Hornet-derived Gremlin. It represented the first American-built sub-compact car.

• Cadillac produced its last DeVille convertible in 1970. When the '71 models debuted, Cadillac transferred its sole convertible offering to the front-wheel-drive Eldorado.

• In racing, stock car driver Buddy

Baker broke all closed circuit speed records when he went 200.447 m.p.h. in a Dodge Charger Daytona at Alabama International Speedway in Talladega, Ala. That record was soon surpassed by Bobby Isaac, who recorded a speed of 201.104 m.p.h., also in a Charger Daytona. That record stood until 1983.

• During 1970, General Motors purchased rights to produce the Wankel rotary engine. Development work began on the GM rotary engine (GMRE), with the intent of putting the rotary engine into production by the mid-70s.

• GM production for the 1971 model year was hampered by a UAW strike during the latter half of 1970 that lasted for 67 days in the United States and 95 days in Canada. The strike resulted in a 1,350,000 unit car-truck production loss for GM.

• Big changes were forthcoming as the '71 models debuted. The muscle car era began to wind down as emissions and safety regulations led to decreases in horsepower. GM and AMC cut engine compression ratios across the board in preparation for low-lead and unleaded gasoline. Ford and Chrysler retained higher compression ratios on many of their engines for one more season.

• Some GM cars came equipped with a new maintenance-free sealed battery. GM cars also featured safer windshields and a disappearing tailgate on station wagons.

• One of the more controversial designs of the '70s debuted — Buick's "boattail" Riviera. Cadillac's Eldorado and Oldsmobile's Toronado also received major restylings for '71.

1970 - Cadillac discontinued its rear-wheel-drive convertible at the end of the model year and introduced a convertible based on the front-drive Eldorado for 1971.

• After a three-year run, AMC dropped its sports car, the two-place AMX, at the end of the '70 model year. AMC retained the AMX monicker for a special edition of the redesigned '71 Javelin.

• The trend toward sub-compact cars continued as Chevy introduced the Vega and Ford the Pinto. The Vega was powered by an innovative linerless aluminum four-cylinder engine, while the Pinto sourced many drivetrain components from Ford's European branches.

• Mercury re-entered the compact car market with a version of the Ford Maverick that resurrected the Comet nameplate. AMC added a Sportabout station wagon to its Hornet line. It was, and would remain for several years, the only American-built compact station wagon.

• "Captive Imports" — foreign-built cars rebadged and sold with American nameplates on them — began to appear during 1970. In the spring of '70, the Mercury Capri, built by Ford of Germany, debuted as a '71 model. Also introduced as a '71 model was the Plymouth Cricket, built in England and sold there as the Hillman Avenger.

• Lincoln dealers got an Italian/American hybrid exotic in the form of the De Tomaso Pantera. Ford announced the Pantera during 1970, delivering the first copies the following year. The mid-engine sports car was powered by Ford's 351-cid Cleveland V-8 and initially sold for around $10,000.

• When the '71 Imperial debuted, it was once again a Chrysler division model and was no longer considered a separate division. Imperial offered a Bendix four-wheel antiskid braking system as optional equipment.

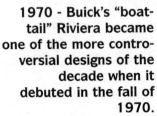

1970 - Buick's "boat-tail" Riviera became one of the more controversial designs of the decade when it debuted in the fall of 1970.

1971

1971 - Chrysler Corp. eliminated the last of its convertible models at the end of the 1971 model year. Pictured is a 1971 Plymouth Barracuda.

1971 - By the end of the 1971 model year, the muscle car movement had virtually died. It was the final season for Chrysler's 440 "six pack" engine, seen here in a Plymouth Road Runner.

• It would be the final year for Chrysler's famed 426-cid Hemi V-8 and its triple-carbureted 440 "Six Pack" engine. Chrysler also retired the 300 nameplate and ceased convertible production at the end of the '71 model year.

• Lincoln celebrated its golden anniversary in 1971.

• Oldsmobile built its 13-millionth automobile in 1971, while Pontiac built its 15-millionth automobile.

• Pontiac added a compact to its line in March, in the form of the Nova-derived Ventura II.

• AMC introduced a Buyer Protection Plan, which offered correction of any factory defect, at no cost to the car's owner, for one year or 12,000 miles.

• Dodge entered the subcompact field with the "captive import" Colt, built by Mitsubishi and introduced during the first half of 1971 as a '72 model.

• On Aug. 15, President Richard Nixon announced a 90-day wage and price freeze. The freeze came as the '72 models were about to debut, and helped boost new car sales. October saw a new car sales record, with more than one million units sold that month. In all, more than

10 million new cars were built during 1971.

• When the '72 models debuted, Ford and Chrysler followed GM's lead of the prior year, and slashed compression ratios across the board. Both companies eliminated big-block V-8s from the option lists on their pony cars.

• Chrysler introduced electronic ignition on some of its cars, eliminating points and condensers from the ignition system. The system consisted of an electronic control unit, a new distributor and an electronic voltage regulator. Pontiac also offered an electronic ignition system for 1972.

• Automakers began the switch from gross horsepower ratings to SAE net horsepower ratings. The latter more accurately reflected the power output of an engine as installed in a car.

• Impact absorbing front bumpers appeared on GM's large cars for '72, in preparation for the stricter bumper standards for '73 model cars.

1971 continued

• Oldsmobile Toronado adopted a disc brake wear indicator, which made noise when it was time to replace the brake pads.

• The Lincoln Continental Mark III was redesigned and rechristened the Mark IV.

• Chrysler began using stainless steel for its radio antennas.

• Buick's "sun coupe" option for the '72 model year featured an unusual canvas folding sunroof. As convertibles began to disappear, more cars offered sliding metal sun roofs as optional equipment.

• AMC began offering Chrysler-built automatic transmissions, in place of the formerly used Borg-Warner units.

• Ford began investigating the possibility of producing the Wankel rotary engine. Both Ford and GM continue their gas turbine engine programs.

1972

1972 - Beginning with the introduction of the 1973 models, all cars, such as this Ford Torino, had to have front bumpers capable of withstanding a five m.p.h. impact.

• Production reached record levels during 1972. For the year, domestic new-car sales topped nine million units for the first time ever.

• In January of 1972, Congress revoked the excise tax on new cars and light trucks. Beginning that month, the government mandated a buzzer/light system for new cars that activated if the driver started the engine without fastening his or her seat belt.

• Cadillac celebrated its 70th anniversary, and Oldsmobile celebrated its 75th anniversary.

• Strikes at GM's Lordstown, Ohio, Vega plant and Norwood, Ohio, Camaro-Firebird-Nova assembly plant hampered production of those models.

• Automakers continued to address quality control issues, as Ford introduced a nationwide guaranteed service program, "No Unhappy Owners."

• GM continued work on its rotary engine program, anticipating the introduction of a rotary-powered Vega in the fall of 1974. Ford also continued exploring the possibilities of the rotary, saying, " ... we don't want to be left at the gate." Chrysler, on the other hand, felt the rotary "will turn out to be one of the most unbelievable fantasies ever to hit the world auto industry."

• President Richard Nixon presented an Eldorado coupe to Leonid Brezhnev of the Soviet Union when Nixon visited the communist nation.

• As the 1973 models debuted, emissions and safety topped the agenda, via new federal mandates. A new emissions-control device, the exhaust gas recirculation (EGR) valve, was installed on engines nationwide. Stronger bumpers were required on passenger cars,

the fronts capable of withstanding a 5 m.p.h. impact, the rears a 2 1/2 mph impact.

• One of the last true muscle cars debuted, when Pontiac released the Super Duty 455 V-8 for its '73 Firebird and mid-sized LeMans and Grand Am. The '73 Trans Am marked the first time that model offered body colors other than blue or white, and was also the first to offer the "screaming chicken" decal on the hood.

• Beginning with the '73 model year, Chrysler made electronic ignition standard on all its new cars.

• GM's new pillared ("Colonnade") styling on its intermediates signaled the beginning of the decline of the hardtop body style. Proposed government roll-over standards were partly responsible for the decline of the hardtop body style.

• Front disc brakes were coming into wide usage by the time the '73 models appeared, and were standard equipment on many 1973 cars. Radial tires were also increasingly becoming standard equipment on new cars.

• The Automobile Manufacturers Association (AMA) changed its name to the Motor Vehicle Manufacturers Association (MVMA).

• Pontiac produced its 16-millionth car in November 1972. New to the Pontiac line for '73 was the sporty Grand Am, which utilized the Colonnade styling of the intermediates.

• Swivelling bucket seats were a novel feature of the Chevrolet Chevelle and Monte Carlo, and Oldsmobile Cutlass. Other features

of the '73s included a digital clock on some Chryslers and windshield washer jets located on the wiper arm of many full-sized Ford products.

• Oldsmobile added a version of the Chevy Nova, called Omega, to its product line. Many compacts and sub-compacts began sporting hatch backs.

1973

1973 - Ford introduced a radically restyled Mustang, dubbed the Mustang II as a 1974 model.

1973 - GM debuted its all-new pillared "colonnade" hardtop intermediates. An addition to the lineup was the Pontiac Grand Am.

1973 continued

• The U.S. auto industry topped all previous production and sales records in 1973, with more than 9.6 million cars sold. Cadillac produced its five-millionth car and the division's 1973 model year sales topped 300,000 units for the first time. Chevy produced a record 3.7 million cars. The one-millionth car to wear the Chrysler badge rolled off the assembly line on June 26, 1973.

• Federal standards for improved safety features continued to impact the auto industry, as all cars manufactured after Jan. 1, 1973, had to have side-door intrusion beams.

• Flamboyant GM executive John Z. DeLorean resigned from his position as Vice President Car & Truck Divisions.

• In October 1973, the Arab oil embargo began, creating the first energy crisis. Member nations of the Organization of Petroleum Exporting Countries (OPEC) embargoed oil shipments to the United States and other countries which supported Israel in the Yom Kippur war. Especially hard hit by the oil embargo were full-size car sales; buyers began to flock to smaller, more fuel-efficient autos.

• The pony car ranks continued to shrink. When the '74 models debuted, the Mustang became the Mustang II, a sub-compact-sized car based on the Pinto chassis. As with the original Mustang, a key player in the development of the Mustang II was Lee Iacocca. Mercury moved in the opposite direction, moving the Cougar to a larger, intermediate chassis.

• American Motors produced its 6-millionth vehicle since the company formed from the merger of Nash and Hudson in May 1954. AMC also began casting some of its own V-8 engine blocks. AMC's all-new '74 Matador followed GM's Colonnade styling trend, while GM extended the treatment to some of its larger cars.

• Ford produced its last convertible during 1973, a Mercury Cougar XR-7 ragtop.

• Ford introduced the Torino Elite as a 1974 model.

• GM introduced a tire specifically built to its own specifications. GM also offered an air bag passive restraint system on some of its full-size cars.

• With the country fully engulfed in the energy crisis, the end of 1973 saw the Big Three idling assembly plants to compensate for unsold inventories, consisting mostly of full-sized cars.

• GM continued development of the Wanke rotary engine but delayed introduction of a production model until 1975.

1974

1974 - AMC's brand-new intermediate was the Matador, shown here in upscale "X" trim.

• The energy crisis continued as 1974 arrived. The OPEC embargo finally ended in April, but gasoline prices remained high. The oil embargo led to a general sales slump for 1974, with new car sales dropping to 7.3 million, a 24 percent decline compared with the previous year.

• In an effort to conserve fuel, President Nixon called for voluntary gas station closings and a 55 m.p.h. national speed limit. As many states began lowering speed limits to 55 m.p.h., cruise control became an increasingly popular option. Fuel economy gauges began to appear in new cars.

• The pony car market virtually disappeared in 1974. The Plymouth Barracuda, Dodge Challenger and AMC Javelin were dropped by their respective makers after the '74 model year, and Chevy discontinued the Z-28 option on the Camaro (it reappeared in '77). Of all the pony cars on the market at the start of the decade, only the Firebird and Camaro survived into 1975. The drastically downsized Mustang II qualified more as a sub-compact economy car than a true pony car, and it lacked the outright performance offered by the Camaro and Firebird.

• During early 1974, Ford abandoned development of the Wankle rotary engine. AMC, on the other hand, expressed an interest in possibly utilizing GM's rotary engine in its upcoming pacer subcompact.

• The muscle car market also gave its final dying gasp. The "original" muscle car, Pontiac's GTO, disappeared at the end of the '74 model year.

• In an ironic twist, GM bought back the tooling for Buick's V-6 engine, which had been sold to Kaiser/Jeep in the '60s and subsequently acquired by AMC when it bought Jeep. By mid-74, a revised version of the V-6 was being produced by Buick.

• As the '75 models debuted, the biggest news was in the area of emissions. Stricter federal standards led to the adoption of catalytic converters on the exhaust systems of many American new cars.

All GM and most Ford, Chrysler and AMC cars got the devices. The catalytic converter required the use of unleaded fuel. Catalytic converters were also partially blamed for new-car prices that averaged $1,000 more than the introduction prices of comparable '74 models. In response to dramatically increased sticker prices, automakers began to offer longer-term loans on new cars.

• Rectangular headlights appeared on some '75 models, marking the first major change in headlight appearance since the adoption of quad headlight systems in 1958.

• GM's High Energy Ignition (HEI) system became standard on all its cars. AMC and Ford also standardized electronic ignition on all of their cars.

• As a fuel saving effort, AMC offered overdrive on six-cylinder equipped Hornets and Gremlins.

• New models from GM included the Pontiac Astre, Olds Starfire, Chevrolet Monza and Buick Skyhawk. New engines for these cars included Buick's revived V-6, a 260-cid V-8 for Olds, and a 262-cid V-8 for Chevrolet. The diminutive

Starfire represented the smallest car sold by Olds since the discontinuation of the Curved Dash model in 1908. Chevy's Monza was to have become GM's rotary-engined car, but GM, after several delays, finally shelved the rotary project during the latter half of '74 because of emissions and cost problems.

• Chrysler introduced the new Cordoba, which Dodge also sold as the Charger. At Ford, new models included the Ford Granada/Mercury Monarch.

• The '75 Chevy Corvette featured a rubber bladder-type fuel cell.

• Lincoln's Continental Mark IV came with four-wheel disc brakes. The Lincoln Continental, Ford Thunderbird and full-sized Mercurys offered four-wheel disc brakes as an option.

• Lincoln and Thunderbird offered "Sure-Track" anti-skid brakes.

• The early months of the '75 model year saw a reversal of the previous year, with sales of larger cars improving and small car sales slumping.

• Ford and GM went completely to radial ply tires for the 1975 model year.

1975

1975 - Ford's Granada was billed as a luxury compact car.

• Sales continued to slump during 1975 — domestic new-car sales dropped 5.3 percent below 1974's level. In an effort to boost sales, the automakers began to offer rebates and cut sticker prices on new cars early in '75. Chrysler

Corporation led the way, offering rebates of up to $300.

• GM announced plans to redesign its entire product lineup by 1980,

1975 - AMC's sub-compact Pacer boasted a large amount of glass and an exceptionally wide body.

1975 continued

and borrowed $600 million towards that end. The automaker also discussed a possible joint development effort with Mazda on the Wankel rotary engine.

• The Bricklin auto company,

formed in 1971, went into receivership during 1975. Chrysler reported losses during the first three quarters of 1975.

• As the push for greater fuel economy continued, the use of lightweight aluminum and plastics in cars increased. Average fuel economy for the industry continued to improve, with the new 1976 mod-

els proving to be 12.8 percent more efficient than the '75s and 26.6 percent better than the '74s.

• By 1975, there were more than 3.8 million miles of roads in the United States, and fuel consumption for the year was estimated at 112.8 billion gallons.

• Mid-year introductions included

1975 - One of the last holdouts from the muscle car era was the Pontiac Trans Am, which continued to offer large-displacement V-8 engines until the end of the decade.

1975 - The Buick Electra was one of several GM models that switched from round to rectangular headlights.

1975 - Chrysler debuted an all-new model called Cordoba.

1975 - The Dodge Aspen was the division's replacement for the Dart line.

1975 - Cadillac's new small car, the Seville, featured fuel injection and a price tag around $12,000.

1975 continued

the Pinto-based Mercury Bobcat, and AMC's all-new sub-compact, the Pacer. The Pacer featured an extremely wide body and 5,615 square inches of glass. AMC invested $60 million in the development of its small car. Also appearing mid-year was Chevrolet's Cosworth Vega. A joint effort with Cosworth of England, the special-edition Vega featured a fuel-injected, dual-over-head cam, 16-valve four-cylinder engine.

• In May, Cadillac introduced its small car, the Seville. Priced at around $12,000, it featured Bendix electronic fuel injection (EFI) as standard equipment.

• Chevrolet began offering a

60,000-mile guarantee on the aluminum four-cylinder engine used for the Vega and several other GM sub-compacts.

• Oldsmobile produced its 16-millionth car during 1975.

• At the end of the '75 model year, GM dropped all its remaining convertible models, with the exception of the Cadillac Eldorado convertible.

• For the '76 model year, Chevy introduced the sub-compact Chevette, and Cadillac offered four-wheel disc brakes on the Eldorado. Pontiac debuted the Sunbird, GM introduced a five-speed overdrive manual transmission, and Chevy introduced a 305-cid V-8. GM expanded the use of rectangular headlights to more of its car lines. Pontiac celebrated its 50th anniversary.

• Chrysler offered two new compacts, the Dodge Aspen and Plymouth Volare. Chrysler's new compacts featured transverse torsion bars for the front suspension, and a modular instrument panel cluster held in place by four screws. Chrysler claimed the latter cut removal time in half.

• Ford resurrected the Cobra moniker for a special version of the Mustang II fastback, dubbed the Cobra II. Lincoln's Continental Mark IV added four special designers series: Cartier, Pucci, Givenchy and Bill Blass.

• Bumpers for the new '76 models were required to withstand a 3 m.p.h. corner impact. Fuel system check valves were mandated for all models to prevent fuel spillage in a rollover. New standards for brakes led to the elimination of front shoe brakes by the end of 1975.

1976

1976 - At the end of the 1976 model year, production of American convertibles was discontinued when the final Cadillac Eldorado rolled off the assembly line.

• The American automobile industry chalked up sales of 8.6 million cars for calendar-year 1976, and GM posted record earnings of $2.9 billion. As more emphasis was placed on fuel economy, the industry began to discontinue production of its largest V-8 engines.

• Chrysler introduced its "lean burn" engine system early in 1976 on 400-cid V-8s installed in intermediate and full-sized cars. It used an underhood computer to regulate spark timing for maximum fuel combustion and efficiency. Chrysler also sold the non-automotive portion of its Airtemp air conditioning division.

• Production of the American convertible was discontinued after the last Cadillac Eldorado convertible rolled off the assembly line in 1976, as Cadillac announced the model would be shelved in '77. Collectors eagerly snatched up the final Caddy convertibles, temporarily inflating their prices. Declining popularity and fear of federal safety standards for rollover crashes brought about the demise of the body style. In 1982 Chrysler revived the convertible with a special soft-top version of the Lebaron.

• Volkswagen announced plans to open an assembly plant in the United States to produce its subcompact Rabbit.

• Congress authorized $160 million for a six-year electric car research and development program.

• Chrysler got a contract from the U.S. Army to build XM-1 tanks. At the end of the '76 model year, Chrysler dropped the long-running Valiant and Dart nameplates in order to expand production of the Volare and Aspen.

• For 1977, GM began "down-sizing" its large cars, as did Ford. The new GM large cars were a foot shorter and 750 pounds lighter than their predecessors. Ford redid its intermediates and also shrank the Thunderbird to intermediate size.

• Ford offered an Extended Service Plan, which extended the warranty on some components for an additional cost.

• Pontiac introduced two new engines which shared a number of common components, a 301-cid V-8 and a 151-cid four-cylinder engine. Cadillac extended its four-wheel disc brake system to the Seville and Fleetwood Brougham. The Oldsmobile Toronado got a new Microprocessed Sensing and Automatic Regulation (MISAR) electronic spark timing system.

• AMC added a station wagon to its Pacer line.

• Chrysler extended use of its lean burn system to the 440-cid and 360-cid V-8s, and added a two-barrel carburetor to the 225-cid Slant Six. A low-slip torque converter appeared in Chrysler automatic transmissions.

• Hot factory accessories for the '77s included citizens band (CB) radios and removable roof panels, known as T-tops. Ford and Chrysler intermediates joined the switch to rectangular headlights on the '77 models.

• By '77, all American cars came equipped with catalytic converters, and the phase-out of leaded gas began.

1976 - Ford drastically downsized its Thunderbird, making it an intermediate for the 1977 model year.

1976 - The Oldsmobile Delta 88 was among the GM full-sized cars that underwent downsizing.

1977

• Domestic new car and truck production reached a new record in 1977, with 12.7 million units sold, eclipsing 1973's record production. Imports grabbed a record 18.5 percent share of new car sales in 1977. Domestic new cars accounted for 9.2 million units produced, better than '76, but still below the record production of 1973.

• Electronics played an increasing role in reducing emissions and improving fuel economy. Many cars began to utilize electronic fuel control systems.

• Uncertainty over upcoming emissions standards dominated the automotive scene during the first half of 1977. Originally, exceedingly tough emissions standards were set to go into effect for the '78 model year. Revisions to the standards stalled in Congress and some wondered whether there would be a '78 model lineup in the fall. Automakers faced the possibility of having to continue to call the new '78 models '77s in order to side-step the new standards. Eventually, less-stringent standards were adopted.

• In April, GM announced it was ending all rotary engine development.

• Recalls became more common during 1977, with a record 12.6 million vehicles recalled for correction related to safety. This was up from 3.5 million vehicles recalled during 1976.

• At mid-year '77, Chevrolet reintroduced the Z/28 package for the Camaro. Other mid-year introductions included the Chrysler LeBaron/Dodge Diplomat, which were Chrysler's entries into the luxury compact market, and the Pontiac LeMans Can Am.

• AMC added a Volkswagen-built four-cylinder engine to the Gremlin's option list. AMC announced plans to purchase four-cylinder engines from Pontiac beginning in the 1980 model year.

• Oldsmobile production for the '77 model year topped one million cars for the first time. One of Oldsmobile's big sales leaders was the Cutlass series.

• Lincoln's answer to the Cadillac Seville, the Versailles, debuted in April 1977. The small luxury car, based on the Ford Granada, carried distinctive Lincoln traits such as the "Continental spare" trunk lid.

• When the '78 models debuted, sticker prices, which had been increasing for several years, rose by roughly six percent. The new model year marked the first time manufacturers had to meet the new Corporate Average Fuel Economy (CAFE) standards. The standard for the '78 model year was 18 m.p.g., with the mileage requirements increasing over the next several years to 27.5 m.p.g. for 1985.

• The new model year marked the 75th anniversary for Ford.

• For the '78 model season, GM extended its downsizing of the previous year to its intermediate cars. For its 25th anniversary, the '78 Corvette featured a new fastback rear window, and a special silver anniversary model was released.

• GM introduced a new diesel V-8 engine, derived from Oldsmobile's 5.7-liter (350-cid) gasoline engine. It was the world's first V-8 passenger car diesel engine. The Cadillac Seville offered a Trip Computer as an option. Buick offered a turbocharged version of its V-6 engine in the Regal and LeSabre sport coupe.

• One of the first wave of American sub-compacts bowed out, as GM discontinued the Chevrolet Vega/Pontiac Astre at the start of the '78 model year. New in the sub-compact field were a four-door version of the Chevy Chevette and the Ford Fiesta. The Fiesta was a front-drive car built in Europe.

• Ford introduced the new compact Fairmont and its Mercury counterpart, the Zephyr, which replaced the Ford Maverick/Mercury Comet. The new AMC Concord was based on the compact Hornet.

• Plymouth and Dodge dropped their respective full-size models for '78. Improving economy in its automatic transmissions, Chrysler Corporation introduced a "lockup" torque converter, which mechanically locked itself to the flywheel once the transmission shifted into high gear. This eliminated fuel-wasting torque converter slip.

• By the beginning of the '78 model year, all of the American auto manufacturers had begun the process of converting to the metric system.

1977 - Dodge's Magnum XE featured a grille reminiscent of the classic Cord 810/812 of the '30s.

1977 - Mercury introduced an all-new compact that resurrected the old Lincoln monicker Zephyr.

1978

1978 - **Volkswagen began producing its Rabbit sub-compact at a plant in Pennsylvania.**

• United States car production continued its comeback during 1978. Domestic new-car output for the year totaled nearly 9.2 million units, coming in just below 1977's level. All North American assembly plants turned out a record 14.7 million cars and trucks, eclipsing the record set the previous year. The imports saw their market share slip to 17.7 percent. GM car and truck sales surpassed seven million units for the first time.

• Chrysler Corp.'s new front-drive sub-compacts, the Omni and Horizon, debuted at the beginning of 1978. They were the first U.S.-built front-drive sub-compacts.

• Ford Motor Company celebrated its 75th anniversary and produced its 150 millionth car, truck or tractor since its inception.

• Financially troubled AMC announced plans to join forces with French manufacturer Renault. Also facing financial difficulties, Chrysler sold much of its European holdings.

• In April, Volkswagen assembled its first U.S.-built Rabbit at its new assembly plant in Pennsylvania. Volkswagen was the first foreign company to establish an assembly plant in the United States since the 1920s.

• Corvette was selected to pace the 1978 Indianapolis 500-mile race, and a special black and silver pace car edition was released. Like the Eldorado convertible of '76, collectors flocked to this model, temporarily inflating prices.

• In July 1978, Henry Ford II, saying "things just didn't work out," fired Lee Iacocca from his position as president of Ford Motor Company. In November, Iacocca was hired as president of Chrysler Corporation and helped guide that firm through its financial troubles.

• In the fall of '78, Oldsmobile opened its new Cutlass assembly plant in Lansing, Mich. At the time, it was the largest car assembly plant in the country.

• For the '79 model year, the CAFE requirements for the industry rose to 19 miles per gallon. The term "gas guzzler" came into increasing usage as more Americans became concerned with fuel economy. Mandated automobile emissions levels were also reduced for the '79 model year.

1978 - The Plymouth Horizon (and its Dodge Omni twin) were Chrysler's first domestically produced sub-compacts, and the company's first front-wheel-drive cars.

1978 - The restyled Buick Riviera adopted the front-drive chassis of the Olds Toronado and Cadillac Eldorado.

• Oldsmobile offered a smaller 260-cid version of its diesel V-8 engine. Availability of diesel and V-6 engines was increased at GM.

• The '79 Lincoln Versailles became the first American car to offer halogen sealed-beam headlights.

• Pontiac released a special edition Firebird Trans Am to commemorate the 10th anniversary of the model.

• The redesigned '79 Buick Riviera joined the all-new Oldsmobile Toronado and Cadillac Eldorado as a front-wheel-drive car. Also new on the block were a downsized LTD and Marquis from Ford, and New Yorker and Newport from Chrysler. Ford brought out a redesigned Mustang and a sister car at Mercury, using the Capri name. AMC replaced the Gremlin with the Spirit.

• A second energy crisis loomed at the end of the year, as OPEC raised oil prices by 14.5 percent in December.

1979

1979 - GM's all-new front-drive 'X cars' debuted at mid-year for the 1980 model year, the Chevy version being called Citation.

• Automobile production took a tumble during 1979. Domestic new-car sales fell to 8.3 million units. Imports, however, had a banner year, with 2.3 million cars sold, capturing a record 21.7 percent share of the U.S. market.

• The big events of the year were Chrysler's financial troubles and the second energy crisis. Lee Iacocca, named chairman of Chrysler Corporation in September, and other Chrysler executives went before Congress seeking a federal loan to bail out the automaker. Chrysler's top brass warned the government the company might close its doors by the beginning of the next year without federal financial help. Congress approved a $3.5 billion aid bill for Chrysler in December 1979.

• OPEC raised oil prices sharply, and this combined with political unrest in Iran and that country's subsequent cut in oil shipments to the United States, led to a second energy crisis and rising gasoline prices. The average gas price at the start of the year was 74 cents per gallon, but rose to $1.14 by the end of the year. Interest in small, fuel-efficient cars rose as a result.

• GM produced its 100-millionth vehicle since its inception in 1911.

• John DeLorean's tell-all book about General Motors, *On a Clear Day You Can See General Motors*, finally reached print four years after being completed by writer J. Patrick Wright.

1979 continued

• In August, Henry Ford II relinquished his position as chief executive officer at Ford, but remained chairman. Philip Caldwell became the new CEO of the automaker.

• AMC finalized its deal to join forces with French Renault. Under the agreement, Renault would invest $150 million in AMC and get a 22.5 percent interest in the independent automaker. Renault's automobiles, beginning with the Le Car, would be sold by AMC in the United States. AMC also pulled the plug on the sub-compact Pacer during 1979. New at the automaker was the four-wheel-drive Eagle, the first volume four-wheel-drive passenger car produced in the United States.

• The last "big-block" muscle car disappeared, as Pontiac dropped its 400-cid V-8 from the Firebird's option list at the end of the '79 model year. The last 400s were assembled in 1978, and used in the '79 Firebirds. Most of those engines went into the special 10th anniversary Trans Ams.

• At mid-year, Chrysler revived the legendary 300 nameplate.

• GM released its all-new "X-body" compact cars in April as 1980 models. The Chevy Citation, Buick Skylark, Oldsmobile Omega, and Pontiac Phoenix were GM's first compact front-wheel-drive cars. With the introduction of the Citation, Chevrolet retired the Nova nameplate.

• Also making news at GM for the 1980 model year were the availability of diesel engines in all GM lines and a new front-wheel-drive "bustleback" Cadillac Seville that

recalled the styling of early '50s Rolls-Royces and Bentleys. The new Seville also featured four-wheel independent suspension and four-wheel disc brakes, and was the first U.S. car to offer a diesel engine as standard equipment.

• Ford downsized the big Lincolns.

• CAFE requirements rose to 20 m.p.g. for the 1980 model year. Gas-guzzler fines were levied on cars with m.p.g. ratings of less than 15 m.p.g.

• Ford downsized the intermediate Thunderbird and Cougar XR-7. New at Ford was a four-speed automatic overdrive transmission, available on some of its larger cars.

• U.S. auto manufacturers offered extended warranty coverage at an additional charge.

• Ford and GM offered several 1980 models with turbocharged engines.

1980

1980 — AMC's 1980 Eagle 4x4 sedan was considered a benchmark four-wheel-drive vehicle.

• Chrysler Corporation announced its "Chrysler Guarantees" program, which included a 30 day/1,000 mile money-back guarantee, a two-year maintenance program for purchase and lease customers, and a no-cost motor club membership for emergency road service.

• Chrysler also introduced its line

of 1981 "K" cars, the Dodge Aries and the Plymouth Reliant.

• Phillip Caldwell became CEO and chairman of Ford Motor Company. This marked the first time in the history of the company that the chairman was not a member of the Ford family.

• The Chevrolet Citation, its front-

wheel-drive model, was selected as the Motor Trend "Car of the Year."

• The upcoming 1981 model year was heralded as the "Year of the Small Car." Ford, Chrysler and General Motors would introduce lines of economical automobiles with front-wheel drive and transverse mounted engines.

1980 — The all-new 1980 Dodge Mirada coupe boasted one of the largest V-8 engines, 360 cubic inches, of any domestic passenger car.

• In the Spring of the year, GM announced it would spend $40 billion to build new factories, upgrade older plants and install equipment with the goal of production capacity equaling six million cars per year by 1984. These would be vehicles of unitized bodies, front-wheel drive with transverse mounted engines.

• Chevrolet introduced a new V-6 engine and discontinued its venerable inline six.

• Dodge introduced a new model, the 1981 Mirada, to replace the discontinued Magnum XE.

• Lincoln's two cars, the Continental and the Mark VI, were both downsized and redesigned.

• Mercury introduced a new four-speed overdrive automatic transmission.

1981

A special-edition 1981 Buick Regal, with a turbocharged engine, served as pace car for the 65th Indianapolis 500.

• Dodge's K-car, Aries, which had been introduced late in 1980, won the Motor Trend "Car of the Year" award. It would become Dodge's sales leader.

• Ford introduced its new compact "world cars," the Escort and the Lynx, under the Lincoln-Mercury marque, as replacements for the Pinto and Bobcat.

• A Buick Regal, with a 4.1 liter V-6 engine, was the pace car for the 65th Indianapolis 500 mile race.

• Chevrolet's new Corvette plant in Bowling Green, Ky., assembled its first Corvette, a 1982 model, June 1.

• The auto industry continued its consideration of use of alternative fuels, specifically methanol.

• General Motors developed new engines for its '82 models. They included a Cadillac-built 125 hp V-8, an Olds-built 3.8 liter diesel V-6, and a Buick-built high-output 2.9 liter V-6. Chevrolet introduced a diesel engine for the Chevette. Cadillac also offered the first variable displacement engine, the V-8-6-4.

• For the '82 selling season, the domestic automakers offered the public 261 models of cars. Cadillac brought out its new subcompact, the Cimarron, in May. It was powered by a four-cylinder engine and a manual transmission.

1981 — Chrysler's K-car series, the Dodge Aries (pictured) and the Plymouth Reliant, proved to be saviors for Chrysler Corporation.

1981 continued

• Oldsmobile debuted its new Ciera, the first Cutlass with front wheel drive.

• The Big Three automakers' losses totaled $1 billion, by the third quarter.

• In a move seen to save automakers as much as $30 million, the EPA tailpipe emissions certification program was cut in cost and complexity. The new requirements broadened the definition of engine family so the manufacturers could add vehicles to a certified engine family and implement ongoing changes without the EPA's prior approval.

• The automobile lease-rental industry continued to grow.

• Borg-Warner introduced a new five-speed manual transmission that became available on the 1982 Pontiac T1000.

• Ford Motor Company introduced a new 3.8-liter, 112 h.p. V-6 engine that was used in several of its models. The engine weighed 311 pounds.

• The introduction of the '82 cars in September was seen as "lackluster" and contributed to the already high domestic new-car inventories.

• Chrysler offered profit sharing to the United Auto Workers.

• The 1981 Imperial featured an all-electronic dashboard.

• The 1981 Olds Sport Omega was the first production vehicle to use "reinforced reaction-injection molding" (plastic) fenders.

• Ford used plastic halogen headlamps.

• Chevrolet used plastic rear springs on the 1982 Corvette to save weight.

• The 1981 Chevrolet Chevette Scooter, priced at $4,673, was America's lowest price U.S. built automobile.

• GM and Ford offered automatic transmissions with overdrive.

• Lincoln debuted its new, downsized 1982 Continental.

• Ford introduced its 5.0 1. V-8 in the 1982 Mustang and Capri.

1982

1982 — Chevrolet introduced the Cavalier compact in '81 for the 1982 model year.

- Buick introduced a convertible in the Riviera line and a specially prepped, turbocharged Grand National Regal ran at Daytona.

- Chevrolet introduced its subcompact, Cavalier, the compact Celebrity, and the newly designed Camaro. Its Pontiac counterpart, the Firebird, also debuted. Some Camaros were fitted with plastic hoods. It also touted the year as "the year of the diesel" and offered the powerplant in five models. The diesel was not well received.

- Slow sales cut auto output to its lowest ebb since 1958. The industry built more than 5,055,000 automobiles in '82, but it fell short of '81's total of 6,280,045. Hardest hit of American makers was American Motors, which fell short of the previous year by some 47 percent. Production of the Big Three automakers was off by the following percentages: Chrysler, 20 percent; General Motors, down 18.40 percent; Ford, a decline of 16.5 percent.

- AMC built a computer into its electronic feedback carburetion system to aid in the diagnostic process.

- Cadillac introduced an aluminum V-8 engine, the 249 cu. in. HT-4100 to replace the variable displacement engine of the year before.

- Chrysler revived the convertible as it introduced its 1982 LeBaron convertible in April. It was the first convertible since the 1976 Cadillac Eldorado.

- Honda began production of automobiles in Marysville, Ohio. It was the first Japanese automobile manufacturer to build cars in the United States.

1982 — Chevrolet redesigned the Camaro for the 1982 model year and gave it a more aerodynamic shape.

1983

- The U.S. automakers rebounded from three poor years to have an excellent year.

- General Motors entered an agreement with Toyota to build small cars together in a plant in California.

- Chrysler Corporation paid back its federally guaranteed loans seven years early.

- The federal government filed a lawsuit against GM alleging the company's X-cars had brake defects.

The National Highway Traffic Safety Administration asked for $4 million in damages and a recall, but GM denied the charges.

- Auto manufacturers sold more than 9.1 million cars, reflecting a 13 percent increase over the previous year's total of just under 8 million.

- Buick debuted its Questor, a concept car used to test electronic ideas and innovations.

- AMC debuted its Alliance, a co-production with Renault. The front-wheel drive car was assembled in Wisconsin, but had engines produced in France. The last independent had to sell off subsidiaries to raise cash in the wake of losses.

- Ford brought back the Mustang convertible in the 1983 model year.

- Sales of Buicks rose enough to move the GM division into fourth place.

- A twin-turbocharged V-6 powered Buick Riviera convertible paced the 67th Indianapolis 500.

- Ford's Escort was the best-selling car in the country and the new aero-styled '83 Thunderbird was a runaway hit, doubling the sales of its predecessor.

1983 continued

• Ford introduced its new compact, Tempo, in May, but as an '84 model. Mercury did likewise with its sister compact, Topaz.

• Chevrolet introduced a Monte Carlo SS late in the model year.

• AMC was the first American auto company to offer an electronically controlled automatic transmission.

• Chrysler and Ford offer "talking dashboards."

• Chrysler added a Town & Country convertible with simulated wood trim to its LeBaron line.

• Dodge introduced its Shelby Charger, a high performance version for the younger clientele.

• Pontiac introduced its 2000 Sunbird convertible.

• A.M. General Corp. received a $1.2 billion contract to build the "Hummer."

• In May, Pontiac introduced its first full-sized car in two years, the Parisienne.

1983 — American Motors Chairman Paul Tippit, right, receives the 1983 *Motor Trend* 'Car of the Year' award from Bob Brown of Petersen Publishing Co. It was given to the 1983 Renault Alliance.

1983 — The Ford Thunderbird was completely redesigned for the '83 model year and had a drag coefficient of .35, the lowest of any personal luxury car.

1983 — Oldsmobile celebrated the 15th anniversary of its Hurst/Olds in the '83 model year with a special edition, limited run version.

1984 — Chevrolet's Cavalier, its best-seller in '83, received a facelift for the 1984 model year, and made available a convertible for the first time since 1975.

1984

• Buick introduced Sequential-port Fuel Injection (SFI) and Multi-port Fuel Injection (MFI) on its 3.8 liter V-6 engines. Some Buick employees carried the torch bearing the Olympic flame through Flint on its way to Los Angeles.

• Chevrolet brought out its new, fourth generation Corvette. It had an all new body and featured stainless steel exhaust headers, anti-theft system and other amenities.

• Chrysler removed Imperial and Cordoba from its lineup and discontinued its workhorse engine, the slant six. The front-drive New Yorker sales rose by a startling 66 percent. Chrysler was tops in the industry in turbo production with most going on Lasers and Dodge Daytonas.

• Ford introduced its Tempo compact along with the Mercury version, the Topaz. Ford also introduced its high performance SVO Mustang.

• Lincoln introduced its all-new Mark VII that was shorter, more aerodynamic and sporty.

• Pontiac introduced its sporty two-seater, the Fiero. It featured plastic "Enduraflex" body panels and mid-engine design.

• Chevrolet's Cavalier was America's best selling car. The Cavalier convertible was introduced.

• Cadillac introduced in April its 1985 front wheel drive models, the DeVille and Fleetwood.

• Chrysler introduced its series of front-wheel-drive minivans under the badges of Dodge Caravan and Plymouth Voyager.

• GM bought EDS, H. Ross Perot's company, for $2.5 billion.

1984 — The all-new 1984 Chevrolet Corvette was available as a coupe only.

1984 — Pontiac Fiero, the first American produced, mid-engine sports car, debuted in 1984.

• Lincoln-Mercury began marketing the British-built 1985 Merkur through its dealers.

• GM and Ford announced they would offer mobile phones in their 1985 model cars.

• GM and Toyota began their joint venture, NUMMI, to produce cars in California. The first product of the venture was the Nova sedan.

• Chrysler acquired a five-percent interest in Italian car maker Maserati.

1984 — Ford debuted the front wheel drive Tempo, pictured, and the companion Mercury Topaz in 1983 as a 1984 model.

1985

1985 — Oldsmobile introduced its first front wheel drive model of the '85 model year, the Ninety-Eight, early in 1984. It was 25 inches shorter than its predecessor.

• In January, GM announced it would build a new car, the Saturn, at a factory in Tennessee. William Hoglund was named president.

• In February, Buick shut down its Flint plant where the rear-wheel drive Regal was built. The plant was changed over to production of the front-wheel drive LeSabre and the first one rolled off the line in September.

• The three major automakers each purchased companies in an effort to expand and diversify. GM purchased Hughes Aircraft for $5 billion.

• General Motors Acceptance Corp. purchased the rights to service the portfolio of Minneapolis-based Norwest Corp., which stood at $11 billion. GMAC also purchased Colonial Group of CoreStates Financial Corp, which had a portfolio of $7.4 billion.

• Chrysler purchased Gulfstream Aerospace Corp, maker of corporate aircraft, for $637 million. Chrysler also purchased Finance America from BankAmerica Corp. for $405 million, and E.F. Hutton Credit Corp. from E.F. Hutton Group for $147 million. Ford bought 81 percent of First Nationwide Financial Corp, the ninth-largest savings and loan association in the nation. Ford also bought New Holland farm equipment company from Sperry Corp. for $330 million. It became part of Ford's Tractor Operations.

1985 — The Dodge Caravan, a runaway best seller in its initial year, returned for the '85 model year as the only front-wheel drive mini-van.

• Chrysler was reorganized into a holding company with four autonomous operating groups.

• The car haulers's strike prompted the auto industry to offer financial incentives to car buyers. It resulted in record numbers of car sales.

• At the end of the '85 model year, Buick ceased production on diesel engine-equipped passenger cars, the X-bodied Skylark, and the "big" Riviera that had been honored as car of the year in 1979.

• New cars for the '86 model year debuted. The revamped, down-sized Riviera featured a Graphic Control Center, an innovative instrument panel.

• The combined car-truck sales hit a record 15.6 million vehicles, with 11 million as cars, the remainder as trucks.

• The Yugo was introduced at $3,990.

• Hyundai Motor America was formed to start in February 1986.

• Chrysler was hit by a UAW strike for 12 days.

• Ford introduced the Taurus sedan. It soon established itself as a sales leader and became one of the most dominant vehicles ever to wear the blue oval.

• Ford offered anti-lock brakes (ABS) as optional equipment on Lincolns.

• Mazda broke ground in Flat Rock, Mich., for a new assembly plant.

• Chrysler and Mitsubishi built a joint-venture plant in Illinois.

1985 — Ford's '86 Taurus debuted in '85 and became one of Ford's best selling products.

1986

- For its twentieth anniversary, Oldsmobile Toronado was redesigned. It was much lighter and shorter than the '85 model. A special anniversary model bore badging and equipment.

- H. Ross Perot of Texas, architect of EDS, became critical of GM and its president, Roger Smith. GM bought class E stock from Perot and aides for $750 million and removed him from chairman's seat of EDS.

- In an effort to enliven a sedate market, auto companies offered low-interest loans (2.9 percent for GM and Ford, 2.1 for Chrysler, zero interest for AMC.) It worked as September sales set records.

- Ford Motor Company reported profits of $2.5 billion for 1985, the second highest in the company's history.

- Chrysler Corporation reported a net profit of $1.64 billion for 1985.

- John Z. DeLorean, one-time engineer and Pontiac division chief, was acquitted of fraud and racketeering charges in December. He had been charged with embezzling $8.5 million from investors in his DeLorean automobile project.

- Toyota announced plans to produce a car in a new plant in Georgetown, Ky.

- Chrysler and AMC announced plans for AMC to build Chrysler, Plymouth and Dodge rear-wheel drive cars in the plant at Kenosha, Wis.

- Chrysler also broke ground for its tech center located in Auburn Hills, Mich. Chrysler introduced its P-cars for 1987, the Plymouth Sundance and the Dodge Shadow.

- Cadillac announced the body for the 1987 Allante would be built in Italy, then shipped by air to Detroit for assembly.

1986 — For the 1986 model year, Buick completely redesigned and downsized its personal luxury entry, the Riviera.

1986 — Chevrolet's 1986 Corvette got a soft convertible top for the first time since 1975. A bright yellow version, below, paced the Indianapolis 500 that year.

1987 — The limited edition '87 Buick Regal Grand National received an increase in horsepower and torque from the previous year. It was introduced in May 1987.

1987

• Chrysler Corporartion purchased American Motors for an undisclosed sum. Dollar estimates of the purchase ran as high as $2 billion. The plum of the deal was acquisition of the Jeep name and line of vehicles. The last auto merger, in 1954 between Hudson and Nash-Kelvinator, formed American Motors.

• Other big-ticket purchases by automakers included Ford's purchase of Aston Martin and Chrysler's additional buy of Lamborghini.

• Henry Ford II passed away Sept. 29 at age 70. He had been chief executive officer from 1945, when he was called out of the Navy to save a foundering company. Ford hired "The Whiz Kids," a 10-man team that helped bring about salvation of the company. Ford held the CEO position until 1979, moved to chairman of the board in '80 and then retired.

• The stock market collapse of Oct. 19 dropped the Dow-Jones Industrial Average by 508 points.

• Ford and General Motors both announced big profits for the preceding year, but Ford's profits topped those of GM. Ford's net profit was $3.29 billion for '86, while GM's was recorded at $2.95 billion. It was the first time since 1924 Ford's bottom line was better than GM's.

• Both Ford and General Motors hammered out labor agreements with the UAW without need of strikes. Job security ranked high among the main issues, and the pact included guaranteed employment provisions.

• Chrysler introduced the LeBaron sedan, coupe and convertible, built on the K-car chassis. The LeBaron replaced the Laser.

• Chevrolet introduced its L-body products, the two-door Beretta and the four-door Corsica.

• The Ford Thunderbird Turbo Coupe was selected as Motor Trend's 'Car of the Year.'

• Ford offered its Tempo/Topaz with the option of driver-side airbags. The car also became available in four-wheel drive. The Tempo and all other Ford passenger cars would be equipped with electronic fuel injection as standard equipment.

• Ford announced the closing of its Romeo tractor plant, the last Ford tractor plant in the United States.

• GM imported a Korean-built subcompact bearing the name Pontiac LeMans.

• Buick brought out the limited-production GNX, the final version of the division's Grand National high performance series.

1987 — The 1987 Ford Thunderbird Turbo Coupe bore a brand new look and was powered by a turbocharged, fuel injected 2.3 liter engine of 190 horsepower.

1988 - The 1988 Eagle Premier was offered in two models: the LX, pictured, for luxury seekers and the ES for those wanting a European sports sedan.

1988

• Consumer confidence and a diverse offering of products brought renewed interest in American-made cars as sales exceeded the previous year's. Combined sales of passenger cars and light trucks exceeded 15 million. Light trucks, in particular, continued their record-setting climb.

• The stock market crash of '87 apparently had no lasting impact on the automotive industry's sales in '88 as they rose more than three percent over '87's sales. The weak U.S. dollar, however, had a negative effect on European and Japanese imports, increasing their prices. Results on sales of imported vehicles were mixed, however.

• GM introduced new products including the Buick Regal, Olds Cutlass Supreme and Pontiac Grand Prix, all of which were built on the GM10 platform. Ford Motor Company brought out new products, the Mazda-made Probe and a new Lincoln Continental, that proved to be successful in their inaugural year.

• Toyota began producing its cars in an assembly plant in Georgetown, Ky.

• The use of computers to control engine, transmission and suspension systems continued to increase. Engineers could design engines with not only power but also fuel economy.

• Chevrolet and Ford announced two powerful new engines. Ford debuted its Yamaha dual overhead cam, 24-valve 220-hp V-6. It would power the '89 Ford Taurus SHO. Ford also introduced a new engine for its rear-wheel drive Thunderbird/Cougar: a supercharged 3.8 liter V-6. Chevrolet unveiled a new engine that would power its high performance ZR-1 Corvette: the LT5 was made of aluminum, displaced 5.7 liters and used a 32-valve, double-overhead cam valve train. The V-8 also featured 16 intake runners instead of the usual eight. Output was listed at 385 h.p.

• Also on the engineering front, Chrysler equipped its Garrett turbocharger with a variable nozzle system to minimize turbo lag and give near immediate response. It would be installed on some of Chrysler's '90 model year products.

• Oldsmobile announced its new

1988 — Chevrolet's 1988 Corsica, introduced in March 1987, was chosen as Family Circle magazine's 'Car of the Year.'

1988 — The 1988 Buick Regal Limited, all new for that model year, was a member of the GM-10 platform used by other GM divisions.

Quad-4 engine, a turbocharged, four-cylinder, 2.3 liter engine with 16 valves, that produced 250 horsepower.

• Buick introduced the Reatta, a sporty, two-place limited edition model for the luxury market.

• Pontiac offered its 6000 STE model with four-wheel drive. The GM division also ceased production of the Fiero, its mid-engined sports car.

• Chrysler closed its plant in Kenosha, Wis. It had been an AMC and Nash manufacturing facility in its long history.

• GM chose the famous Waldorf-Astoria hotel in Manhattan as the venue in which to debut the company's new technology.

• To better serve its customers, Cadillac began to offer a roadside assistance program.

• Ford offered electrically heated windshields for quicker de-icing.

1989

1989 — Introduced in '88, the Mazda-produced 1989 Ford Probe, shown here in GT trim, was also offered in GL and LX models.

• The George Bush administration came out tough on the auto industry by demanding that automakers sell alternative-fueled cars with a target of .5 million of them by 1995 and double that amount from 1997 to 2004. In Congress, seven CAFE bills were introduced in an effort to push higher the corporate average fuel economy. They called for an increase in the average to 50 m.p.g. by early in the 21st century.

• Ford Motor Company bought an ailing Jaguar of Coventry, England, for $2.56 billion.

• Sales of automobiles and trucks for the 1989 calender year were down, on the average, slightly more than 5 percent.

• Ford Escort was the top-selling model of the year, edging out the Honda Accord.

• Oldsmobile introduced more products for the 1990 model year than in any other year in its history.

• Chevrolet's 1989 Corvette was offered with a six-speed manual

1989 continued

transmission, that was a cooperative venture between Chevrolet and ZF (Zahnradfabrik Friedrichshafen) of Germany.

• The number of states with mandatory seatbelt usage laws reached 33.

• Chrysler sold its stake in Mitsubishi Motors and purchased Thrifty Rent-a-Car. The company also introduced a 3.3 liter, V-6 engine of its own design and manufacture for 1990 model year vehicles. The 1989 Dodge Shelby Shadow was fitted with compression-molded plastic composite wheels. Chrysler re-introduced the Imperial for the 1990 model year.

• The AMC Talon became available as front-wheel drive or a four-wheel drive vehicle.

• Ford brought out the new version of the Lincoln Town Car for the 1990 model year. Lincoln-Mercury dealers discontinued selling the import Merkur.

• The states in the northeastern part of the country banded together to demand stricter, California-style emission standards.

• Chevrolet introduced its ZR-1 Corvette, a special high-performance version of the American sports car.

• GM introduced four-door models to the Pontiac Grand Prix, Buick Regal and Olds Cutlass Supreme lines.

• Michelin bought the Uniroyal Tire Co. for $1.5 billion.

1990

• Robert C. Stempel became the chairman, chief executive and chief operating officer of GM, taking over for Roger Smith. Stempel was the first engineer to ascend to GM's top post.

• GM marketed the Saturn automobile in October after seven years of preparation.

• Car production, at 6,078,306, was down slightly more than 11 percent from 1989 production.

• The cost of anti-lock braking systems was decreased by Chrysler. GM adopted the use of electronically controlled struts that varied shock damping in several Cadillacs and Oldsmobiles.

• Safety and ride improvements were implemented. The number of cars with air bags increased sharply.

• The Middle East crisis forced the price of gasoline upward.

• Congress passed a clean air bill that mandated stricter tailpipe standards and, for the first time, alternate-fueled cars.

• Contract talks between the Big 3 automakers and the UAW concluded peacefully following some speculation of a strike. Chrysler's agreement stipulated the St. Louis minivan plant would be the first U.S. assembly plant to function on a three-shift, 35-hour work week, and the workers would be paid for 40 hours.

• Auto manufacturing saw an increased utilization of computerization as well as plastic parts. GM's Saturn was built using numerous plastic body parts.

• Cadillac became the first manufacturer to use traction control, which was built in to the 1990 Cadillac Allante. The GM luxury automaker became the first U.S. automaker to receive the U.S. Commerce Department's "Malcolm Baldridge Quality Award."

• Harold "Red" Poling became

1990 — The sporty 1990 Mustang 5.0 was available as a GT hatchback, pictured, or as an LX convertible.

1990 — The 1990 Chevrolet Beretta was the official pace car for the 74th running of the Indianapolis 500. Chevrolet produced 7,500 Beretta Indy coupes.

chairman of Ford Motor Company March 1.

• GM bought a 50 percent share of the Swedish auto manufacturer Saab.

• Lincoln-Mercury sold the Australian-built Capri.

• Ford introduced a new 4.6 liter, SOHC (single-overhead cam) V-8 engine in the Lincoln Continental

Town Car. Ford also brought out new models of the Escort and Mercury Tracer.

• Gear Inc., a new venture by GM and Chrysler, was the first manufacturing partnership to involve two major U.S. automakers.

• GM unveiled its experimental electric car, the "Impact," at the Los Angeles car show.

• Buick introduced its '91 Park Avenue models as the first GM luxury car to use the electronically controlled, four-speed automatic transaxle.

• Dodge offered the twin-turbocharged Stealth.

• CAFE increased to 27.5, up from 26.5 m.p.g.

1990 — For the 1990 model year, Lincoln presented the Continental with a bolder grille, revised hood ornament and new taillamps.

1991 — The 1991 Ford Thunderbird Super Coupe featured a supercharged V-6 engine.

1991

• 1991 proved to be an off year for sales of autos and light trucks. Sales dropped some 12 percent to 12.3 million. With the drop Ford, GM and Chrysler bathed communally in red ink as losses were set at $7.5 billion.

• In response to heavy losses, GM began a cost cutting campaign that included layoffs of nearly 80,000 employees and closings of at least 20 plants.

• Chrysler's efforts to emerge from heavy losses included sales of its interests in Diamond-Star, FinanceAmerica and E.F. Hutton Credit Corp.

• General Motors built a concept car that would not only squeeze 100 miles per gallon of fuel, but also zip from 0-60 in under eight seconds. It was called the "Ultralite" and it weighed 1,400 pounds It was built with a carbon fiber body and powered by a two-stroke engine.

• Chrysler began its production of the new Viper at its new plant on Mack Avenue, in Detroit. The new sports car featured a V-10 engine.

• Buick reintroduced the full-sized Roadmaster. It had been absent from the Buick line since 1958. Buick also offered a supercharged V-6 engine in the Park Avenue.

• Chrysler Corporation became the first automaker to make airbags standard in all models of passenger vehicles.

• Cadillac introduced a redesigned Seville for its '92 line.

1991 — The all-new Dodge Stealth R/T was inspired by the Dodge Intrepid concept car.

1992 — The Roadmaster returned to the Buick lineup in the form of the '91 Roadmaster Estate Wagon and the '92 Roadmaster Sedan.

1992

• GM's new Saturn automobile was the only buoyant portion of the giant automaker as the five other divisions lost money. Saturn, GM's newest offering, sold very well and turned a profit in the process.

• After a dismal 1991, Chrysler bounced back to record net profits of $723 million in 1992. Brisk sales of the Chrysler's new LH vehicles and the Jeep Cherokee were strong contributors to the turnaround.

• GM and Ford both lost money in 1992. GM's losses totaled $4.45 billion, while Ford's approached $400 million.

• The Big Three experienced changes at the helm. At Chrysler, Lee Iacocca retired and Robert Eaton, formerly of GM, took over in the top spot.

• At GM, early in April, outside directors, led by John Smale of Proctor & Gamble Co., changed personnel: Executive committee chairman Robert Stempel was removed and replaced by Smale. Stempel, who retained the CEO and chairman posts, subsequently resigned in October. Jack Smith became president after Lloyd Reuss was moved from the presidency down to executive vice-president. Reuss subsequently retired.

• At Ford, president Philip Benton retired; however at the time of his retirement, a successor had not been named.

• The one-price, no-haggle practice was adopted by some dealerships across the country.

• A '92 Cadillac Allante, with the Northstar V-8, paced the Indianapolis 500 mile race. The Northstar engine was designed for short-term emergency operation with no coolant.

• GM entered a contract with Nissan to supply the latter with engine cylinder blocks.

• Mercury entered a venture with Nissan to co-design and build the Mercury Villager.

• The three U.S. automakers formed the United States Council for Automotive Research (USCAR).

• Chrysler moved its headquarters from Highland Park, Mich., (its home since 1925) to Auburn Hills, Mich.

• The average price of a 1992 model automobile was $16,700. The average price of a 1980 model was $7,574.

• For the '93 model, the horsepower on the ZR-1 Corvette was raised to 405. For the same model year, Saturn would add a station wagon to its line up. Also for '93 Pontiac and Chevrolet would introduce the redesigned Firebird and Camaro, respectively. The 1993 Cadillac Fleetwood Brougham would be the longest car in the U.S. at 225 inches.

• Ford introduced a completely, sleekly redesigned Lincoln Mark VIII for the '93 model year.

1992 — The 1992 Dodge Viper RT/10 came onto the scene in '91 with an 8 liter, 400 horsepower V-10 engine. It was the pace car for the 75th Indianapolis 500 in 1991.

1993

1993 — The all-new Ford Probe, a joint venture with Mazda, featured a 2.0 liter, twin overhead camshaft engine.

• Chrysler, with its new products and under the leadership of Chairman Robert Eaton and President Robert Lutz, had an average sales increase of 21 percent. Jeep led the way with a 55 percent increase.

• The North American Free Trade Agreement, NAFTA, a pact between the United States, Canada and Mexico, was approved in November, despite opposition from organized labor and a faction led by H. Ross Perot. NAFTA set up a $6 trillion per year trading block with the three nations.

• Chrysler's first Neon rolled off the Belvidere, Ill., assembly line Nov. 10.

• Buick unveiled its all new Riviera late in November. It was built on GM's G-platform, that would be shared by the Oldsmobile Aurora as a 1995 model.

• Harold "Red" Poling, chairman of Ford Motor Co., retired Nov. 1 and turned over his position to Alex Trotman. Poling had been in the automobile industry 42 years.

• Saturn, GM's newest automobile, celebrated its 10th anniversary in November. It had sold nearly 229,000 vehicles in the '93 model year.

• The 100th anniversary of the Duryea automobile was observed Sept. 11 at Greenfield Village, Dearborn, Mich., with the driving

of an exact replica of J. Frank Duryea's automobile. It was built by Richard Stevens, a high school teacher from Springfield, Mass., Duryea's hometown.

• The CAFE (corporate average fuel economy) rating rose to 28.3.

• Ford sent an executive team to Japan to assist Mazda in solving management problems.

• Ford celebrated its 90th birthday.

• GM offered power sliding doors on some of its minivans.

• The Chevrolet Geo Metro XFI was the year's mileage champ in America at 55 m.p.g.

• German automakers announced

1993 — The 1993 Chevrolet Camaro Z-28 served as the pace car for the 77th Indianapolis 500.

1993 — The 1993 Chrysler Eagle Vision TSi was introduced in '92 along with two other LH series cars, the Chrysler Concorde and the Dodge Intrepid.

plans to build plants in the United States, Mercedes-Benz in Vance, Ala., and BMW in Spartanburg, S.C.

• The MVMA (Motor Vehicle Manufacturers Association) became the American Automobile Manufacturers Association (AAMA). Andrew H. Card, Jr., became the president of the AAMA.

• Brand new models for the 1994 model year included Plymouth /Dodge Neon, Oldsmobile Aurora and a completely redesigned Ford Mustang. The Neon was equipped with an intake manifold made of glass-filled nylon.

• The U.S. government, Ford, GM and Chrysler formed a super car project called the Partnership for a New Generation of Vehicles to develop a car that will get 80 m.p.g.

• Chrysler sold Lamborghini.

1994

1994 — Chevrolet revived its Impala SS for the '94 model year and gave it life with a Corvette LT1, 260 horsepower V-8 engine.

• Chrysler put its new subcompact Neon on sale early in January.

• Ford announced in November it would reorganize itself under a program called Ford 2000 as put forth by Chairman Alex Trotman. The company planned to become the world's leading automaker by: growth in existing and emerging markets; building more products, but with fewer platforms and power trains, to earn more profit per vehicle. The changes would start January 1995.

• Sales of automobiles by General Motors, Ford and Chrysler soared and their factories produced cars as fast as they could for the entire year. Demand for products was high as factories struggled even at full capacity to meet it.

• Chrysler's products continued an upward sales trend with Grand Cherokees and pickup trucks leading the way. Chrysler's profits hit an all-time record high of $3.7 billion.

• Ford introduced its subcompact Aspire as a replacement for the Festiva. It also introduced (Sept.

1994 — The 1994 Chrysler LHS sedan stood as flagship of the line with a 214 horsepower SOHC V-6 engine and anti-lock brakes.

1994 continued

29) the Ford Contour/Mercury Mystique compacts to replace the Ford Tempo/Mercury Topaz.

• Cadillac's longtime divisional headquarters and assembly plant on Clark Avenue, aka "Clark Street," was demolished.

• Ford Motor Company became the first of the Big 3 to sign an agreement to build automobiles in Vietnam. An agreement was reached with Song Con Diesel to build Ford cars and trucks near Hanoi.

• Chevrolet reintroduced the Impala SS. Built on the Caprice platform, the Impala SS featured a higher horsepower engine and distinctive paint and trim.

• Oldsmobile offered an onboard navigation system on its LSS model.

• Cadillac provided a factory-backed warranty on pre-owned Cadillacs.

• BMW Manufacturing Corp. of Germany opened an assembly plant in November in Spartanburg, S.C.

• The first Saturn homecoming in Tennessee drew 38,000 people.

• Most U.S. automakers were now using the new ozone-friendly refrigerant, HFC-134A, replacing CFC-12 in air conditioning units.

• Chrysler introduced new '95 models, the Chrysler Cirrus/Dodge Stratus and the Dodge Avenger/Plymouth Sebring.

1995

1995 — Power for the 1995 Lincoln Continental came from a 4.6-liter V-8 engine.

• The new Lincoln Continental was introduced at the Detroit Auto Show

• In March, Toyota built its one millionth engine at its plant in Georgetown, Ky. The plant opened in 1989 to produce four-cylinder engines. It added V-6 engine production in 1994.

1995 — The Buick Riviera was all new for the 1995 model year.

• Saturn built its one millionth automobile June 1.

• General Motors assembly plant at Hamtramck, Mich., with its robotic assembly lines, produced its one millionth vehicle in September. It opened in the early '80s.

• George Romney, former CEO of American Motors Corporation and principal proponent of the American compact car, died in July at age 88. Romney, former three-term governor of Michigan, made a bid for the presidency in the '60s. He was appointed to former President Nixon's cabinet as secretary of housing and urban development. Romney was also former managing director of the Automobile Manufacturers Association, a forerunner of the American Automobile Manufacturers Association.

• The United Auto Workers, the International Association of Machinists and the United Steelworkers of America signed an agreement that would unite the three unions by the year 2000. The union unification was seen as a move to gain more political clout and increased effectiveness at the bargaining table.

• German automaker Mercedes Benz began building an assembly plant in Vance, Ala., with plans for production in early 1997.

• After a $4.2 billion investment, Ford's Jaguar division in Coventry, England, finally showed its first profits since 1988, the year before Ford bought the company.

• The U.S. Government initiated trade sanctions on Japanese luxury model automobiles in May.

• Kirk Kerkorian, a billionaire investor from Las Vegas, Nev., along with former Chrysler chairman, Lee Iacocca, attempted to take over Chrysler Corporation.

• Nissan announced it would spend $30 million to build a new engine assembly plant in Decherd, Tenn.

• General Motors announced in January it would discontinue making its large-platform rear wheel drive cars by the close of the 1996 model year. Cars affected are: the Chevrolet Caprice/Impala SS, the Buick Roadmaster and the Cadillac Fleetwood. Dwindling demand was cited as the reason for discontinuance.

• The Big 3 automakers reported record earnings on sales in 1994. The total was $13.9 billion. Ford's earnings were $5.3 billion, GM $4.9 billion, Chrysler $3.7 billion.

• New models were introduced by the Big 3. Ford debuted is all-new designs of the Ford Taurus and Mercury Sable. GM introduced its newly styled Saturn, and Chrysler showed for the first time its Plymouth Breeze.

1996 — Ford's Taurus received a complete redesign for the 1996 model year.

1996 — The 1996 Plymouth Breeze sedan helped lead the resurgence of the Plymouth nameplate in the mid-90s.

1996

• A UAW strike at the Delphi Chassis Systems plant, Dayton, Ohio, idled 26 GM plants for 17 days.

• The automobile industry centenial marked the 100th anniversary of the beginning of the automobile industry in the United States. The industry began when the Duryea brothers produced 13 vehicles from the same set of plans - the first mass produced vehicle - in their Duryea Motor Wagon Company workshop in Springfield, Mass., in 1896.

• The centennial of the American automobile industry was observed in Detroit and Dearborn, Mich., with a week-long celebration in mid-June. There was a variety of activities involving numerous car clubs, including the largest, the Antique Automobile Club of America, Hershey, Penn., and such Motor City institutions as Henry Ford Museum, Greenfield Village, the Detroit Historical Museum, the National Automotive History Collection at the Detroit Public Library, and others. Capping off the centennial celebration was a car show featuring 1,500 restored examples of the Motor City's finest iron, and a parade of 101 historic

vehicles, one from each of the industry's first 100 years, as well as the current model year.

• The American Automobile Centennial week concluded with a formal reception and dinner in downtown Detroit. Comedian/car fan Jay Leno served as master of ceremonies for the gala and grand marshal of the parade.

• Chrysler introduced a coupe version of the Viper, the GTS-R.

• GM became the first auto manufacturer to warranty tires.

• GM announced it would move from its headquarters since 1929 to new corporate location in downtown Detroit in the Renaissance Center.

• In March, the California Air Resources Board (CARB) postponed

its zero emission (electric) vehicle mandate from 1998 to 2003. CARB's action came after findings that then-current battery technology would not result in vehicles with the range and performance to meet the needs of a wide range of consumers.

• GM announced plans to begin marketing its dedicated electric vehicle , the two-seater sports car known as the EV1, in Southern California and Arizona in fall of 1996. Ford and Chrysler were developing battery-powered versions of vehicles for marketing.

• The federal government and the auto industry, led by AAMA, began a renewed effort to encourage international harmonization of safety and emmision standards for vehicles.

Personalities

In the 19th century, the nearest thing to a practical form of personalized transportation was the horse and buggy. But there were men in America who envisioned something better. It was the imagination, resourcefulness and determination of men such as these that brought to America four million miles of modern roads and streets traveled by more than 100 million cars, trucks and buses.

Edgar and Elmer Apperson

Walter Austin

Carl Breer

APPERSON, Edgar
1870-1959

On July 4, 1894, drove his first car, manufactured on assignment for Elwood Haynes, with whom he and his brother Elmer later formed Haynes-Apperson Auto Company ... after dissolution of Haynes-Apperson, Edgar and his brother formed Apperson Brothers Motor Car Company to manufacture the Apperson "Jack Rabbit" ... following his brother's death, Edgar sold to a syndicate in 1924 ... in 1946 made the initial member of industry's "Hall of Fame."

APPERSON, Elmer
1861-1920

Collaborated with brother Edgar on the manufacture of Elwood Haynes' first car ... partner in both the Haynes-Apperson and the Apperson Brothers Motor Car Company ... died while watching auto race at Los Angeles Speedway.

AUSTIN, Walter S.
1866-1965

Along with his father, built the Austin Highway King in a little shop in Grand Rapids, Michigan, 1901-1918 ... the Austin was a luxury car with some models costing $6,000 and up ... his major contributions include inventions covering the four-speed planetary transmission with steering post shift, double cantilever springs, and two-speed axle.

BENDIX, Vincent
1883-1945

In 1907 organized an auto firm, and sold some 7,000 Bendix motor buggies before the company failed ... developed the starter drive which bears his name, first selling it to the Eclipse Machine Company in 1913 ... became a leader in the aircraft field, and sponsor of the Bendix-Transcontinental Air Races.

BREER, Carl
1883 - 1970

Breer, along with Owen Skelton and Fred Zeder came to be known as the "Three Musketeers." ... they worked together for 33 years ... known primarily for their engineering innovations at Chrysler Corp. from the '20s through the '50s ... the three-man engineering team created the foundation on which Walter P. Chrysler built the corporation bearing his name ... Breer, along with Skelton, joined Fred M. Zeder at Studebaker in 1915 and formed the nucleus of Studebaker's engineering department ... Chrysler persuaded the "three engineering musketeers" to join him at Willys in 1920 ... when Willys went into receivership, Breer, Skelton, and Zeder formed their own consulting firm ... they subsequently went with Chrysler's Maxwell-Chalmers firm and Chrysler Corp. came into being ... at Chrysler the team of three men created the innovative Chrysler Airflow cars, Fluid Drive transmission, four-wheel hydraulic brakes, downdraft carbu-retor and other engineering feats ... became director of Chrysler's engineering research institute.

BRISCOE, Benjamin
1869-1945

Founded the Briscoe Manufacturing Company in 1887 ... in 1903 joined with Jonathan Maxwell to form the Maxwell-Briscoe Motor Company ... in 1910 organized the United States Motor Company, a short-lived (1912) aggregation of some 130 separate firms ... left United States Motor Company in 1912, and in 1913 organized the Briscoe Motor Company and the Argo Motor Company to manufacture cyclecars.

BRISCOE, Frank
1875-1954

Founder and president of Brush Runabout Company ... also connected with brother Benjamin with Briscoe Manufacturing Company ... other endeavors included interests in Maxwell-Briscoe, United States Motor Company, and Briscoe Motor Company.

Vincent Bendix

Benjamin Briscoe

David Dunbar Buick

Lee Chadwick

Hugh Chalmers

Roy D. Chapin

BUICK, David Dunbar
1855-1929

Instrumental in devising a technique for applying enamel to cast iron ... using the money he received from his plumbing ventures, Buick in 1902 founded the Buick Manufacturing Company to work on a valve-in-head engine ... having perfected the engine, he organized Buick Motor Car Company in 1903 with the backing of the Briscoe brothers ... the company was unsuccessful, and on Nov. 1, 1904, William Durant bought the controlling interest.

CHADWICK, Lee S.
1875-1958

Engineering genius who held close to 200 patents, many in automotive field ... built his first two cars in 1899 while superintendent of the Boston Ball Bearing Company ... when company was sold in 1900, became general superintendent of the Searchmont Motor Company ... built the Chadwick, 1903-1911 ... first car to use a supercharger, 1906 ... in racing competition, one of the fastest cars of its day ... credited with developing a carburetor employing a variable gasoline flow for different throttle openings ... president of Perfection Stove Company, 1923-1952.

CHALMERS, Hugh
1873-1932

Worked for National Cash Register from the time he was 14, rose to vice president before he was 30 ... in 1907 bought the Thomas half of the Thomas-Detroit Company ... by 1909 had complete control of Chalmers-Detroit, then renamed the Chalmers Motor Company ... Chalmers backed Harry W. Ford's Saxon Motor Company in 1913 in a spectacular, though eventually unsuccessful, attempt to challenge the Model T ... became chairman of the board of Chalmers when it was leased to Maxwell in 1917, a position he held until his retirement in 1922.

CHAPIN, Roy D.
1880-1936

First worked for Ransom E. Olds as a photographer and gear filer ... while still in Olds' employ, drove a 1901 curved-dash model to New York for the second annual National Auto Show ... left Olds in 1906 to organize along with Howard E. Coffin, Thomas-Detroit Company later Chalmers-Detroit Company ... in 1909, again with H.E. Coffin, Chapin with the backing of J.L. Hudson left Chalmers-Detroit to organize and head Hudson Motor Car Company ... backed movement for good roads as chairman of numerous highway institutions ... served as Secretary of Commerce under President Herbert Hoover in 1932. Roy's son, Roy D. Chapin, Jr. became general manager and then was named chairman of the AMC board and chief executive officer in January 1967. Chapin, Jr. retired as CEO in 1977.

Louis Chevrolet

J. Walter Christie (L)

Walter P. Chrysler

CHEVROLET, Louis
1878-1941

Came to the United
States from Switzerland
in 1900 to sell a wine
pump which he had
invented ... drove with
brothers Gaston and
Arthur ... raced against
Barney Oldfield ... his
racing style attracted
William C. Durant, who
engaged Chevrolet as
team driver for Buick ...
designed the first models
of the Chevrolet for the
Chevrolet Motor Car
Company in 1911 ...
president of Frontenac
Motor Company, which,
in addition to race cars,
made a racing conversion
for the Model T Ford.

CHRISTIE, John W.
1886-1944

First builder of a successful front wheel drive
automobile ... Christie
racers, competing on
tracks in the United
States and abroad from
1904 to 1910, proved
soundness of Christie's
engineering concepts ...
manufactured fire engine
tractors, 1912-1916 ...
developed an armored
tank in the 1930's capa-
ble of cross-country

speeds of 50 m.p.h. ...
tested and liked by
United States military but
rejected by War
Department ... Christie's
designs were sold abroad
... British and Russians
promptly began manufac-
turing Christie tanks in
large numbers.

CHRYSLER, Walter P.
1875-1940

Left his job as works
manager for American
Locomotive in 1911 to
join Buick Motor
Company ... when he left
General Motors for Willys
in 1920, Chrysler was
president of Buick and
first vice president of
General Motors ... at
Willys Chrysler was exec-
utive vice-president
engaged primarily in sav-
ing the company from
bankruptcy ... almost
simultaneously, he was
attempting to salvage the
foundering Maxwell-
Chalmers Company ... by
1922 Willys was back on
its feet, and Chrysler
turned his full attention
to the Maxwell-Chalmers
situation ... in 1924 he
brought Maxwell-
Chalmers out of the

woods with the introduc-
tion at the National
Automobile Show of the
new Chrysler models ...
shortly thereafter, Chase
Securities Corporation
agreed to lend Maxwell
$50 million, and the cor-
poration that was to
become Chrysler was on
its way ... the years following 1924 brought
continuing success to the
Chrysler Corporation.

CLIFTON, Colonel
Charles
1853-1928

In 1897 left Ball, Lewis
and Yates Coal Mining
Company to become sec-
retary and treasurer for
George N. Pierce
Company ... remained
treasurer after a 1909
reorganization which saw
the formation of Pierce-
Arrow Motor Car
Company ... in 1916,
Colonel Clifton became
president of Pierce-
Arrow, and in 1919 was
named chairman of its
board of directors ...
apart from his duties
with Pierce-Arrow,
Colonel Clifton served as
president of National

Automobile Chamber of
Commerce from its birth
in 1913 until March 2,
1927, when he resigned
his active post to serve in
an honorary capacity.

COLE, Edward N.
1909-1977

Born in Michigan on
Sept. 17, 1909, Ed Cole
graduated from the GM
Institute in 1933 and
joined Cadillac's engi-
neering department. Rose
through the ranks to
become chief engineer at
Chevrolet in May 1952
... Developed the revolu-
tionary Chevy V-8, and
oversaw the introduction
and development of the
Corvette drivetrain ...
Designed and spearhead-
ed the innovative rear-
engined, air-cooled
Corvair ... became gener-
al manager of Chevrolet,
executive vice president

Col. Charles Clifton

Powel Crosley, Jr.

Horace Dodge

John Dodge

of General Motors and, finally, president of GM, a rare achievement for an engineer. After his retirement in 1974, he continued his first love, engineering ... first at International Huskey and then at Checker Motors in Kalamazoo, Mich., where he was named president. He died in a plane crash May 2, 1977.

CROSLEY, Jr., Powel 1886-1961

Considered by many to be well ahead of his time ... claim to fame in the automobile industry was a series of diminutive economy cars boasting 50 mile-per-gallon gas mileage ... native of Cincinnati, Crosley first attempted entering the automobile business prior to 1910, but met with no success ... made a name for himself in radios and also refrigerators with the novel feature of shelves in the door (known as the "Shelvador") ... in 1939, Crosley returned to the automotive field with a tiny economy car powered by a two-cylinder engine ... after World War II, Crosley introduced a more conventional, but still tiny,

car powered by a unique sheetmetal four-cylinder engine. By way of comparison, the Crosley was more than a foot shorter than the Volkswagen Beetle ... in the seller's market of the late 40's, Crosley production peaked at 28,000 units in 1948, but interest soon waned ... problems with the engine and buyer resistance to small cars spelled the end for Powel Crosley's cars, despite a broad range of models offered ... in 1952, Crosley sold the automobile company and production ended.

CUMMINS, Clessie L. 1888-1968

Developed first high-speed light-weight diesel engine ... founder of the Cummins Engine Company ... credited with revolutionizing the highway transportation industry by adapting the sometime cumbersome marine diesel engine to truck use ... demonstrated the automotive capabilities of the diesel by installing a four-cylinder marine diesel engine in a Packard automobile chassis in 1929 and driving it from Indianapolis to New York

... in 1931 one of Cummins' diesel-powered trucks was driven from New York to Los Angeles ... Cummins retired as president and board chairman of Cummins Diesel in 1956.

DOBLE, Abner 1890-1961

Built his first steam car at the age of 16, and in his spare time as a student at MIT he designed and built several more ... in 1914 he drove a prototype model to Detroit where he found recognition and backing ... four years later 80 Doble Detroit Steam cars had been built ... in 1920 he founded Doble Steam Motors in the San Francisco area ... much of Doble's fame came as a result of the prominence of his clientele ... Hollywood stars and starlets of the day along with royalty from Europe and Asia absorbed much of his modest production ... in later years Doble spent much of his time abroad working as a steam power consultant to locomotive manufacturers and other firms ... he returned to the U.S. in 1950 ... ill health forced him into retirement in the early 1950's.

DODGE BROTHERS, John, 1864-1920; Horace, 1868-1920

After working as machinists for several companies, the brothers developed a ball bearing bicycle and organized Evans and Dodge Bicycle Company to manufacture it ... after numerous financial transactions, their company was absorbed by a Canadian firm and the Dodges went to Detroit to open a machine shop ... in 1901 and 1902 they made transmissions for the Olds Motor Works ... in 1903 Henry Ford offered each of the brothers 50 shares of stock in his new company, provided they would manufacture engines for him ... although criticized by friends for doing so, the Dodges accepted Ford's terms, becoming the owners of one-tenth of the newly formed Ford Motor Company ... in 1919 they received $25,000,000 for their original $20,000 investment ... the Dodge Brothers left Ford to found their own company, Dodge Brothers, Inc., and manufactured their Dodge Brothers car.

Frederick Duesenberg

William C. Durant

Charles Duryea

J. Frank Duryea

DORRIS, George P. 1874-1968

With the help of his brother, Dorris built his first car in Nashville, Tennessee, in 1897 ... helped found the St. Louis Motor Carriage Company in St. Louis, Missouri, in 1898 ... when firm moved to Peoria, Illinois, in 1906, Dorris established the Dorris Motor Car Company in St. Louis ... Dorris cars were always of advanced design, some with overhead valve engines and custom bodies ... the company also made a line of trucks and buses ... production of all vehicles stopped in 1926.

DUESENBERG, Frederick Samuel 1877-1932

By 1902 Duesenberg's racing experience had won him a position as test driver for the Rambler Company ... in 1904 he designed his own car, a racer, which was manufactured by the Mason Auto Company until 1910 ... about that time, Duesenberg designed his famous horizontal valve engines and

introduced them to the racing world ... in 1913 the Duesenberg Motor Company was organized, producing a multitude of engines for the war effort ... following the war, Fred and brother August organized Duesenberg Brothers Incorporated to manufacture the racing machines which in 1919 captured all the world's records up to 300 miles in every class from 161 to 450 cubic inches ... although E.L. Cord bought control of his company in 1927, Duesenberg remained active in racing until his death, the result of a driving accident.

DURANT, William Crapo 1860-1947

At 25, Durant teamed with Dallas Dort to form the Durant-Dort Carriage Company, manufacturers of two-wheeled carts ... in 1904 Durant bought out and reorganized Buick Motor Car Company ... after a 1908 attempt to merge Buick, Maxwell-Briscoe, Ford, and Reo proved unsuccessful, Durant on September 16, 1908, launched the General

Motors Co. ... in the next two years, Durant bought in quick succession Cadillac, Olds, Oakland, Carter, Elmore, Ewing, Welch and several other lesser auto producers ... financial difficulties forced Durant out of General Motors in 1910, but by 1915, after his spectacular success with Chevrolet, "Fabulous Billy" was back to take over the corporation he had founded ... Durant remained at the head of GM until 1920, when a depression saw the corporation's stock tumble from $400 to $12 a share despite his attempts to turn the tide ... 1920 saw a management reorganization at General Motors leaving Durant on his own to start over again ... and start he did, participating in a series of enterprises ranging from Durant, Dort, and Star cars to Flint cars and finally Mason trucks ... the 1929 depression, however, all but ended Durant's financial undertakings, and he lived in comparative obscurity until his death.

DURYEA, Charles E. 1861-1939

Started in the bicycle business ... by 1891 had secured financial backing for a carriage-engine combination of his own design ... September 22, 1893, was recorded in the Springfield *Evening Union* as the official debut of the first Duryea car, whose creation is still lost in controversy between Charles E. and brother J. Frank ... after proving the vehicle's reliability in numerous races, the brothers went into business as the Duryea Motor Wagon Company in 1896 ... two years later both Duryeas left the company, and Charles E. organized the Duryea Power Company of Reading, Pennsylvania, which manufactured a three-cylinder car until 1914 ... after 1914 Duryea devoted much of his time to the writing of textbooks about the automobile.

DURYEA, J. Frank 1870-1967

Shares credit with his brother Charles for designing and building

Andrew L. Dyke

Albert Russel Erskine

Virgil Exner

America's first marketable gasoline-powered automobile ... the Duryea brothers road tested their first car in Springfield, Massachusetts, in 1893 ... in 1895 James drove a Duryea Motor Wagon to victory in the first American automobile race ... averaged 7 1/2 m.p.h. over a snow-covered course between Chicago and Evanston, Illinois ... James subsequently manufactured the Stevens-Duryea from 1901 to 1915, when he sold his stock in the company and retired.

DYKE, Andrew L. 1876-1959

Organized first automobile parts and supply business in America in St. Louis, Missouri, in 1899 ... Dyke developed and manufactured (1900) what is regarded as first American float-feed carburetor ... published *Dr. Dyke's Anatomy of the Automobile*, one of America's first how-to-do-it books for owner-mechanics (1904) ... from 1910 to 1952, edited and published the highly respected *Dyke's Automobile and Gasoline Engine Encyclopedia* ... Dyke established or became active in many early car producing firms: St. Louis, Dyke-Britton, D.L.G., Dorris ... from 1899 to 1904 Dyke sold kits from which buyers could assemble their own cars ... conducted one of America's first correspondence schools for auto mechanics.

EATON, Robert 1940 - —

The current chairman and chief executive officer of Chrysler Corporation ... joined Chrysler March 16, 1992, as vice-chairman and chief operating officer and a member of the company's board of directors ... As Chrysler's CEO, Eaton successfully thwarted a corporate takeover bid in 1995 by investor Kirk Kerkorian and associates

... was selected as the Automotive Hall of Fame '95 "Industry Leader of the Year" ... came from an engineering background and was president of General Motors in Europe before joining Chrysler ... born in Colorado and educated in Kansas.

ERSKINE, Albert Russel 1871-1933

Became treasurer of Studebaker in 1910 ... became first vice president in 1913, and president in 1915 ... in 1928, as president, Erskine witnessed the greatest sales in the company's history up to that time ... in that same year, he negotiated the Pierce-Arrow-Studebaker merger.

EXNER, Virgil 1909 - 1973

Although he designed automobiles for a number of companies, Exner's name is most closely associated with Chrysler Corp. and its "Forward Look" cars he designed during the late

'50s ... started designing advertising brochures for Studebaker, and did his first automotive design work at GM ... after a tumultuous period working for Raymond Loewy's design studio and penning designs for Studebaker, Exner ended up at Chrysler ... during the early '50s, he was responsible for the designs of many of the company's show cars, but it was in the mid-50s that his designs came to the forefront on production cars ... his fin-bedecked, longer, lower, wider Chrysler products of 1957 caused a sensation in the industry, and left Ford and GM scrambling to catch up to Chrysler's design lead ... but as the fin fad waned, Exner's designs fell from favor, and he left Chrysler in the early '60s ... in the years between his departure from Chrysler and his death in 1973, Exner continued to design cars, turning his attention toward a series of neo-classic designs based upon the great classics of the '20s and '30s.

The Fisher Brothers: (L-R) Alfred J., Lawrence P., Charles, T., Fred J., William A., Howard A. and Edward F.

FISHER BROTHERS,
Frederic J., 1878-1941
Charles T., 1880-1963
William A., 1886-1969
Lawrence P., 1888-1961
Edward F., 1891-1972
Alfred J., 1892-1963
Howard A., 1902-1942

With skills acquired from their father, a master carriage maker, and $50,000 in capital, Frederic and Charles established the Fisher Body Company in 1908, and in succeeding years Lawrence, Alfred and Howard were brought into the business ... Frederic and Charles realized that motoring would remain a seasonal activity until motorists could be protected from the elements ... they began campaigning for closed bodies, and in 1910 their efforts were rewarded when 150 closed bodies were ordered by the Cadillac

Motor Company ... in December of that year the Fisher Closed Body Company was formed ... in 1916 the two companies were merged into the Fisher Body Corporation ... the brothers sold their corporation to General Motors, their biggest customer, in 1926 for an estimated $208 million of General Motors stock ... the brothers became key General Motors officials, helping to run the firm's newly acquired Fisher Body Division ... Lawrence became president of the Cadillac Motor Car Company, one of General Motors' biggest divisions ... Frederic and Charles, both GM vice-presidents, retired in 1934 to devote their time to personal business interests and philanthropic organizations.

FLANDERS, Walter E. 1871-1923

One of the auto industry's first mass-production experts ... in 1907 Flanders headed an Ohio firm which secured a contract for 1,000 Ford crankshafts ... in 1908 firm produced 10,000 units for Ford ... Ford was so impressed that he hired Flanders as production manager ... left Ford in 1909 to found the E.M.F. Co., whose cars were distributed by Studebaker ... served for a short time as vice president and general manager of Studebaker ... left Studebaker in 1911 and started the Flanders Manufacturing Company and subsequently the United States Motor Company ... latter included Maxwell, Stoddard-Dayton, Brush, Alden Sampson truck

Walter E. Flanders

and component manufacturers ... eventually Maxwell and another Flanders-based company, Chalmers, formed the nucleus of Chrysler Corporation.

FORD, Edsel 1893 - 1943

Although his father, Henry Ford, never permitted him to fully control Ford, Edsel still managed to exert consid-

Edsel Ford

Henry Ford

Henry Ford, II

Herbert H. Franklin

erable influence over the cars bearing his family's name ... this was especially true in the area of design, where he had a hand in the shaping of the Model A Ford, Lincoln-Zephyr, and the Lincoln Continental ... the only child of Henry Ford, Edsel was born in 1893, and upon his graduation from Detroit University School in 1912 he began a full-time career with Ford Motor Co. ... by 1919, Edsel was president of Ford, but Henry Ford still called most of the shots ... may have disagreed with many of his father's policies, but he seldom took a stand against his father ... the increasingly strained relationship with his father took its toll on his health ... surgery for stomach ulcers in 1942 revealed he had cancer ... Edsel Ford died the following year ... oldest son, Henry Ford II, took over the reins of the company and guided it through the difficult times following World War II.

FORD, Henry
1863-1947

As a youngster Ford showed his mechanical aptitude by constructing a steam engine when he was 15, and became an expert watch repairman before he was 20 ... his first car, built while he was an engineer with the Edison Illuminating Company, made its first successful run in 1896 ... in 1899 he resigned from Edison to become chief engineer for the Detroit Automobile Company, remaining with them until 1902 ... in that year, Ford left Detroit Automobile (later reorganized as the Henry Ford Company, and finally the Cadillac Automobile Company) because of policy differences ... six months later he organized Ford Motor Company ... a proponent of light, serviceable cars, Ford on Oct. 1, 1908, introduced the Model T and produced in the 19 years that followed over 15 million "Tin Lizzies" ... 1927 marked the end of "T" production, followed by the Model A ... Ford established a $5 minimum wage in 1914, increasing it to $6 in

1922, introduced the eight-hour day and profit-sharing in 1914, and adopted a 40-hour week in 1926 ... Mr. Ford played an active role in the management of the Ford Motor Company until 1945, when his grandson Henry Ford II was named president of the company.

FORD, Henry II
1917 - 1987

Following the death of Edsel Ford, the Ford Motor Co. stood at a critical juncture ... Henry Ford no longer possessed the mental ability to adequately run the company, and Edsel's widow, Eleanor, did not want to see Harry Bennett placed in charge by the senior Ford ... through her extensive stock ownership in the company, she was able to see to it that her oldest son, Henry Ford II, ascended to the company presidency in 1945 at the age of 28 ... Known as "The Deuce," Ford, with the help of a talented staff of executives known as the "whiz

kids," guided his grandfather's company back to profitability after the troubled times of the mid-40s ... remained firmly in control of the company over the next three decades, reminding those questioning his decisions that his name was on the building ... an era ended when The Deuce retired from his position as chief executive officer in 1979 ... he remained chairman, but retired from that position the following year.

FRANKLIN, Herbert H.
1867-1956

Started out as a reporter on the weekly Coxsackie, New York, *Herald* and eventually became owner of the paper ... sold it in 1893 to form the H.H. Franklin Manufacturing Company, which pioneered in die casting ... in 1902 placed the Franklin air-cooled car on the market ... it pioneered in many progressive and innovative design features ... under

Joseph W. Frazer

Charles J. Glidden

Ray A. Graham

Elwood G. Haynes

Franklin's guidance the firm's production climbed from 12 the first year to 11,000 in 1923, and nearly 15,000 by 1930.

FRAZER, Joseph W. 1892 - 1971

A high-bred, well educated Tennessean who came to be known as one of the greatest salesmen in the auto industry ... while with Chevrolet in the '20s, Frazer worked as the division's treasurer and helped establish General Motors Acceptance Corp. (GMAC) ... worked for Pierce-Arrow, Maxwell and Chrysler and counted Walter P. Chrysler as a personal friend ... named the Plymouth, Chrysler's entry into the low-priced field ... left Chrysler to become president and general manager of Willys Overland, then president and chairman of Graham-Paige ... in 1945 he formed a corporation with Henry J. Kaiser to build automobiles bearing their names.

GLIDDEN, Charles Jasper 1857-1927

In 1900 Glidden retired from active business life, having accumulated a comfortable fortune during his association with the Bell Telephone Company ... in 1903 he made a motor tour of the major countries of Europe, followed a year later by an auto journey around the world, the first of its kind ... during the latter trip, Glidden conceived the idea of organizing a series of motor tours around the United States to promote the infant auto industry ... the first Glidden Trophy was awarded to Percy Pierce in 1905, the last to a team of Metz cars in 1913 ... while in existence the Glidden Tour was conducted annually (with the exception of 1912) and served to capture the imagination of its spectators, while at the same time stimulating their interest in the burgeoning auto industry ... in his later years he

devoted much of his time to promoting interest in aviation.

GRAHAM, Ray A. 1887-1932

Along with brothers Robert C. and Joseph C., began in the glass manufacturing business, using machines invented by Joseph ... while managing the family's farm properties, Ray became interested in the possibilities of light weight trucks and invented a rear axle to be used under a Ford chassis ... after their glass company merged with the Owens Bottle Company, Joseph and Robert joined Ray to form the Graham Brothers Truck Company, builders of truck bodies ... in 1921 the brothers made an agreement with Dodge allowing them to build a truck carrying the Graham nameplate, but using Dodge engines and transmissions ... to keep the arrangement permanent, Dodge bought majority interest in

Graham Brothers six months after the original agreement, and the Grahams became officials of Dodge Brothers ... their association with Dodge was brief, lasting only until 1927 when they left to buy and reorganize Paige-Detroit, forming the Graham-Paige Motors Corporation.

HAYNES, Elwood G. 1857-1925

Haynes' car, among the first built in the United States, was constructed with the aid of the Apperson Brothers and successfully tested in 1894 ... four years later he started Haynes Automobile Company; initially successful, it went out of business in 1925 ... aside from his manufacturing endeavors, Haynes was a prominent metallurgist, pioneering in the use of aluminum in motor cars as well as in developing several important structural alloys.

Lee Iacocca

Thomas B. Jeffery

Edward "Ned" Jordan

IACOCCA, Lee
1924 - —

Few men in the auto industry are able to make a name for themselves as a top executive of more than one manufacturer ... Lee Iacocca is such a man, having risen to the upper levels of Ford Motor Co., and then, after being unceremoniously dismissed by Henry Ford II, assuming a lead role at Chrysler Corp. ... started with Ford and rose quickly through the company ranks ... a shrewd marketer, Iacocca played a major role in the "safety campaign of 1956, along with the development of the Mustang, the Lincoln Continental Mark III and the Mustang II ... by the late '70s, Iacocca seemed poised to take over as head of Ford Motor Co. upon Henry Ford II's retirement ... personal differences between the two men led to Iacocca's dismissal in 1978 ... within months, he had been hired as president of beleaguered Chrysler Corp., and became the company chairman the following year ... was instrumental in securing federal loan guarantees that kept Chrysler afloat through difficult times in the early '80s ... by the latter half of that decade, Chrysler was once again a profitable company. Iacocca aligned himself with billionaire Kirk Kerkorian in a bid to take over Chrysler Corp. It was unsuccessful ... Iacocca retired from Chrysler in Dec 1992.

JEFFERY, Thomas B.
1845-1910

Came to the United States in 1863, and in 1879 began to manufacture bicycles under the trademark "Rambler" ... Jeffery, who invented the clincher tire in 1881, began experimenting with motor vehicles as early as 1897, but it wasn't until 1900 that he successfully produced one ... in that year, he sold his bicycle business and purchased a factory in which he began to manufacture G & J cars (later known as Rambler cars) in 1902 ... Jeffery remained president of Thomas B. Jeffery Company, later the Nash Motors Company, until his death.

JORDAN, Edward "Ned"
1882-1958

Entered the auto industry as advertising manager for the Thomas B. Jeffery Company ... Jordan remained with the Jeffery Company until 1916 when he organized his own company, the Jordan Motor Car Company ... although production was low — Jordan refused to build more than 5,000 "Playboys" in any single year, the company always showed a profit, largely as a result of its advertising program ... instituted by Jordan himself it was the first to stress the esthetic value of the car and make an appeal to the prospective buyer's sense of adventure and glamour ... the company prospered until the 1929 market crash ... after the Depression, Jordan worked as an advertising consultant, and in 1950 began writing a weekly column in the *Automotive News*.

Henry B. Joy

JOY, Henry Bourne
1864-1936

Served as president of the Fort Street Depot Company from 1896 to 1907 ... while with Fort Street Depot, Joy became interested in W.D. Packard's auto company, initially as an investor, eventually becoming president of Packard in 1901 ... while with Packard, he also championed the movement for good roads as president of the Lincoln Highway Association ... Joy remained president of Packard until 1916, at which time he became chairman of the board ... ill health forced him to retire several years before his death.

Henry J. Kaiser

Charles F. Kettering

Charles Brady King

William S. Knudsen

KAISER, Henry J.
1882 - 1967

From humble beginnings in New York, he made a fortune in sand and gravel in the Pacific Northwest ... he worked on the Hoover, Bonneville and Grand Coulee Dam projects and built ships, known as the Liberty Ships, during World War II ... following the war, he experimented with fiberglass bodied cars and front wheel drive cars ... formed a corporation with Joe Frazer in 1945 to build cars bearing their names.

KETTERING, Charles F.
1876-1958

Began his career as an engineer for National Cash Register ... after working at NCR for five years, left to organize Delco Laboratories for the purpose of developing an ignition system ... one of his first customers was Henry Leland, president of Cadillac, who, after ordering 8,000 ignition systems, later called upon Kettering to perfect the electric self-starter that appeared on the 1911 Cadillac ... in 1916 he sold his interest in Delco to the United Motors Corporation ... in 1920, "Boss Ket" became the head of the General Motors research laboratories, contributing toward the development of such things as quick-drying paint and Ethyl gasoline ... Kettering went into a purely nominal retirement in 1947, remaining with General Motors as a director and research consultant until his death in Dayton, Ohio.

KING, Charles Brady
1868-1957

Like Ford, King first became interested in self-propelled vehicles upon seeing one at the 1893 Columbian Exposition, where he had gone to exhibit some of his own inventions ... preceding the 1896 debut of his first practical vehicle, King in 1895 had organized American Motor League, a pioneer association to promote better roads ... King also designed the 1902 "Silent Northern," a vehicle which featured three-point suspension and an integral engine-transmission assembly ... he organized the King Motor Car Company in 1910, and in 1916 turned his efforts to the design of aircraft engines.

KNUDSEN, Semon E.
1912- –

Semon Emil "Bunkie" Knudsen was the son of William S. Knudsen, a prominent automotive engineer ... worked his way up through the ranks at General Motors ... at age 44, in 1956, became the youngest general manager of a GM automotive division taking the top spot at Pontiac ... changed the image of Pontiac from a stodgy old woman's car to a stylish, race bred, wide track performer ... In November 1961 Knudsen was made general manager of Chevrolet. Under his leadership Chevrolet's production increased by nearly one million cars in four years ... resigned from General Motors January 1, 1968 ... became president of Ford Motor Company in February, 1968 and remained for 18 months ... formed Rectrans to build mobile homes. It became part of White Motor Corporation and Knudsen joined the firm as chairman of the board and chief executive officer in May 1971. He remained with White until December 1980. Knudsen served as chairman of the Motor Vehicle Manufacturers Association (MVMA) in 1977-78.

KNUDSEN, William S.
1879-1948

Joined the Ford Motor Company in 1912 as manager of the company's 27 plants ... during

Semon E. Knudsen

Henry M. Leland

Alvan Macauley

Howard C. Marmon

World War I, Knudsen was in charge of manufacturing Eagle boats for the Navy ... before leaving Ford in 1921 he had installed assembly plants in several foreign countries ... resigned from Ford to become general manager of Ireland and Matthews Manufacturing Company, but in less than a year he was called to Chevrolet Motor Company ... two years later he became president and general manager of Chevrolet, as well as vice president of General Motors ... under Knudsen's guidance, Chevrolet in 1928 switched from a four to a six-cylinder engine, and within a year had produced well over one million of the new models ... after becoming president of General Motors in 1937, Knudsen in 1940 resigned his office to take a position on the National Defense Advisory Commission ... during the war he served with several government agencies, usually acting as a co-ordinator and general "trouble

shooter" ... so thorough was his work that in 1944, Knudsen, then a three star general, received the Army's Distinguished Service Medal.

LELAND, Henry M. 1843-1932

Spent his younger years working in the factories of several well-known firearms manufacturers learning first-hand the technique of parts interchangeability, a method he employed so successfully in the auto industry ... after a series of ventures that ran from inventing the mechanical hair clipper to manufacturing engines, Leland in 1902 reorganized the Henry Ford Company, which became the Cadillac Motor Car Company ... while with Cadillac, Leland was responsible for the company's introduction of such innovations as standardized parts, electric starting, and automatic ignition advance ... Leland left Cadillac in 1917, and some years later organized the Lincoln Motor Car

Company, which was purchased by Ford in 1922.

MACAULEY, Alvan 1872-1952

Began his career as a patent attorney, holding various positions with National Cash Register and American Arithmometer, predecessor of Burroughs Corporation ... Macauley joined Packard as general manager in 1910 ... three years later he was made vice president, and in 1916 became president of Packard ... under Macauley's guidance, Packard, as well as becoming a leading auto producer, specialized in the development of engines, contributing such things as the Liberty engine of World War I, the first engine specifically designed for a tank and first production diesel aircraft engine ... Macauley, a director of the National Automobile Chamber of Commerce from 1913, became its president in 1928, an office he held until 1946 ... he was made chairman of the board of Packard in

1939, serving in that capacity until retiring in 1948.

MARMON, Howard C. 1876-1943

Worked as an associate with his father in a flour mill machinery business that was eventually absorbed in the auto industry ... became vice president in charge of engineering at the Marmon Motor Company in 1902 ... designed the Marmon automobile as well as the 1911 Indianapolis Race winning Marmon "Wasp" ... invented the duplex down draft manifold and pioneered in the use of weight saving aluminum in V-16 engines ... served as president of the Society of Automobile Engineers during the years 1913-1914, and in 1931 was awarded a medal for the outstanding automotive design of the year, the Marmon Sixteen ... developed the Liberty engine during World War I ... selected as the only American honorary member of the British Society of Automotive Engineers.

George W. Mason

Charles W. Matheson

Jonathan D. Maxwell

Samuel A. Miles

MASON, George Walter
1891-1954

Entered the auto industry in 1913 with Studebaker ... a year later, he joined Dodge, leaving in 1915 to become purchasing agent for the American Auto Trimming Company ... during World War I Mason acted as a co-ordinator for the Army Ordinance Department ... in 1919 accepted a position with Irving National Bank in New York ... in 1921 Mason returned to the auto industry, taking a position with Maxwell-Chalmers Corporation, then being reorganized by Walter P. Chrysler ... a year later he was named general works manager, holding that position until leaving Chrysler to become vice president of Copeland Products, Incorporated, in 1926 ... although elected president of Copeland in 1927, Mason in 1928 left to become president of Kelvinator Corporation ... in 1936, an offer of the presidency of Nash Motors ultimately resulted in the formation of the Nash-Kelvinator Corporation with Mason as president and Charles W. Nash board chairman ... with Nash's death in 1948, Mason, at that time president of the Automobile Manufacturers Association, also became board chairman of N-K ... when the Nash-Kelvinator-Hudson Motor Car Company merger in 1954 was completed, Mason became president and chairman of the newly formed American Motors Corporation.

MATHESON BROTHERS,
Charles W., 1876-1940
Frank, 1872-1967

They built the Matheson between 1903 and 1913 ... in 1921, after spending a year as New York sales representative for Dodge Brothers, Charles became vice president of that company ... three years later he became vice president and sales director for General Motors' Oakland Motor Car Company ... after resigning his post with General Motors, Charles assumed a similar position with Kelvinator ... In 1928 he moved on to Chrysler Corporation, becoming vice president in charge of sales ... 10 years later he left Chrysler to become president and general manager of Reo Motor Car Company, a position Charles Matheson held until his death.

MAXWELL, Jonathan Dixon
1864-1928

Like many other automobile manufacturers, Maxwell got his start in the bicycle business, operating a repair shop with Elmer Apperson ... he assisted Elmer Apperson and Elwood Haynes in building the latter's first car ... in 1903 Maxwell teamed with Benjamin Briscoe to organize the Maxwell-Briscoe Company, producers of a $500 two-cylinder runabout ... aside from his manufacturing accomplishments, Maxwell was an inventor of note, assisting in the design of the Oldsmobile and Northern automobiles and inventing the thermo-siphon cooling system ... he served as vice president of the United States Motor Company before retiring from the auto industry in 1913.

METZ, Charles
1864-1937

Organized the Waltham Manufacturing Company to build bicycles ... later associated with the Orient Oil Bicycle and the Orient Buckboard companies ... in 1909 Metz purchased the Waltham factory, and began to manufacture the low priced Metz "22" ... a team of three of his cars won the 1913 Glidden Tour with a perfect score ... throughout his association with the auto industry, Metz championed the movement toward smaller, lower-priced cars, at one time going so far as to devise a plan for shipping component parts to dealers for assembly ... Metz Company was dissolved in 1922, at which time Mr. Metz retired from the industry.

Charles W. Nash

Ransom E. Olds

James W. Packard

MILES, Samuel A.
1862-1932

Dean of American automobile shows ... born in England ... came to America and edited cycling publications, promoted bicycle shows, and helped found *Motor Age* magazine ... staged the first Chicago auto show in 1901 ... soon became manager of the New York and Chicago shows ... general manager of the National Association of Automobile Manufacturers in 1903 ... served about a year (1913-14) as first manager of the National Automobile Chamber of Commerce ... then devoted himself exclusively to the shows until his death.

NASH, Charles W.
1864-1948

Started his career working in the Durant-Dort carriage works, where he developed the straight-line conveyor-belt system, a standard item in today's auto assembly plants ... when Durant left the wagon business to start Buick,

Nash went along with him and in 1910 became president of that company ... Buick so prospered under Nash's leadership that in 1912 he was made president of General Motors, a position he held until 1916 ... in that year Nash purchased the Thomas B. Jeffery Company and in 1917 began to manufacture Nash cars ... Nash remained president of the Nash Motor Company until 1930 when he became chairman of the board ... shortly thereafter, merger negotiations with the Kelvinator Corporation were completed, and the Nash-Kelvinator Corporation was formed with George Mason as president and Charles W. Nash as chairman of the board.

OLDS, Ransom E.
1864-1950

After successful experiments with steam vehicles as early as 1886, Olds completed his first gasoline-powered vehicle in 1894 ... encouraged by the interest shown in his vehicle, Olds organized Olds Motor

Vehicle Company in 1897 ... this first endeavor was not successful; the company was reorganized in 1899 as the Olds Motor Works ... in 1901 Olds developed his famous "curved dash runabout" priced at $650, making it the first really low-priced car ... after a 1901 fire destroyed the Detroit plant, the company moved to its Lansing location ... two years later Olds sold his interest in the Olds Motor Works, later Olds Division of General Motors, and organized the Reo Motor Car Company ... seemingly not content with helping to found an industry, Olds continued his experiments with the internal combustion engine, contributing, among other things, the first practical power mower.

PACKARD, James Ward
1863-1928

Organized the Packard Electric Company in

1890 ... by 1893 Packard had drawn the plans for his first auto, but financial difficulties delayed its production until 1899 ... after experiments with the initial car proved successful, Packard in 1900 organized New York and Ohio Automobile Co. ... with increased capital, the company moved to Detroit in 1903 and became Packard Motor Company ... Packard, prior to this time president, became chairman of the board, a post which he held until retiring in 1915.

PAIGE, Fred O.
1864-1935

Organized Paige-Detroit Motor Company in 1909 to produce two-cycle automobiles ... Paige was president of the company until 1910, at which time Harry Jewett assumed control ... in 1927 the Graham Brothers acquired control of Jewett's interests, and the company became Graham-Paige.

George N. Pierce

Albert Pope

Alfred P. Reeves

PIERCE, George N.
1846-1910

Father of the Pierce-Arrow car and one of the founders of Pierce-Arrow Motor Company ... began career in 1872 as a member of a firm producing birdcages and iceboxes ... in the 1880's the company began manufacturing bicycles and tricycles ... the first little Pierce motorette was the outcome of experimenting Pierce had started in the 1890's ... president and director of Pierce at the time of his retirement in 1908.

POPE, Albert Augustus
1843-1909

After serving in the Civil War, Pope organized in 1879 a company to manufacture bicycles, a venture which was to earn for him the title "the founder of American bicycle industries" ... following his highly successful bicycle ventures, Pope began to manufacture electric runabouts through the Columbia Electric Company in 1896 ... within a few years, he controlled the Pope-Toledo, Pope-Harford, and Pope-Waverly Companies ... however, with auto success on one hand, Pope faced a crisis on the other in the form of a decline of his bicycle business, eventually forcing the Pope Manufacturing Company into receivership.

PORTER, Finley R.
1872-1964

Chief engineer of the Mercer Company, 1910-1915, and designer of the Mercer Raceabout ... Porter left school at the age of 11 and took correspondence courses in mechanical engineering ... became head of his own company at Port Jefferson, Long Island, where the manufacture of F.R.P. autos started in 1914 ... only a few made ... however, F.R.P. designs later formed the basis for one of America's most powerful and expensive cars of its period, the Porter, 1920-1922 ... chief engineer of Curtiss Air Craft Corporation, Engine Division, 1919 ... consulting engineer with Bendix Corporation during World War II.

REEVES, Alfred P.
1876-1962

Began as a bicycle writer in Brooklyn ... managed bicycle races, later auto races ... when popularity of the bicycle declined, Reeves became one of country's first automotive editors, starting in 1902 with the *New York Evening Mail* ... his managerial talents were widely recognized throughout the industry ... in 1906 selected to manage the American Motor Car Manufacturers Association ... in 1909, the Association of Licensed Automobile Manufacturers ... appointed general manager of the National Automobile Chamber of Commerce in 1914 ... name of association changed to Automobile Manufacturers Association in 1934, and six years later its head- quarters were moved to Detroit ... Reeves continued as advisory vice president and manager of the New York office ... instrumental in forming AMA's patent cross-licensing agreement ... known as "Mr. Auto Show" for having had a part in producing every National Auto Show from 1900 to 1940.

REUTHER, Walter
1907 - 1970

A pioneer in the establishment of the United Auto Workers, an organization of which he was president for 24 years ... Reuther, a West Virginia native, took his union education from his own father, Valentine Reuther ... a socialist, the elder Reuther, organized a trade union of brewery workers ... shared with his two brothers, Victor and Roy, a dedication to social, political and economic reforms ... became a skilled machinist and worked for Ford before going to Europe with his brothers to train auto workers there ... they returned in 1935 and Walter subsequently began his work as a

Andrew Riker

George W. Romney

George B. Selden

Alfred P. Sloan, Jr.

union organizer ... was elected local 174's president and rose from there ... subsequent union activities solidified the position of the UAW and raised the standard of living of automotive workers ... became president of the CIO (Congress of Industrial Organizations) in 1952 ... died in a plane crash in 1970.

RIKER, Andrew L.
1868-1930

Built an electric tricycle in 1884 at the age of 16 ... after graduation from Columbia Law School formed his own company which began producing a full line of electric passenger and commercial vehicles in New Jersey in 1899 ... deserted the electric field in 1902 and joined Locomobile to help design their first gasoline car ... until about 1920 vice president and chief engineer of Locomobile ... Riker helped organize S.A.E. ... served as its first president ... chairman of the Mechanical Branch of the Association of Licensed Automobile Manufacturers.

ROMNEY, George W.
1907-1996

Born in Chihuahua, Mexico of Mormon American parents ... began his automotive career in 1939 as manager of the Automobile Manufacturers Assn. in Detroit ... joined Nash-Kelvinator in 1948 ... The compact Rambler was developed and marketed, starting in 1950, under his leadership ... Nash and Hudson merged in 1954 to form American Motors and Romney became its president and remained there until 1962 ... ran for governor in Michigan and was elected to three terms ... made a bid for the Republican presidential nomination in 1968 ... served as secretary of housing and urban development in the first Nixon administration ... died of a heart attack in 1996.

SELDEN, George Baldwin
1846-1932

A veteran of the Civil War, he became a patent attorney in 1871 ... having a keen interest in

mechanics, Selden unsuccessfully experimented with engines of his own design during the years 1873-1875 ... by 1876, he was working on the design for a self-propelled vehicle using an engine operating on the Brayton cycle ... Selden had developed a three-cylinder-Brayton type engine by 1877, and proceeded to design the road locomotive disclosed in his patent application of May 8, 1879 ... although never successful in obtaining the funds to build the proposed machine, Selden was granted his patent — No. 549,160 "Road Machine" Nov. 5, 1895 ... on Nov. 4, 1899, he sold the patent on a royalty basis to W.C. Whitney of Columbia Electric who successfully brought suit against a number of automobile manufacturers before the now historic appeal judgment Jan. 11, 1911 (Electric Vehicle Company vs. C.A. Buerr) wherein the patent was held valid but not infringed by virtue of the fact that all manufacturers were using Otto, not Brayton, type engines ... Selden

unsuccessfully entered other auto firms before his death.

SKELTON, Owen
1886 - 1969

(See Breer, Carl)

SLOAN, Alfred P., Jr.
1875-1966

President of General Motors from 1923 to 1936 ... started as a draftsman with Hyatt Roller Bearing in 1895 ... soon headed company and in 1916 at Durant's urging merged a group of accessories companies, including Hyatt, to form United Motors Corporation ... latter corporation soon became part of General Motors ... Sloan's administrative genius welded the loosely-knit General Motors units into world's largest, most profitable auto making concern ... stepped down as board chairman of General Motors in 1956 ... devoted full time to various philanthropies ... Sloan established Sloan Foundation in 1934 ... later, the Sloan-Kettering Institute for Cancer Research.

John F. Smith

Charles E. Sorensen

Francis E. and Freelan O. Stanley

John M. Studebaker

Harry C. Stutz

SMITH, John F. (Jack) 1938 - —

John F. "Jack" Smith, Jr. became chairman of the General Motors Board of Directors on January 1, 1996 ... also the chief executive officer and president of GM ... was elected to the latter two positions on November 2, 1992 ... born and educated in Massachusetts, Smith began his career with GM in his home state at the Fisher Body facility in Framingham ... formerly held positions as comptroller of GM (1980) and former president and general manager of General Motors of Canada Ltd. (1984) and president of General Motors Europe (1987).

SORENSEN, Charles E. 1881-1968

Vice president and director of Ford Motor Company ... Henry Ford's close associate and consultant ... born in Denmark and came to America at age of four ... joined Ford in 1905 as a patternmaker and soon demonstrated a genius for production ... helped develop the conveyor systems, assembly lines, and other innovations which established Ford as a front-runner in industrial mass production ... credited with basic design of many Ford facilities throughout the world, including the Willow Run plant, which produced bombers during World War II ... left Ford in 1944 and served a year as president of Willys-Overland, Inc.

STANLEY BROTHERS, Francis E., 1849-1918 Freelan O., 1849-1940

In 1893, the twin brothers invented the Stanley dry plate process which revolutionized photography ... they were co-designers of the Stanley Steamer — 1897 — and the world-record-holding steamer of 1906 (Ormond Beach, 127.66 m.p.h.) ... as owners of the Stanley Motor company they directed the business until retiring in 1917.

STUDEBAKER, John Mohler 1833-1917

In 1858 bought brother Henry's share of the Studebaker Brothers (Wagon) Company which then became C. (for brother Clem) and J.M. Studebaker Company ... the company entered the auto industry as a body maker in 1899 ... in 1902 produced its first vehicle, an electric car ... in 1908 Studebaker contracted to market the entire output of the E-M-F Company ... in 1911 the two firms merged to form the Studebaker Corporation, which produced the first car with a Studebaker name plate in 1912 ... John M. Studebaker served as chairman of the corporation until his death.

STUTZ, Harry C. 1871-1930

After winning recognition among the early auto manufacturers with the invention of an improved rear axle, Stutz became successively sales manager for the Schebler Carburetor Company, engineer for the Marion Motor Car Company, and designer of the famous "American Underslung" for the American Motor Car Company ... in 1910 he entered into the Stutz Motor Parts Company and in 1911 organized the Ideal Motor Company to manufacture Stutz cars ... two years later the companies merged to form the

Edwin R. Thomas

Alex Trotman

Preston Tucker

William K. Vanderbilt, Jr.

Stutz Motor Car Company with Stutz as president ... although he sold his interest in Stutz Motor Car Company in 1919, Harry Stutz later joined Henry Campbell, his partner in the Stutz Motor Parts Company, in the H.C.S. Motor Car Company, again as president ... Stutz remained president of H.C.S. until his retirement.

THOMAS, Edwin Ross 1850-1936

Started the E.R. Thomas Motor Company of Buffalo in 1900 ... the company was quite successful, and Thomas remained its president until his decision to retire in 1911, when he sold his holding to the United States Motor Company ... although successful as an auto maker, Thomas probably gained his greatest fame as the designer-builder of the "Thomas Flyer," winner of the 1908 New York to Paris (via California, Siberia and Europe) Race ... despite the fact that he officially retired in 1911, Thomas

was active in numerous enterprises until his death.

TROTMAN, Alex 1933 - —

Became chairman of the board of directors and chief executive officer of Ford Motor Company in November 1993 ... as chairman and CEO, Trotman initiated Ford 2000, a program to completely restructure the company ... prior to '93, Trotman served as president and chief operating officer of the Ford Automotive Group ... born in Middlesex, England, and educated in Edinburgh, Scotland, Trotman served in the Royal Air Force before joining Ford of Britain in 1955 ... has served Ford Motor Company throughout the world and is past president of Ford Asia-Pacific and past president and chairman of Ford of Europe.

TUCKER, Preston 1903 - 1956

Considered to be one of the last automotive renegades ... succeeded in

building only 51 automobiles but made quite a name for himself in the process ... had been involved in a variety of jobs relating to the automobile industry, and after World War II he began formulating plans to build his own automobile ... Tucker's automobile would be more advanced than anything other automakers produced at the time ... a variety of wild claims circulated about the car as Tucker began building the company ... promises included an engine in the rear, a third headlight up front, disc brakes, aerodynamic shape, a heavily padded, crash-proof interior, etc. ... plans called for establishing production in a Chicago plant which had been used for war production ... when prototypes finally emerged, but failed to include all the fabulous features Tucker had hyped, things unraveled ... the Securities and Exchange Commission (SEC) began an investigation into possible stock fraud, and in 1949 Tucker and seven associates went on trial

for mail fraud conspiracy and violation of securities laws ... they were acquitted of the charges, but Tucker's automotive venture had folded.

VANDERBILT, William K., Jr. 1878-1944

Heir to vast wealth who did much to help the automotive industry in its formative years ... originated (1904) and sponsored the Vanderbilt Cup Races in an effort to bring to America the motoring impetus spawned by the Gordon Bennett Cup Races in Europe ... a racing driver of highest ability ... established several world's road and straight-away records in the 1902-1904 period ... Vanderbilt's personal records and his cup races did much to inspire American manufacturers to build cars which could and did successfully challenge European dominance.

Rollin H. White

Childe Harold Wills

John N. Willys

Alexander Winton

Walter C. White

Windsor T. White

WHITE BROTHERS,
Windsor T., 1866-1958
Rollin H., 1872-1962
Walter C., 1876-1929

The brothers began their careers working for the White Sewing Machine Company, owned by their father ... Rollin and Windsor did experimental work on steam engines and produced the first steam powered White automobile in 1900 ... in 1901 Walter was sent to London to demonstrate the car and establish a niche in the European market ... he returned to the United States in 1904 and continued to demonstrate the company's vehicles in races and hill climbs ... in 1906 the White Company was organized, with Windsor as president, to handle the automotive line ... the brothers introduced their first gasoline car in 1909, and in 1910, their first gasoline powered truck ... in 1915 the White Motor Company was formed with Windsor as president ... Rollin left the company in 1914, founded the Cleveland Plow company and manufactured tractors ... he re-entered the automotive industry in 1923 producing the Rollin car until 1925 ... in 1921 Walter assumed the presidency of the White Motor Company as Windsor was made Chairman of the Board.

WILLS, Childe Harold 1878-1940

Spent the years 1900-1903 working for the Boyer Machine Company and nights as a draftsman for Henry Ford's new organization ... when the Ford Motor Company was formed, Wills was made production manager and chief engineer ... he gained fame from his development of the use of vanadium steel for commercial purposes, and is credited with introducing molybdenum steel in auto construction ... in 1919 Wills, by then a millionaire, left Ford, and in 1920 organized his own company, Wills-St. Claire ... never particularly successful, the company went out of business in 1927 ... in 1933, Wills became chief metallurgist for Chrysler, a position he held until his death.

WILLYS, John North 1873-1933

In 1906 he organized the American Motor Car Sales Company to sell the entire output of the Overland Company ...

during panic of 1907 he acquired the manufacturing facilities of the Pope-Toledo Company in an effort to revive the sinking Overland concern ... the company was moved to Toledo with Willys as president and in 1908 the production of Willys-Overland totaled 4,000 units ... by 1915 Willys-Overland production reached 94,500, second only to Ford ... after a post-war bankruptcy threat was averted by Walter P. Chrysler, the company prospered, and in 1929 John N. Willys sold his holdings for $21 million ... hard times after the market crash prompted Willys to return to the company in 1932, but his attempts to save it from bankruptcy were unsuccessful, and Willys-Overland went into receivership in 1933 ... in 1953 the firm became part of Kaiser Industries Corporation.

WINTON, Alexander 1860-1932

Started the Winton Bicycle Company in 1890, ten years after his

Fred M. Zeder

arrival in the United States ... in 1896 Winton built his first car, which he sold to a Pennsylvania engineer the following year ... he organized the Winton Motor Carriage Company in 1897 ... by 1905 he had produced an eight-cylinder motor vehicle, one of the first ... other contributions to the industry include the development of a practical storage battery, design of a successful speed governor, and four years before his death, perfection of a light, oil burning aircraft engine ... he remained president of the Winton Motor Car Company until it suspended production in 1924 ... organized the Winton Engine Company which made marine, rail and industrial diesel engines — the latter firm was purchased by General Motors in 1930 and became the Cleveland Diesel Division.

ZEDER, Fred M.
1886-1951

(See Breer, Carl)

Roll Call

More than 5,500 makes of cars and trucks have been produced by some 2,000 manufacturers in the United States since the dawn of the auto age. Some were trial models, some were produced for one year only, others have a longer story. Listed below are the names of the more than 3,000 makes that can be documented, with known years of production. The fact that more than one manufacturer may have used a specific name at the same time or at different times is not indicated. Model names, such as Corvair (Chevrolet) and Valiant (Chrysler), are not listed. A final dash (–) means to date.

A

Abbott, 1909-18
Abbott-Cleveland, 1917
Abbott-Detroit, 1909
Abbott-Downing, 1919
A.B.C., 1906-11, 1922, 1939
A.B.C. Steamer, 1901
Abenaque, 1900
Abendroth & Root, 1907-13
Able, 1916
Abresch-Cramer, 1910-11
Acadia, 1904
Acason, 1915-26
Ace, 1919-22
A.C.F., 1926
Acme, 1902-1910
Acorn, 1910
Adams, 1906-7, 1911-12, 1924
Adams-Farwell, 1903-13
Adelphia, 1921
Adette, 1947
Admiral, 1914
Adria, 1921
Adrian, 1902-3
Advance, 1910
A.E.C., 1914-16
Aero, 1921
Aerocar, 1905-8, 1948, 1950
Aero-Type, 1921
Aetna, 1915, 1922
Ahrens-Fox, 1911-33
A.I.C., 1913
Airphibian, 1946, 1952
Airscoot, 1947
Airway, 1948-49
Ajax, 1901-3, 1914, 1920-21,
  1925-26
Ajax Electric, 1901-3
Akron, 1901, 1912-13
Alamobile, 1902
Aland, 1917
Albany, 1907-8
Alco, 1905-14
Aldo, 1910
Aldrich, 1897-98
Alena, 1922
Algonquin, 1913
All American, 1919, 1923
Allegheny, 1908
Allen, 1914-22
Allen & Clark, 1908-9
Allen Cyclecar, 1914

Allen-Kingston, 1907-10
Allfour, 1919
Allis-Chalmers, 1914-17
Allith, 1908
All Power, 1917-21
Allstate, 1951-53
Alma, 1913
Alpena, 1911-13
Alsace, 1919-20
Alstel, 1915-17
Alter, 1915-17
Altha Electric, 1900-1
Altham, 1896-1901
Altman, 1898
Alxo, 1905
Amalgamated, 1905
Ambassador, 1921-25, 1966—
Amco, 1917-21
America, 1911
American, 1900-3
American Austin, 1930-37
American Auto, 1904
American Auto Vehicle, 1907
American Bantam, 1937-41
American Beauty, 1915-16, 1920-21
American Berliet, 1905-7
American Coulthard, 1905-7
American Electric, 1899-1900
American Fiat, 1915
American Gas, 1895
American Knight, 1919
American Mercedes, 1905-7
American Mors, 1906-9
American Motor, 1902-3, 1905-6
American Motors, 1970—
American Napier, 1904
American Populaire, 1904
American Power Carriage, 1900
American Simplex, 1905-10
American Six, 1916-17
American Southern, 1921
American Steam, 1922-23
American Steamer, 1900
American Tri-Car, 1912
American Underslung, 1906-14
American Voiturette, 1899
Americar, 1940-42
Ames, 1898, 1910-16
Amesbury, 1898
Amos, 1913
Amoskeag Fire Engine, 1867-1906
Amplex, 1910-15
Ams-Sterling, 1917

AMX, 1968—
Anchor, 1909-11
Anderson, 1908, 1916-25
Anderson Electric, 1907-19
Andover, 1914-17
Andrews, 1895
Anhut, 1910-11
Ann Arbor, 1909-11
Ansted, 1927
Anthony, 1897
Apex, 1920-22
Apollo, 1906-7
Appel, 1909
Apperson, 1902-25
Apple, 1909, 1915-16
Appleton, 1922
Arbenz, 1911-18
Arcadia, 1911
Ardsley, 1905-6
Argo-Borland Electric, 1914
Argo-Case, 1905
Argo Electric, 1911-16
Argo Gas, 1914
Argonne Four, 1919-20
Ariel, 1905-7
Ariston, 1906
Armleder, 1914
Arnold Electric, 1895
Arrow, 1907, 1914
Artzberger, 1904
Asardo, 1962
Aster, 1960-7
Astor, 1925
Astra, 1920
Atco, 1920-22
Atlantic, 1915
Atlas, 1904-13
Auburn, 1903-36, 1968—
Auburn Motor Buggy, 1908
Aultman, 1901
Aurora, 1906-8
Austin, 1901-20, 1930
Austin Steamer, 1894
Auto-Acetylene, 1899
Auto-Bug, 1910
Autobuggy, 1906
Autocar, 1897-1912
Autocycle, 1907, 1913
Auto Dynamic, 1901
Auto Fore Car, 1900
Auto-Go, 1900
Autohorse, 1917-21
Auto-King, 1900

Automatic, 1906, 1921-25
Automobile Forecarriage, 1900
Automobile Voiturette, 1900
Automotor, 1901-4
Auto Motor, 1912
Auto Red Bug, 1924
Auto-Tricar, 1914
Autotwo, 1900
Auto Vehicle, 1903
Avanti, 1962—
Avanti II, 1965-90
Average Man's Runabout, 1906
Avery, 1921
Avery Tractor, 1942

B

Babcock, 1910-12, 1914
Babcock Electric, 1906-12
Bachelle Electric, 1901
Backhus, 1925
Bacon, 1901-3
Badger, 1910-12
Bailey, 1907-10
Bailey-Electric, 1907-15
Bailey-Klapp, 1915
Bailey-Perking, 1907
Baker-Bell, 1913-14
Baker & Elberg Electric, 1894
Baker Electric, 1899-1915
Baker R & L Electric, 1915-20
Baker-Steam, 1917
Baker Steamer, 1921-23
Balboa, 1924
Baldner, 1902-6
Baldwin, 1900-1
Ball, 1902
Ballard, 1894
Baltimore, 1900
Balzer, 1894
Banker, 1905
Banker Bros., 1896
Banker Electric, 1905
Banner, 1910-11, 1915
Bantam, 1914
Barbarino, 1923
Barby, 1910
Barker, 1912
Barley, 1905-24
Barlow, 1924
Barlow Steamer, 1922
Barnes, 1905, 1912
Barnhart, 1905
Barrett & Perret Electric, 1895

Barrows Electric, 1897
Barrows Motor Vehicle, 1897
Bartholomew, 1901-20
Bartlett, 1921
Barver, 1925
Bateman, 1917
Bates, 1903-5
Bauer, 1914, 1925
Bauroth, 1899
Bayard, 1903
Bay State, 1906-7, 1922-23
B.D.A.C., 1904
Beacon, 1933
Beacon Flyer, 1908
Beardsley, 1901-2
Beardsley Electric, 1914-17
Beau-Chamberlain, 1901
Beaver, 1913-23
Beck, 1921
Bedelia, 1909
Beebe, 1906-7
Beech Creek, 1915-19
Beggs, 1918-23
B.E.L., 1921-23
Belden, 1907-10
Bell, 1907, 1911-23
Bellefontaine, 1908-17
Belmont, 1908, 1910, 1912, 1916
Bemmel & Burnham, 1908
Bender Special, 1918
Bendix, 1907-9
Benham, 1914
Ben-Hur, 1917
Benner, 1908-9
Benson, 1901
Benton, 1913
Benton Harbor Motor Carriage,
  1896
Berg, 1902-7
Bergdoll, 1910-13
Berg Electric, 1921
Berkley, 1907
Berkshire, 1905-12
Berliet, 1905
Bertolet, 1908-12
Berwick Electric, 1904, 1926
Best, 1900
Bethlehem, 1906-8, 1917
Bethlen, 1909
Betz, 1919
Beverly, 1905-7
Bewis, 1915
Bewman, 1912

Beyster-Detroit, 1910-11
B.F., 1912
Bi-Autogo, 1913
Bicar, 1912
Biddle, 1915-20
Biddle-Crane, 1922-23
Biddle-Murray, 1906-8
Billy Four, 1910
Bimel, 1911, 1915-17
Binney-Burnham, 1902
Birch, 1917-24
Bird, 1896-97
Birmingham, 1921-22
Birnel, 1911
Black, 1891, 1907-10
Black Crow, 1907, 1909
Black Diamond, 1904-5
Blackhawk, 1903, 1929-31
Blackstone, 1916
Blair, 1911
Blaisdell, 1903
Blakeslee Electric, 1906
Blemline, 1898
Bliss, 1906
B.L.M., 1906-7
B.L.M.C., 1907-9
Block Bros., 1905
Blomstrom, 1904-6
Blood, 1905
Blue Streak, 1908
Bluffelimber, 1901
Blumberg, 1918
Board, 1912
Bobbi-Car, 1947
Boggs, 1903
Boisselot, 1901
Bollee, 1908
Bollstrom, 1920
Bolte, 1901
Bonner, 1908
Booth, 1896
Borbein, 1904-8
Borland Electric, 1913
Borland-Grannis, 1912-16
Boss, 1903-9
Boston, 1900
Boston & Amesbury, 1902
Boston Electric, 1907
Boston-Haynes Apperson, 1898
Boston High Wheel, 1908
Bour-Davis, 1915-23
Bourne, 1917
Bowling Green, 1912

Bowman, 1921
Boyd, 1911
Bradfield, 1929
Bradford, 1920
Bradley, 1920
Bramwell, 1902-3
Bramwell-Robinson, 1899
Brasie Cyclecar, 1914
Brazier, 1902-4
Brecht, 1901-2
Breer Steam Car, 1900
Breese & Lawrence, 1905
Bremac, 1923
Brennan, 1908
Brew-Hatcher, 1904-5
Brewster, 1934-36
Brewster-Knight, 1916-25
Bricklin, 1974-75
Bridgeport, 1922
Briggs, 1933
Briggs-Detroiter, 1910-18
Briggs & Stratton, 1922
Brighton, 1896, 1914
Brightwood, 1912
Brintel, 1912
Briscoe, 1914
Bristol, 1902-3, 1908
Broc Electric, 1909-16
Brock, 1920-21
Brockville-Atlas, 1911
Brogan, 1946
Brook, 1920-21
Brooks, 1908
Brooks Steamer, 1924
Brothers, 1908
Brown, 1899-1900, 1909, 1912, 1914, 1916, 1922
Brown-Burtt, 1904
Brownell, 1910
Brownie, 1915
Browniekar, 1908-9
Brown Steamer, 1888
Brown's Touring Cart, 1898
Brunn, 1906-10
Brunswick, 1916
Brush Runabout, 1906-12
Bryan Steam, 1918
Buck, 1925
Buckeye, 1905-17
Buckeye Gas Buggy, 1895
Buckles, 1914
Buckmobile, 1903-4
Buddie, 1921

Buddy, 1925
Buffalo, 1900-2, 1907, 1912-15
Buffalo Electric, 1900-12
Buffington, 1900
Buffman, 1900
Buffum, 1900-6
Bug, 1914
Buggyaut, 1909
Buggycar, 1907-10
Bugmobile, 1907-9
Buick, 1903—
Bull Dog, 1924
Bundy Steam Wagon, 1895
Burdick, 1909-11
Burford, 1916
Burg, 1910-15
Burns, 1908-12
Burroughs, 1914
Burrows, 1915
Burtt, 1917-23
Bus, 1917
Bush, 1917-23
Bushbury, 1897
Bushnell, 1912
Busser, 1915
Butler, 1908, 1914
Buzmobile, 1917
Byrider, 1908-9
Byron, 1912
B.Z.T., 1915

C

C.A.C., 1912-16
Cadillac, 1902—
California, 1912
California Cyclecar, 1914
Californian, 1920
Call, 1911
Calorie, 1904
Calvert, 1927
Cameron, 1907-20
Campbell, 1917-19
Canada, 1911
Canadian, 1921
Canda, 1900-1
Cannon, 1904
Cantone, 1905
Cantono Electric, 1905-7
Capital, 1902
Capitol, 1912, 1920
Carbon, 1902
Car Deluxe, 1907
Cardway, 1923

Carhart Steamer, 1872
Carhartt, 1911-16
Carlson, 1904-10
Carnation, 1913-15
Carnegie, 1915-16
Carpenter Electric, 1895
Carrison, 1908
Carroll, 1912-13
Carroll Six, 1920-21
Carter, 1907-12, 1916
Cartercar, 1908-15
Cartermobile, 1924
Carthage, 1924
Casco, 1926
Case, 1910, 1920
Casey, 1914
Cass, 1915
Cato, 1907
Cavac, 1910
Cavalier, 1913, 1927
Caward-Dart, 1924
Cawley, 1917
C.B., 1917
Ceco, 1914
Celt, 1927
Centaur, 1902-3
Central, 1905
Central Steam, 1905-6
Century, 1900-4, 1927
Century Electric, 1901, 1912-16
Century Steam, 1901
C-F, 1907-8
C.G.V., 1903
Chadwick, 1906-16
Chalfant, 1906-12
Chalmers, 1910-23
Chalmers-Detroit, 1908-10
Champion, 1902, 1909, 1915, 1921-25
Champion Electric, 1899
Chandler, 1913-28
Chapman, 1899-1901
Charter Car, 1904
Charter Oak, 1917
Chase, 1907
Chatham, 1907
Checker Cab, 1921—
Chelsea, 1901-4, 1915
Chevrolet 1909, 1911—
Chicago, 1899-1910, 1917
Chicago Commercial, 1905-7
Chicago Electric, 1912-14
Chicago Motor Buggy, 1908

Chicago Steamer, 1905
Chief, 1908-9, 1947
Christie, 1904-10
Christman, 1901-2
Chrysler, 1924—
Church, 1901-3, 1910-11, 1914
Church Electric, 1912-13
Churchfield, 1911-15
Cincinnati, 19-03
Cino, 1909-13
Circa-Hermann, 1914
Cla-Holme, 1923
Clapps Motor Carriage, 1898
Clark, 1898-1903
Clarke Carter, 1909-13
Clark Electric, 1912
Clark-Hatfield, 1908-9
Clarkmobile, 1903-7
Clarkspeed, 1926
Clark Steamer, 1901
Classic, 1917-21
Clear & Dunham, 1905
Cleburne, 1912
Clegg Steamer, 1885
Clendon, 1908
Clermont, 1903
Clermont Steamer, 1922
Cleveland, 1902-9, 1919-25
Cleveland Cycle Car, 1913
Cleveland Electric, 1900
Climax, 1907
Climber, 1919-23
Clinton, 1923
Cloughley, 1902-3
Club Car, 1911
Clyde, 1919
Clymer, 1908
Coates-Goshen, 1908-11
Coats Steam, 1922-23
Coey, 1911
Coey Flyer, 1913
Coggswell, 1912
Colburn, 1907-11
Colby, 1911-14
Cole, 1909-25
Collier, 1917
Collinet, 1922
Collins, 1920-21
Collins Electric, 1901
Colly, 1901
Colonial, 1921-22
Colonial Electric, 1912-13,
  1917-18

Colt, 1908
Columbia, 1899-1907, 1916-24
Columbia Cyclecar, 1914
Columbia Electric, 1895,
  1899-1904, 1906-18
Columbia Gas, 1900
Columbia Knight, 1911
Columbia Motor Carriage, 1897
Columbian, 1914-17
Columbia & Riker, 1901
Columbia Steamer, 1900
Columbia Taxicab, 1915
Columbia Wagonette, 1901
Columbus, 1902-4
Columbus Electric, 1905-14
Comet, 1907, 1916-36, 1946
Comet Cyclecar, 1914
Comet Electric, 1921
Commander, 1921-22
Commer, 1912
Commerce, 1916
Commercial, 1902-9, 1927
Commodore, 1921-22
Commonwealth, 1903, 1917-21
Compound, 1904
Concord, 1916
Conestoga, 1918
Conklin Electric, 1895
Connersville, 1914
Conover, 1907-8
Conrad, 1900-3
Consolidated, 1903-6, 1916
Continental, 1907-9, 1912,
  1914-15, 1933-34
Continental Mark II, 1955-57
Cook, 1921
Copley, Minor, 1907
Coppock, 1907-12
Corbett, 1907
Corbin, 1903-12
Corbitt, 1911-14
Cord, 1929-32, 1935-37, 1965-66
Corinthian, 1922-23
Corl, 1911
Corliss, 1917
Cornelian, 1913
Correja, 1908-14
Cort, 1914
Cortland, 1911, 1916-24
Corweg, 1947
Corwin, 1905-7
Cory, 1907
Cosmopolitan, 1897-1910

Co-Tay, 1920
Cotta, 1901
Country Club, 1904
Couple-Gear, 1905
Courier, 1904, 1909-12, 1922-23
Covel Electric, 1912
Covert Motorette, 1902-7
Covic, 1930
Coyote, 1909
C.P., 1908
Craig-Hunt, 1920
Craig-Toledo, 1906-7
Crane, 1912-15
Crane & Breed, 1912
Crane-Simplex, 1915-17, 1923-24
Crawford, 1905-30
Crescent, 1900-18, 1923
Cresson, 1915
Crestmobile, 1901-5
Cricket, 1914
Criterion, 1912
Croce, 1914
Crock, 1909
Croesus Jr., 1906
Crofton Bug, 1959
Crompton, 1903
Crosley, 1939-52
Cross Steam Carriage, 1897
Crouch, 1900
Crow, 1910-22
Crowdus, 1901
Crow-Elkhart, 1911
Crown, 1908-10, 1914
Crown-Magnetic, 1920
Crowther-Duryea, 1915-18
Croxton, 1911
Croxton-Keeton, 1909-14
Crusader, 1923
Crusier, 1918-19
Cucmobile, 1907
Cull, 1901
Culver, 1905, 1916
Cummins, 1930
Cunningham, 1909-33, 1951
Cunningham Steamer, 1901
Curran, 1928
Curtis, 1921-22
Curtis Steamer, 1866
Custer, 1921
Cutting, 1909-13
Cuyahoga Electric, 1909
C.V.I., 1907-8
Cyclecar, 1914

Cycleplane, 1914-15
Cyclomobile, 1920

D

D.A.C., 1923
Dagmar, 1923-30
Daimler, 1900-7
Dain, 1912
Daley Steam Wagon, 1893
Dalton, 1911
Daniels, 1912, 1915-23
Danielson, 1914
Dan Patch, 1911
Darby, 1909-10
Darling, 1901, 1917
Darrin, 1946
Darrow, 1903
Dart, 1911
Dart Cyclecar, 1914
Dartmobile, 1922
Davenport, 1902
Davids, 1902
DaVinci Pup, 1925
Davis, 1909, 1911-28, 1947-50
Davis Cycle Car, 1913
Dawson, 1904
Day, 1911-14
Dayton, 1904-14
Day Utility, 1914-16
Deal, 1908-11
Dearborn, 1910-11, 1919
Decatur, 1912
Decauville, 1909-12
Decker, 1902-3
Decross, 1914
De Dion Bouton, 1888-1904
De Dion Motorette, 1900
Deemotor, 1923
Deemster, 1923
Deere, 1916
Deere-Clark, 1906-7
Deering, 1918
Deering Magnetic, 1918
Defiance, 1919
DeKalb Jr., 1916
Delage, 1922
De LaVergne Motor Drag, 1896
Delling Steam Car, 1924-29
Del Mar, 1949
Delmore, 1923
Delorean, 1981-83
Delta, 1916

Deltal, 1914
DeLuxe, 1906-9
DeLuxe Electric, 1905
DeMars, 1905
DeMartini, 1919
DeMot, 1910-11
DeMotte, 1904
Denby, 1922
Deneen, 1917
Denegre, 1920
Dependable, 1919
Derain, 1911
Derby, 1924
Desberon, 1901
DeSchaum, 1908-10
Desert Flyer, 1908
DeShaw, 1910
De Soto, 1913-14, 1928-60
De Tamble, 1909, 1912
Detroit, 1904-7, 1916
Detroit-Chatham, 1912
Detroit-Dearborn, 1909
Detroit Electric, 1906-23, 1930
Detroiter, 1912
Detroit Speedster, 1914
Detroit Steamer, 1918
DeVaux, 1931-32
Dewabout, 1899
Dey, 1895
Dial, 1923
Diamond, 1907
Diamond-Arrow, 1907
Diamond T., 1905-11
Diana, 1925
Dictator, 1913
Diebel, 1900-1
Diehl, 1923
Differential, 1921, 1932
Dile, 1914-16
Dillon Steam, 1920
Direct Drive, 1917
Disbrow, 1917-18
Dispatch, 1911-19
Dixie, 1912, 1917
Dixie Flyer, 1916-24
Dixie Tourist, 1908-10
Dixon, 1922
D.L.G., 1907-8
Doble-Detroit, 1919
Doble Steam Car, 1918-32
Dodge, 1914—
Dodge-Graham, 1929
Dodgeson Eight, 1926

Dodo, 1909, 1912-13
Dolly Madison, 1915
Dolson, 1904-7
D'Olt, 1921-26
Dorris, 1905-25
Dort, 1915-24
Double Drive, 1920
Douglas, 1918-19
Dover, 1929
Dowagiac, 1908
Downing, 1914-17
Downing-Detroit, 1913
Doyle, 1900
Dragon, 1906-8, 1921
Drake, 1921
Drednot, 1913
Drexel, 1916-17
Driggs, 1921-23
Driggs-Seabury, 1915
Drummond, 1916
Dudgeon Steam, 1853, 1866-67
Dudley Electric, 1915
Dudly, 1914-15
Duer, 1907-10, 1925
Duesenberg, 1920-37
Dunmore, 1917-18
Dunn, 1914-17
Duplex, 1908-9
duPont, 1919-32
Duquesne, 1903-6, 1912
Durable Dayton, 1916
Durant, 1921-31
Durocar, 1907
Duryea, 1893-97, 1907-12
Duryea-Gem, 1917
Duryea Lightcar, 1915
Dusseau, 1912
Duty, 1920
Duyo, 1914
D. & V., 1903
Dyke, 1902-4
Dymaxion, 1933-35

E

Eagle, 1906-7, 1909, 1924
Eagle Cyclecar, 1914-15
Eagle-Macomber, 1917
Eagle Rotary, 1917-18
Earl, 1907-8, 1921-23
Eastern, 1910
Eastern Dairies, 1925
Eastman, 1899

Easton, 1907-13
Eaton, 1898
Eck, 1903
Eckhardt & Souter, 1903
Eclipse, 1901-2, 1908
Economy, 1906, 1908-11, 1917-22
Economycar, 1914
Eddy, 1902
Edmond, 1900
Edsel, 1957-59
Edwards-Knight, 1912-14
E.H.V., 1903-6
Eichstaedt, 1902
E.I.M., 1916
Eisenhuth, 1896
Eisenhuth-Compound, 1903
Elbert, 1915-16
Elbert Cyclecar, 1914-15
Elcar, 1915-31
Elcar-Lever, 1930
Elco, 1915
Elcurto, 1921
Eldredge, 1903
Electra, 1913
Electric Vehicle, 1897
Electric Wagon, 1897
Electrobat, 1895
Electrocar, 1922
Electronomic, 1901
Elgin, 1916-24
Elinore, 1903
Elite, 1906, 1909
Elite Steamer, 1901
Elk, 1913
Elkhart, 1908-16, 1922
Elliot, 1897, 1902
Ellis, 1901
Ellsworth, 1908, 1917
Elmira, 1920
Elmore, 1901-12
Elston, 1895
Elvick, 1895
Elwell-Parker, 1909
Elysee, 1926
Emancipator, 1909
Emblem, 1910
Embree-McLean, 1910
Emerson, 1907
E.M.F., 1908-12
Emmerson & Fisher Motor Wagon, 1896
Empire, 1898, 1910-19
Empire State, 1901

Empress, 1906
E.M.S., 1908
Endurance-Steam, 1922-23
Enger, 1909
Enger-Everitt, 1906-17
Englehardt, 1901
Engler, 1914
Entz, 1914
Epperson, 1912
Erbes, 1915-16
Erie, 1897, 1916-20
Erie & Sturgis, 1897
Ernst, 1896
Erskine, 1926-30
Erving, 1911-13
Ess Eff, 1912
Essex, 1906-8, 1919-32
Essex Steam Car, 1901
Etnyre, 1910-11
Euclid, 1903-4, 1907
Eugol, 1921
Eureka, 1907-9
Evans, 1904, 1912, 1914
Evansville, 1907-11, 1914-17
Everitt, 1909, 1911
Everybody's, 1908-9
Ewing, 1908-10
Excelsior, 1910

F

Facto, 1920
Fageol, 1916
Fageolbus, 1916
Fairbanks-Morse, 1909
Fairmount, 1906-7
F.A.L., 1909-14
Falcar, 1909, 1922
Falcon, 1908, 1914, 1922, 1938-43
Falcon Cycle Car, 1913-14
Falcon-Knight, 1926-29
Famous, 1908-9, 1917
Fanning, 1899-1903
Fargo, 1913
Farmack, 1915-16
Farmer, 1907
Farmobile, 1908
Farner, 1922
Fast, 1904
Fauber Auto Cycle Car, 1914
Fawick, 1910
Fay, 1912
Federal, 1907-9

Federal Steamer, 1905
Fee, 1908-9
Fenton, 1914
Fergus, 1917, 1920-21
Ferris, 1920-22
Fey, 1898-1905
Fiat, 1915
Fidelity, 1909
Field Steam, 1887
Fifth Avenue Coach, 1924
Finch, 1902
Findley, 1910, 1912
Firestone-Columbus, 1907-15
Fischer, 1902-04, 1914
Fish, 1908
Fisher, 1924
Flagler, 1914
Flanders, 1910
Flanders Electric, 1911, 1915-16
Flexbi, 1904
Flexible, 1932
Flint, 1902-4, 1910-12, 1923
Flyer, 1913, 1933
Flying Auto, 1947, 1950
Fool-Proof, 1912
Foos, 1913
Ford, 1896, 1903—
Fordmobile, 1903
Forest, 1902
Forest City, 1906-9
Forster Six, 1920
Fort Wayne, 1911
Foster Steam, 1900-3
Fostoria, 1906-7, 1916
Fournier, 1902
Four Traction, 1907-9
Four Wheel Drive, 1902-7
Fox, 1921-23
Frankfort, 1922
Franklin, 1902-34
Frantz, 1900-2
Frayer, 1904
Frayer-Miller, 1904-8
Frazer, 1946-51
Fredonia, 1902-4
Fredrickson, 1914
Freeman, 1901, 1931
Freemont, 1923
Freighter, 1917
French, 1913
Friedberg, 1908
Friedman, 1900-3
Friend, 1920-23

Frisbee, 1921
Fritchle Electric, 1907-22
Front-Away, 1917
Front Drive, 1921
Frontenac, 1908, 1917-22
Frontmobile, 1917-19
F.R.P., 1914-16
F.S., 1912
Fuller, 1908-11
Fulton, 1908-9, 1917
F.W.D. Car, 1910

G

Gabriel, 1912
Gadabout, 1914-16
Gaeth, 1898, 1902-10
Gale, 1904-10
Galt, 1914
Gardner, 1919-31
Garford, 1907-8
Garoscope, 1917
Gary, 1915
Gas-Au-Lec, 1905-6
Gas Engine, 1905-6
Gasmobile, 1900-2
Gasoline Motor Carriage, 1897
Gatts Horseless Carriage, 1905
Gawley, 1895
Gay, 1915
Gaylord, 1911-14
Gearless, 1907-9, 1921-23
Gearless Steamer, 1919-22
Gem, 1917-18
General, 1903-4, 1912
General Cab, 1929
General Electric, 1898-1901
General Vehicle, 1906-19
Genesee, 1911-12
Geneva, 1901-3, 1911, 1917
Gerlinger, 1917
German-American, 1902
Geronimo, 1918-21
Gersix, 1915
Ghent, 1917-18
Gibbs, 1903-5
Gibson, 1899
Gifford-Pettit, 1907-8
Gillette, 1916
G.J.G., 1909-15
Gleason, 1910-15
Glide, 1901-20
Globe, 1917, 1921
Glover, 1911, 1921

Goethemobile, 1902
Golden Eagle, 1906
Golden Slate, 1902
Golden State, 1928
Golden West, 1919
Goodspeed, 1922
Goodwin, 1923
Gopher, 1911
Gove, 1921
Grabowsky, 1908-13
Graham, 1930-41
Graham Electric, 1903
Graham-Fox, 1903
Graham Motorette, 1903-5
Graham-Paige, 1927
Gramm, 1901
Gramm-Bernstein, 1912
Gramm-Logan, 1908-10
Grand, 1912
Grand Rapids, 1913
Granite Falls, 1912
Grant, 1913-22
Grant-Ferris, 1901
Grass-Premier, 1923
Graves-Condon, 1899
Gray, 1916, 1922-26
Gray-Dort, 1917
Great, 1903
Great-Arrow, 1903
Great Eagle, 1911
Great Smith, 1907-12
Great Southern, 1911-14
Great Western, 1908-16
Greeley, 1903
Green Bay Steamer, 1877
Greenleaf, 1902
Greenville, 1925
Gregory, 1948
Gregory Front Drive, 1922
Grensfelder, 1901
Greuter, 1899
Greyhound, 1921-23, 1929
Gride, 1903
Grinnell, 1910-15
Griswold, 1907-8
Grout, 1898-1914
Grout-Steamer, 1906
Gurley, 1901
Guy-Vaughan, 1912
G.W.W., 1919
Gyroscope, 1908

H

Haase, 1903-4
Hackett, 1915-20
Hackley, 1905-6
H.A.L., 1916-18
Hale, 1917
Hal-Fur, 1919
Hall, 1903-4, 1915, 1917
Halladay, 1907-15, 1919-20
Hall Gasoline Trap, 1895
Halsey, 1901-9
Halton, 1901
Hambrick, 1908
Hamely, 1903
Hamilton, 1917-22
Hamilton-Holmes, 1921
Hammer, 1905-6
Hammer-Sommer, 1903-4
Handley, 1923
Handley-Knight, 1921-23
Hanger, 1915
Hanover, 1921-23
Hansen, 1902
Hansen-Whitman, 1907
Hanson, 1918-23
Harberer, 1910-13
Harder, 1911
Harding, 1911
Hardinge, 1903
Hardy, 1903
Hare, 1918
Harper, 1907
Harrie, 1925
Harrigan, 1922
Harris, 1893, 1898
Harrisburg, 1922
Harrison, 1906-7, 1912
Harris Six, 1923
Harroun, 1916-21
Hart-Kraft, 1908
Hartley, 1898
Hartman, 1898
Harvard, 1915-22
Harvey, 1914
Hasbrouck, 1899-1901
Haseltine, 1916
Hassler, 1917
Hatfield, 1906-8, 1916-24
Hathaway, 1924
Haupt, 1909
Haven, 1917
Havers, 1911-14

Haviland, 1895
Havoc, 1914
Hawk, 1914
Hawkeye, 1917, 1923
Hawkins, 1915
Hawley, 1907
Hay-Berg, 1907-8
Haydock, 1907-10
Hayes-Anderson, 1928
Haynes, 1894-1924
Haynes-Apperson, 1895
Hayward, 1913
Hazard, 1914
H.C.S., 1920-26
Healey, 1951
Healy Electric, 1911
Hebb, 1918
Heifner, 1921
Heilman, 1908
Heine-Velox, 1906-8, 1921
Heinzelman, 1908
Hendel, 1904
Henderson, 1912-14
Henley, 1899
Hennegin, 1908-9
Henney Hearse, 1922
Henrietta, 1901
Henry, 1911-12
Henry J, 1950-54
Henrylee, 1912
Hercules, 1907. 1914
Hercules Electric, 1902
Herff-Brooks, 1914-16
Herreshoff, 1909-15
Herreshoff-Detroit, 1914
Herschmann, 1904
Hershell-Spillman, 1901, 1904-7
Hertel, 1895-1901
Hertz, 1926
Heseltine, 1917
Hess Steam, 1902
Hewitt, 1905-13
Hewitt-Lindstrom, 1900
Heymann, 1898
H & F, 1911
Hickenhull, 1904
Hicks, 1900
Hidley, 1901
Higdon & Higdon Horseless
   Carriage, 1896
Highlander, 1922
Highway Knight, 1920
Higrade, 1919

Hill, 1907-8
Hillsdale, 1908
Hill's Locomotor, 1895
Hilton, 1908
Hinde & Dauch, 1906-8
Hines, 1908
Hinkel, 1925
Hobbie, 1909-10
Hodge Steamer Fire Engine, 1840
Hodgson, 1902
Hoffman, 1931
Hoffman Gas, 1901
Hoffman Steam, 1902-4
Holden, 1915
Holland Steam, 1905
Holley, 1899-1904
Hollier, 1916-20
Holly, 1910-17
Holmes, 1908, 1918-22
Holmes Gastricycle, 1895
Holsman, 1902-10
Hol-Tan, 1906
Holton, 1921
Holtzer-Cabot, 1895
Holyoke, 1903
Holyoke-Steam, 1899-1903
Homer, 1908
Homer Laughlin, 1916-18
Hoosier Scout, 1914
Hoover, 1917
Hopkins, 1902
Hoppenstand, 1948
Horner, 1917
Horsey Horseless Carriage, 1899
Hoskins, 1921
Houghton, 1916
Houghton Steamer, 1900-1
Houk, 1917
Houpt, 1909
Houpt-Rockwell, 1910
House, 1920
House-Steamer, 1901
Howard, 1901, 1903-6, 1913-17
Howard Gasoline Wagon, 1895
Howe, 1907
Howey, 1907
H.R.L., 1921
Huber, 1894
Hudson, 1909-57
Hudson Steam, 1904
Hudson Steam Car, 1901
Huebner, 1914
Huffman, 1920-26

Hughes, 1899
Hunt, 1905
Hunter, 1921
Huntington, 1907
Huntington-Buckboard, 1889
Hupmobile, 1908-41
Hupp-Yeats, 1911-19
Hurlburt, 1922
Huron, 1921
Hurryton, 1922
Huselton, 1914
Hustler Power Car, 1911
Hydro-Car, 1901
Hydromotor, 1917
Hylander, 1922

I

Ideal, 1902-9, 1912, 1914
Ideal Electric, 1910-11
I.H.C., 1907-8
Illinois Electric, 1901, 1909-14
Imp, 1913, 1915
Imperial, 1900, 1903-5, 1907-8,
   1912-16, 1926–
Independence, 1912
Independent, 1911, 1915-16,
   1920, 1927
Indian, 1922
Indiana, 1910, 1921
Indianapolis, 1899
Ingersoll-Rand, 1921
Ingram-Hatch, 1917-18
Inland, 1920
Innes, 1921
International, 1948
International Auto Wagon, 1900
International Harvester, 1907–
International Harvester Auto Buggy,
   1907-12
Inter-State, 1908-19
Interurban Electric, 1905
Intrepid, 1903-4
Iowa, 1908-9, 1919
Iroquois Buffalo, 1906-8
Iroquois Seneca, 1905-8
Irvin, 1902
Iverson, 1908
Izzer, 1910

J

Jackson, 1899, 1902-23
Jacks Runabout, 1900

Jacquet Flyer, 1921
James, 1911
Janney, 1906-7
Jarvis-Huntington, 1912
Jaxon, 1903
Jay, 1907-9
Jay-Eye-See, 1921
Jeannin, 1908-9
Jeep, 1941–
Jeffery, 1902-16
Jem Special, 1922
Jenkins, 1901, 1907-15
Jersey City, 1919
Jetmobile, 1952
Jewel, 1911
Jewell, 1906-9
Jewett, 1906, 1922-27
J.I.C. see Jay-Eye-See
Joerns, 1911
Johnson, 1905-13
Johnson Steamer, 1901
Joliet, 1912
Joly & Lambert, 1916
Jones, 1916-20
Jones-Corbin, 1902-7
Jones Steam Car, 1898
Jonz, 1909-12
Jordan, 1916-30
J.P.L., 1914
Juergens, 1908
Jules, 1911
Julian, 1925
Julian-Brown, 1925
Jumbo, 1918
Junior, 1925
Junz, 1902
Juvenile, 1906-7

K

Kadix, 1913
Kaiser, 1946-55
Kaiser Darrin, 1952-54
Kalamazoo, 1914, 1922
Kane-Pennington, 1894
Kankakee, 1919
Kansas City, 1905-7
Karbach, 1908-9
Kardell, 1918
Kato, 1907
Kauffman, 1909-10
Kavan, 1905
Kaws, 1922

K-D, 1913-14
Kearns, 1908-17
Keasler, 1922
Keene, 1900-2
Keeton, 1908
Keldon, 1920
Keller, 1947-49
Keller Cyclecar, 1915
Keller-Kar, 1914
Kelley-Springfield, 1918
Kellogg, 1903
Kelly, 1911
Kelsey, 1902, 1922-24
Kelsey Friction, 1921-24
Kelsey Motorette, 1910-13
Kelsey & Tilney, 1899
Kendle, 1912
Kenilworth, 1923
Kenmore, 1909-12
Kennedy, 1898, 1911
Kensington, 1899-1903
Kensington Steam, 1908
Kent, 1916-17
Kent's Pacemaker, 1900
Kentucky, 1915-24
Kenworthy, 1920-22
Kermet, 1900
Kermoth, 1908
Kerns, 1914
Kerosene Surrey, 1900
Kessler, 1921
Kess-Line, 1922
Keystone, 1900, 1909-10, 1918-19
Keystone-Motorette, 1896
Keystone Steamer, 1909
Kiblinger, 1907-9
Kidder, 1901
Kidney, 1910
Kimball, 1922
Kimball Electric, 1912
King, 1896, 1909, 1911-24
King Midget, 1945–
King-Remick, 1906
Kingston, 1907-8
King Zeitler, 1919
Kinnear, 1913
Kinney, 1922
Kirk, 1903-5
Kirkham, 1906
Kirksell, 1907
Kissel, 1906-31
Kleiber, 1925-30
Klemm, 1917

Kline, 1909-23
Kline-Kar, 1916
Kling, 1907
Klink, 1907-9
Klock, 1900
Klondike, 1918
K & M, 1908
Knickerbocker, 1901, 1912
Knight & Klibourne, 1906-9
Knight Special, 1917
Know, 1900
Knox, 1900-15, 1922
Knox-Landsen, 1904
Knudson, 1899
K.O., 1921
Kobusch, 1906
Koehler, 1910-12, 1919
Komet, 1911
Konigslow, 1901-4
Kopp, 1911
Koppin, 1914
Kosmos, 1909
Kraft Steam, 1901
Kramer, 1915
Krastin, 1902-3
Krebs, 1913
Kreuger, 1904
K-R-I-T, 1909-15
Kron, 1915
Krueger, 1904-6
Kuhn, 1918
Kunz, 1902-5
Kurtis, 1954
Kurtis-Kraft, 1949-55
Kurtz, 1921-26

L

Laconia, 1900
Lad's Car, 1914
LaFayette, 1920-24, 1934-39
La France, 1910
La France-Republic, 1925
La Marne, 1920-21
La Marne Jr., 1919
Lambert, 1891, 1904, 1908
Lamphen, 1904
Lampher, 1909
Lamson, 1917
Lancamobile, 1899
Lancaster, 1900-1
Lancer, 1960–
Landover, 1917-18

Landshaft, 1913
Lane, 1920
Lane Steamer, 1899-1911
Langan, 1898
Langer, 1896
Lansden, 1904-10
La Petite, 1905-6
Larchmont, 1900
Larre-Bee-Deyo, 1920
Larsen, 1908
Larson, 1910
La Salle, 1927-40
La Salle Niagara, 1906
Lasky, 1916
Laughlin, 1916-18
Laurel, 1916-21
Lauth-Juergens, 1907-9
Lavigne, 1914
Law, 1902, 1912
Lawson, 1900
Lawter, 1909
L.C.E., 1914
L & E, 1922
Leach, 1899
Leach-Biltwell, 1920-23
Leader, 1911
Lear, 1903-9
Lebanon, 1906-7
Lebgett, 1903
Lee Diamond, 1911
Lehigh, 1926
Lehr, 1908
LeJeal, 1902
Lenawee, 1904
Lende, 1908-9
Lengert, 1896
Lennon, 1909
Lenot, 1912-22
Lenox, 1911
Lenox Electric, 1908
Leon Mendel, 1890
Leon Rubay, 1923
Leslie, 1918
Lesperance, 1911
Lethbridge, 1907
Lever, 1930
Lewis, 1898, 1901, 1913-16
Lewis Airmobile, 1937
Lexington, 1909-26
Liberty, 1916-23, 1926
Liberty-Brush, 1912
Light, 1914

Lima, 1915
Limited, 1911
Lincoln, 1908, 1910-11, 1914, 1920–
Lincoln Continental, 1939-48, 1957–
Lincoln Zephyr, 1935-42
Lindsay, 1908
Lindsley, 1908
Linn, 1929
Linscott, 1916
Lion, 1910-12
Lippard, 1912
Little, 1911-14, 1921
Littlemac, 1930
L.M.C., 1919
Locke Steamer, 1902
Locomobile, 1899-1930
Locomobile Steamer, 1899
Logan, 1905-8, 1914
Lomax, 1913
Lombard, 1921
London, 1922
Lone Star, 1920-23
Long, 1875, 1923
Long Distance, 1900
Longest, 1912
Loomis, 1896-1904
Lord, 1913-14
Lord Baltimore, 1912-13
Lorraine, 1907-8, 1920-21
Los Angeles, 1913
Louisiana, 1900
Lowell, 1917
Lowell-American, 1908-9
Loyal, 1920
Lozier, 1904-17
Lozier Steamer, 1900-1, 1912
L.P.C., 1914-16
Luck Utility, 1913
Ludlow, 1915
Luedinghaus-Espenschied, 1919
Luitwieler, 1909
Lulu, 1914
Lutz, 1917
Luverne, 1906-17
Luxor Cab, 1920-26
Lyman, 1904, 1909
Lyman & Burnham, 1903-4
Lyon, 1911
Lyons-Atlas, 1914-15
Lyons-Knight, 1914

M

Maccar, 1914
McCarron, 1929
McCormick, 1899
McCrea, 1906-8
McCue, 1909-10
McCullough, 1899
McCurdy, 1922
MacDonald, 1920-23
MacDonald Steamer, 1923
McFarlan, 1910-28
McGee Steamer, 1937
McGill, 1922
McIntyre, 1909-15
Mack, 1900–
McKay Steam, 1900
Mackenzie, 1914
Mackle-Thompson, 1903
McLaughlin, 1911, 1916
McLean, 1910
McNabb, 1910
MacNaughton, 1907
Macomber, 1913
Macon, 1917
Macy-Roger, 1895
Madison, 1915-21
Magic, 1922
Magnolia, 1903
Mahoning, 1904-5
Maibohm, 1916-22
Maine, 1915-18
Mais, 1911
Maja, 1908
Majestic, 1913, 1917-18, 1925
Malcolm, 1915
Malcolm-Jones, 1914
Malcomson, 1906
Malden Steam, 1902
Malvern, 1905
Manexall, 1921
Manhattan, 1907, 1921
Manistee, 1912
Manlius, 1910
Manly, 1919
Mann, 1895
Mansfield, 1919
Mansur, 1914
Maplebay, 1908
Maple-Leaf, 1921
Marathon, 1908-15
Marble-Swift, 1903-5

Marion, 1901, 1903-15
Marion-Handley, 1916
Marion-Overland, 1910
Maritime, 1913
Mark-Electric, 1897
Marlan, 1920
Marlboro, 1900
Marlin, 1964-67
Marmon, 1903-33
Marmon-Herrington, 1932
Marmon & Nordyke, 1902
Marquette, 1912, 1929-30
Marr, 1903-4
Marron, 1903
Marsh, 1898-99, 1905, 1920-23
Marshall, 1919-21
Martin, 1910, 1920, 1926, 1931, 1954
Martin-Wasp, 1919-24
Marvel, 1907
Maryland, 1908-10
Maryland Electric, 1914
Mascotte, 1911
Mason, 1906-15, 1922
Mason Steamer, 1898
Massachusetts, 1901
Massillon, 1909
Master, 1918
Mather, 1901
Matheson, 1903-13
Mathews, 1907
Mathewson, 1904
Mathis, 1930-31
Matilda, 1894
Maumee, 1906
Maxen, 1913
Maxfer, 1919
Maxim, 1912, 1920, 1928
Maxim-Goodridge, 1908
Maxim Motortricycle, 1895
Maxwell, 1904-25
May, 1912
Mayer, 1899, 1913
Mayfair, 1925
Maytag, 1911
M.B., 1910
Mead, 1912
Mearo, 1909
Mecca, 1915
Mechaley, 1903
Mechanics, 1925
Med-Bow, 1907-8
Medcraft, 1907-8

Media, 1900, 1907
Meech-Stoddard, 1924
Meiselbach, 1904-9
Melbourne, 1904
Mel Special, 1923
Menard, 1921
Menges, 1908
Menominee, 1915
Mercedes, 1902
Mercer, 1909-25, 1931
Merchant, 1914
Merciless, 1906
Mercu, 1909-29
Mercury, 1904, 1910, 1914-18, 1922, 1930, 1938–
Merit, 1920-23
Merkel, 1905-6
Merz, 1914
Messerer, 1901
Metcar, 1901
Meteor, 1902-3, 1908-9, 1914, 1921
Metropol, 1914-15
Metropolitan, 1917, 1922-23
Metz, 1909-21
Metzcar, 1909-12
Metzger, 1909
Meyer, 1922
Michelet, 1921
Michigan, 1903-7, 1910-13
Michigan Hearse, 1914
Michigan Steamer, 1908-9
Middleby, 1908-12
Midgley, 1905
Midland, 1908-13
Midwest Tractor, 1918
Mier, 1908-10
Mieusset, 1907
Mighty Michigan, 1913
Milac, 1916
Milburn Electric, 1915-24
Miller, 1903, 1907-8, 1912-13, 1921
Miller Special, 1907-8
Mills, 1876
Mills Milwaukee, 1900
Milwaukee, 1925
Milwaukee Steam, 1900-2
Minneapolis, 1919
Mino, 1914
Mission, 1914
Mitchell, 1903-23
Mobile, 1902

Mobile Steamer, 1899-1903
Mobilette, 1913-15
Mock, 1906
Model, 1903-9
Modern, 1907-10, 1912
Modoc, 1911
Moehn, 1895
Moeller, 1911
Mogul, 1912
Mohawk, 1903-4, 1914
Mohler, 1901-5
Mohler & DeGress, 1901-5
Moligan, 1920
Moline, 1904-17, 1920
Moline-Knight, 1913, 1918
Moller Cab, 1920
Monarch, 1903-9, 1914-16
Moncrief, 1901
Mondex-Magic, 1914
Monitor, 1910, 1915
Monroe, 1915-22
Monsen, 1908-9
Moody, 1900
Mooers, 1900
Moon, 1905-31
Moore, 1902-3, 1906-7, 1916-20
Moorespring Vehicle, 1890
Moorespring Vehicle Steam, 1888
Mora, 1906-11
Morgan, 1897, 1908-9
Morlock, 1903
Mor-Power, 1921
Morris-London, 1920-23
Morrison Electric, 1891
Morris Salom Electrobat, 1895-97
Morrissey, 1925
Mors, 1901, 1906
Morse, 1904, 1909, 1915-16
Morse Cyclecar, 1914-15
Morse Steam Car, 1904-6
Mort, 1925
Motor Buggy, 1908-10
Motorcar, 1906-8
Motorette, 1906, 1910-11, 1946
Mountain Road, 1917
Mt. Pleasant, 1914-16
Mover, 1902
Moyea, 1903-4
Moyer, 1912-15
M.P.C., 1925
M & P Electric, 1912-13
M.P.M., 1915
Mueller, 1896

Mueller-Benz, 1895
Mueller-Trap, 1901
Mulford, 1909
Multiplex, 1913
Muncie, 1903, 1906
Munsing, 1908, 1913
Munson, 1900
Muntz Jet, 1951
Murdaugh, 1900
Murray, 1901, 1916-20
Murray-Max Six, 1921-26
Muskegon, 1918
Mustang, 1948
Mutual, 1914-19
Myer B. & F., 1912
Myers, 1904

N

Nadig, 1889
Nance, 1911-12
Napier, 1904-12
Napoleon, 1916-18
Narragansett, 1915
Nash, 1917-57
Nash Healey, 1951-54
Natco, 1912
National, 1900-24
National Electric, 1900
National Sextet, 1920
Nebraska, 1926
Neilson, 1907
Nelson, 1905, 1917-20
Nelson-Brennen-Peterson, 1914-15
Nelson & Le Moon, 1915-20
Neustadt, 1912
Neustadt-Perry, 1903
Nevada, 1908
Nevin, 1927
Newark, 1912
Newcomb, 1921
New Era, 1902, 1916
New Haven, 1899, 1911
New Home, 1901
New Orleans, 1920
New Perry, 1903
Newport, 1916
New Way, 1907
New York, 1900, 1907, 1926
Niagara, 1903, 1915
Nichols-Shepard, 1912
Niles, 1916, 1921
Noel, 1913

Nolan, 1924
Noma, 1919-23
Nonpareil, 1913
Northern, 1903-8
Northway, 1921
Norton, 1901-2
Norwalk, 1912-22
Novara, 1917
Nucar, 1929
Nyberg, 1912-14

O

Oakland, 1907-31
Oakman, 1898-1900
Obertine, 1915
O'Connell, 1928
Odelot, 1916
Offenhauser, 1934
Ogren, 1907, 1915-20
Ohio, 1909-18
Ohio Electric, 1900-15
Ohio Falls, 1911-15
Okay, 1907
Okey, 1903-8
Oldfield, 1917
Old Hickory, 1915
Old Reliable, 1912, 1926
Oldsmobile, 1896–
Olds Steam Car, 1896
Oliver, 1911, 1935
Olympian, 1917-20
Olympic, 1913, 1922
Omaha, 1912-13
Omar, 1908-10
Omort, 1927
Only, 1909-11
Only Car, 1911-15
Oregon, 1916
Orient, 1900
Orient-Auto-Go, 1900
Oriole, 1927
Orion, 1900
Orleans, 1920
Orlo, 1904
Ormond, 1904
Orson, 1911
Oscarlear, 1905
Oshkosh, 1926
Oshkosh Steamer, 1877
Otto, 1909
Ottokar, 1903-4
Otto-Mobile, 1911-12

Overholt Steam, 1912
Overland, 1903, 1906-09
Overman, 1899-1902
Owatonna, 1903
O-We-Go, 1914
Owen, 1899, 1910
Owen Magnetic, 1915-20
Owen-Schoenieck, 1915
Owen-Thomas, 1908
Owosso, 1911
Oxford, 1905-6

P

Pacific, 1914
Pacific Special, 1911
Packard, 1899-1958
Packers, 1911
Packet, 1915, 1917
Page, 1907-9, 1923
Page-Toledo, 1910
Paige, 1910
Paige-Detroit, 1909-28
Pak-Age-Car, 1925
Palace, 1912
Palmer, 1906, 1912
Palmer-Moore, 1905
Palmer-Singer, 1907-14
Pan, 1918-20
Pan-American, 1902-4, 1917-21
Panda, 1954
Panther, 1908
Paragon, 1906, 1917, 1922
Paramount Cab, 1924
Parenth, 1921
Parenti, 1920-21
Parker, 1919, 1922
Parkin, 1903-9
Parry, 1911
Parsons, 1906
Partin, 1913
Partin-Palmer, 1913-17
Pasco, 1908
Pastora, 1913
Paterson, 1908-24
Pathfinder, 1911-18
Patrician, 1917
Patriot, 1922
Patterson-Greenfield, 1916
Pawtucket, 1901-2
Payne-Modern, 1906
Peabody, 1907
Peck, 1897

Peerless, 1900-32
Peerless Steam, 1902-9
Peet, 1923-26
Peets, 1908
Pelletier, 1906
Penford, 1924
Peninsular, 1915
Penn, 1911-13
Pennant, 1923
Pennnington, 1890, 1894
Pennsy, 1917-18
Pennsylvania, 1907-13, 1916-17
Penn-Unit, 1911
People's, 1901
Perfection, 1906-8
Perfex, 1912
Perry, 1895
Peru, 1938
P.E.T., 1913
Peter Pan, 1907, 1914
Peters, 1921-24
Peters-Walton, 1914
Petrel, 1908-12
Phelps, 1902-5
Phianna, 1917-20
Philadelphia, 1924
Philion, 1892
Phipps, 1911-12
Phipps-Johnston, 1909
Phoenix, 1900
Pickard, 1908-12
Pickwick, 1930
Piedmont, 1908, 1918-20
Pierce, 1903
Pierce-Arrow, 1901-38
Pierce Motorette, 1901
Pierce-Racine, 1903-11
Pierce-Stanhope, 1903
Piggins, 1909-10, 1912
Pilgrim, 1916-18
Pilliod, 1916
Pilot, 1911-23
Pioneer, 1909-11, 1914-15, 1917,
    1920
Pirate, 1907
Pirsch, 1910
Piscorski, 1901
Pitcher, 1920
Pittsburgh, 1896-99, 1905-11
Pittsburgh Electric, 1905-11
Pittsburgher, 1919
Pittsfield, 1907
Planche, 1906

Plass Motor Sleigh, 1895
Playboy, 1946-49
Plymouth, 1910, 1928–
P.M.C. Buggyabout, 1908
Pneumobile, 1914-15
Pokorney, 1904-5
Polo, 1927
Pomeroy, 1902
Ponder, 1916, 1922
Pontiac, 1906-9, 1926–
Pope, 1895-99
Pope Columbia, 1897
Pope-Hartford, 1897-1914
Pope Motor, 1903-8
Pope-Robinson, 1902-4
Pope-Toledo, 1901-9
Pope Tribune, 1902-9
Pope-Waverly, 1903-8
Poppy Car, 1917
Porter, 1900, 1920-22
Port Huron, 1918
Portland, 1914
Poss, 1912
Postal, 1907-8
Powell, 1912
Powercar, 1909-11
Poyer, 1913
Practical, 1906-9
Prado, 1921
Pratt, 1911-16
Praul, 1895
Preferred, 1920
Premier, 1903-26
Premocar, 1920
Prescott, 1901-5
Preston, 1921-23
Price, 1908
Pridemore, 1914
Primo, 1906, 1911
Prince, 1902
Princess, 1905, 1914-18
Princeton, 1923
Progress, 1912
Prospect, 1902
Prudence, 1912
Publix, 1946
Pullman, 1907-8
Pungs-Finch, 1904-10
Pup, 1948
Puritan, 1917
Puritan Steam, 1902

Pyramid, 1902

Q

Quakertown, 1915
Queen, 1902-6
Quick, 1899
Quinlan, 1904
Quinsler, 1904

R

R.A.C., 1911-12
Racine, 1895
Rae, 1909
Rae Electric, 1898
Railsbach, 1914
Rainier, 1905-11
Ralco, 1904
Raleigh, 1920
Rambler, 1900, 1902-13, 1957-69
Randall, 1903-6
Randall Steamer, 1902-3
Randolph Steam, 1908-10
Ranger, 1907, 1910-11, 1921-22
Ranier, 1911
Rassel, 1911
Rassler, 1907
Rauch & Lang Electric, 1905-24,
    1927-30
Rayfield, 1911-15
R.C.H., 1911-14
Read, 1913-14
Reading, 1912-18
Reading Steamer, 1960
Real, 1915
Rebel, 1968–
Reber, 1902-3
Red Arrow, 1915-16
Red Ball, 1924
Red Bug, 1928
Red Devil Steamer, 1866
Red Jacket, 1907
Redshield, 1911
Red Wing, 1928
Reed, 1909
Reese, 1921
Reeves, 1897, 1908-11
Regal, 1908-18
Regas, 1903-5
Regent, 1917
Reid, 1903-5
Reiland & Bree, 1928
Reinertsen, 1902

Relay, 1904
Reliable, 1906-9
Reliable-Dayton, 1908-9
Reliance, 1903-9, 1917
Remel-Vincent Steam, 1923
Remington, 1901-4, 1912, 1915-16
Rennoc, 1918
Reno, 1908
Renville, 1911
Reo, 1904-36
Republic, 1911-15
Revere, 1917-25
Rex, 1914-15
Reya, 1918
Reynolds, 1920
Rhodes, 1908
Richard, 1914-18
Richards, 1914
Richelieu, 1922-23
Richmond, 1908-12, 1915
Richter, 1902
Rickenbacker, 1922-27
Ricketts, 1902
Ricketts Diamond, 1909
Rickmobile, 1948
Riddle, 1916, 1922-24
Rider-Lewis, 1908-9
Riess-Royal, 1922
Riker Electric Stanhope, 1896-99
Riker Gasoline, 1900
Riley & Cowley, 1902
Rinker Electric, 1898
Riper, 1917
Ripper, 1903
Ritz, 1915-16
Riviera, 1907
R & L Electric, 1920
R.M.C., 1908
R.O., 1911
Roadable, 1946
Road Cart, 1896
Roader, 1911-12
Road King, 1922
Road Plane, 1945
Roadster, 1903, 1915
Roamer, 1916-25
Robe, 1923
Roberts, 1904
Roberts Six, 1921
Robie, 1914
Robinson, 1900-2, 1914
Robson, 1908-11

Roche, 1920-26
Rochester, 1901
Rockaway, 1902-3
Rockcliff, 1905
Rocket, 1913, 1924
Rockette, 1946
Rock Falls, 1920
Rockford, 1903, 1908
Rock Hill, 1916
Rockne, 1931-33
Rockwell, 1908
Rodgers, 1903-5, 1921
Roebling, 1909
Roger, 1903
Rogers, 1895, 1911-12
Rogers & Hanford, 1901-2
Rogers Steamer, 1899
Rollin, 1923-25
Rolls-Royce (U.S.), 1920-31
Roman, 1909
Romer, 1921-24
Roosevelt, 1929-31
Root & Van Dervoort, 1904
Roper-Steamer, 1865
Roper Steam Vehicle, 1894
Ross, 1905-9, 1915-18, 1929
Rossler, 1907
Rotarian, 1921
Rotary, 1904-5, 1916-17, 1922
Rovan, 1914
Rovena Front-Drive, 1926
Rowe, 1911
Rowe-Stuart, 1922
Royal, 1904, 1914
Royal Electric, 1905
Royal Tourist, 1904-12
Rubay, 1922-24
Ruggles, 1905
Ruler, 1917
Rumley, 1920
Runabout, 1902
Runner, 1913
Rush, 1918
Rushmobile, 1902
Russell, 1902-3, 1910
Russell-Knight, 1914
Rutenber, 1903
Ruxton, 1929-31
R & V Knight, 1919-24
Ryder, 1908-11
Rylander, 1914

S

Safety, 1909, 1917
Safety Steamer, 1901
Safeway, 1925
Saf-T-Cab, 1926
Saginaw, 1916-17
St. Cloud, 1921
St. Joe, 1909
St. Johns, 1903
St. Louis, 1899-1907, 1922
Salisbury Motorcycle, 1895
Salter, 1909
Salvador, 1914-15
Sampson, 1904-11, 1919
Samson, 1919-23
Sanbert, 1911
Sandow Cab, 1925
Sandusky, 1903-4, 1911
Sanford-Herbert, 1911
Santos Dumont, 1902-4
Saturn, 1991–
Savage, 1912
Sawyer, 1913
Saxon, 1914-22
Saxon-Duplex, 1920
Sayer, 1917
Sayers & Scoville, 1907-24
Scarab, 1935-40, 1946
Schacht, 1905-13
Schaefer, 1910
Schaum, 1900-1
Schebler, 1908
Schleicher, 1895
Schloemer, 1889
Schlosser, 1912
Schlotterback, 1912
Schmidt, 1910
Schnader, 1914-18
Schoening, 1895
Schwartz, 1920
Scientific, 1921
Scioto, 1911
Scootmobile, 1947
Scott, 1901, 1921
Scott-Newcomb Steam, 1921
Scout, 1961–
Scripps, 1911
Scripps-Booth, 1914-22
Scripps-Booth Cyclecar, 1914
Seagrave, 1912, 1921
Searchmont, 1900-3

Sears, 1908-9
Sebring, 1909-12
Seitz, 1911
Sekine, 1923
Selden, 1906-14
Sellers, 1909
Sellew-Royce, 1909
Seminole, 1928
Senator, 1906-11
Seneca, 1917-24
Serpentina, 1915
Serrifile, 1921
Servitor, 1907
Seven-Little-Buffaloes, 1908
Severin, 1920-22
S.F., see Ess Eff
S.G. Gay, 1915
S.G.V., 1910-15
Sha, 1920
Shadburn, 1917-18
Shad-Wyck, 1917
Shain, 1902-3
Shamrock, 1917
Sharon, 1915
Sharp, 1915
Sharp-Arrow, 1909-11
Shaum, 1905-8
Shavers Steam Buggy, 1895
Shaw, 1900, 1914-21
Shawmut, 1905-9
Shay, 1978-81
Shelby, 1902-3, 1917
Shelby American, 1965–
Sheldon, 1905
Sheridan, 1921
Shoemaker, 1908-9
Sibley, 1911
Sibley-Curtis, 1912
Siebert, 1907-9
Sigma, 1914
Signal, 1915
Signet, 1913
Silent, 1906
Silent Knight, 1912
Silent Sioux, 1910
Silver Knight, 1906
Simmons, 1910
Simms, 1920
Simonds Steam Wagon, 1895
Simplex, 1905-19
Simplex-Crane, 1915
Simplicity, 1907-11
Simplo, 1909-10

Sinclair, 1921
Sinclair-Scott, 1906-7
Singer, 1916
Single Center, 1908-10
Sintz, 1897, 1903-4
Sizer, 1911
S.J.R., 1915-16
Skelton, 1920-23
Skene, 1900-1
S. & M., 1913
Small, 1915, 1919-22
Smith, 1905-12
Smith & Mabley, 1905-7
Smith Motor Wheel, 1909
Smith Spring Motor, 1896
S.N., 1921
Snyder, 1908-9
Sommer, 1908
Soules, 1905-8
South Bend, 1919
Southern, 1908-10, 1922
Southern Six, 1921-22
Sovereign, 1907
Spacke, 1915-19
Spartan, 1907
Spaulding, 1902-3, 1911-16
Special, 1906
Specialty, 1898
Speed Wagon, 1918
Speedway, 1904
Speedway Special, 1918
Speedwell, 1907-15
Spencer, 1914, 1921
Spencer Steamer, 1862, 1901
Spenny, 1915
Sperling, 1921
Sperry, 1903
Sphinx, 1914-16
Spicer, 1903
Spiller, 1900
Spillman, 1907
Spoerer, 1909-14
Sport, 1921
Spracke, 1921
Sprague, 1896
Springer, 1904-6
Springfield, 1900-1, 1903-4, 1909-10
Sprite, 1914
Squier Steam, 1899
S.S.E., 1917
S & S Hearse, 1907
Stafford, 1911-15
Stahl, 1910

Standard, 1902-5, 1909, 1916-23
Standard Eight, 1917
Standard Electric, 1911-14
Standard Electrique, 1903
Standard Six, 1910-11
Standard Steamer, 1900
Standish, 1925
Stanhope, 1903, 1905
Stanley, 1903
Stanley Steamer, 1897-1924
Stanley-Whitney, 1899-1902
Stanmobile, 1901
Stanton-Steam, 1901
Stanwood, 1920-22
Star, 1904, 1914, 1917, 1922-28
Starbuck, 1914
Starin, 1903
States, 1915-16, 1918
Static, 1923
Staver, 1907-14
Steamobile, 1901-2
Steam Vehicle, 1900-3
Stearns, 1898-1929
Stearns-Electric, 1900-4
Stearns-Knight, 1911
Stearns Steam Car, 1900-4
Steco, 1914
Steele, 1915
Steel Swallow, 1907-8
Stegeman, 1911
Steinhart-Jensen, 1908
Stein-Koenig, 1926
Steinmetz, 1920
Stephens, 1916-24
Stephenson, 1910
Step-N-Drive, 1929
Sterling, 1909-11, 1915, 1921-23
Sterling-Knight, 1921-25
Sternberg, 1909
Stetson, 1917
Stevens, 1915
Stevens-Duryea, 1902-15, 1919-24
Stewart, 1895, 1915
Stewart-Coates, 1922
Stickney Motorette, 1913
Stilson, 1908-10
Stoddard, 1911
Stoddard-Dayton, 1904-13
Storck, 1902
Storms, 1915-16
Stoughton, 1919
Stover, 1909
Strathmore, 1900-1

Stratton, 1901-2, 1908-9, 1923
Streator, 1905-8
Stringer Steam, 1901
Strobel & Martin, 1910
Strong & Rogers, 1900
Strouse Steam, 1915
Struss, 1897
Studebaker, 1902-66
Sturges, 1895
Sturgis-Erie, 1898
Sturtevant, 1904-7
Stutz, 1912-34
Stuyvesant, 1911-12
Suburban, 1910-12
Success, 1906-9, 1920
Sullivan, 1904
Sultan, 1906-12
Sultanic, 1913
Summit, 1907
Sun, 1915-17
Sunset, 1906-7
Super Cooled, 1923
Superior, 1908, 1918
Super Kar, 1946
Super Traction, 1923
Supreme, 1917, 1922, 1930
Swanson, 1911
Sweany Steam Carriage, 1895
Synnestvedt, 1904-8
Syracuse, 1899, 1905

T

Taft Steam, 1901
Tait, 1923
Tally-Ho, 1914
Tarkington, 1922
Tarrytown, 1914
Tasco, 1947
Taunton, 1901-2, 1904
Taylor, 1921
Teel, 1913
Templar, 1918-25
Temple, 1899
Templeton-Dubrie, 1910
Tennant, 1915
Terraplane, 1932-39
Terwilliger Steam, 1904
Tex, 1915
Texan, 1919
Texas, 1918-21
Texmobile, 1921
Thermot Monohan, 1919

Thomart, 1921
Thomas-Detroit, 1906-8
Thomas Flyer, 1902-12
Thompson, 1902-4, 1907-8
Thomson, 1901-8
Thor VI, 1909-10
Thorne, 1929
Thornycroft, 1901-3
Thorobred, 1901
Thresher, 1900
Thunderbird, 1954–
Tiffany, 1913
Tiffin, 1914
Tiger, 1914
Tiley, 1904, 1907-10
Tincher, 1904-9
Tinkham, 1899
Titan, 1916, 1919
Titan Vim, 1925
Tjaarda, 1934
Toledo, 1902, 1909-10, 1915
Toledo Steamer, 1903
Tonawanda, 1900
Toquet, 1905
Torbensen, 1902-8
Touraine, 1912-16
Tourist, 1903
Tower, 1918
Town Car, 1909
Towne Shopper, 1948
Trabold, 1921
Tractmobile Steam, 1900
Traffic, 1914
Transit, 1912
Trask-Detroit, 1922
Traveler, 1914-15, 1924
Traveller, 1906-7, 1910
Traverse City, 1918
Traylor, 1920
Trebert, 1907
Triangle, 1918
Tribune, 1913
Tri-Car, 1907, 1955
Tricar, 1912
Tricolet, 1905
Tri-Moto, 1901
Trinity Steam, 1900
Triplex, 1905
Triumph, 1900-1, 1906-11, 1920
Trojan, 1916
Trombly, 1911
Troy, 1908-9

Trumbull, 1914-16
Tucker Mobile, 1900
Tucker Torpedo, 1946-47
Tudhope, 1913
Tulcar, 1915
Tulsa, 1917-21
Turnbull, 1918
Turner, 1902-4
Twin City, 1910
Twin Coach, 1927
Twombly, 1910, 1914-16
Twyford, 1902-8

U

Ultimate, 1920
Ultra, 1908-11, 1918
Union, 1902-5, 1908-9, 1912, 1917
United, 1902-4, 1916
United Motor, 1902
Unito, 1908
Universal, 1912, 1917, 1919
University, 1907
Unwin, 1907
Upton, 1903-6
Urgan, 1913
U.S., 1908
U.S. Auto, 1899-1918
U.S. Carriage, 1910-18
U.S. Long Distance, 1900-4
U.S. Motor Car, 1908
U.S. Motor Vehicle, 1899-1901
Utility, 1910, 1918

V

Valley Dispatch, 1927
Van, 1904
Van Auken, 1914
Vanderbilt, 1921
Van Dyke, 1912
Vanell Steam Carriage, 1895
Van L., 1911
Van Wagoner, 1900
Vaughn, 1905, 1913-14, 1923
V.E.C., 1903
Veerac, 1911
Velie, 1908-29
Vernon, 1916-20
Verrett Motor Wagon, 1896
Versare, 1928
Vestal, 1914
Veteran, 1921

Viall, 1917
Victor, 1906-15, 1921
Victoria, 1900
Victors, 1923
Victor Steamer, 1900
Victory, 1920
Viking, 1908, 1929-30
Vim Cyclecar, 1915
Virginian, 1911
Vixen Cyclecar, 1914-16
Vogel, 1909
Vogue, 1918-22
Vogul, 1918
Voiturette, 1914
Voltra, 1917
Voltz, 1915
Vreeland, 1920
Vulcan, 1913-15, 1920

W

Waco, 1915
Wade, 1913
Wagenhals, 1910-15
Wagner, 1902
Wagonette, 1901
Wahl, 1914
Waldron, 1909-11
Walker, 1911
Wall, 1901-4
Wallworth, 1905
Walter, 1904-9, 1921
Waltham, 1898, 1900-9, 1922
Waltham Orient, 1901
Walther, 1903
Walton, 1902
Walworth, 1905
Ward, 1920
Ward Electric, 1914-16
Ward La France, 1919
Ward Leonard, 1901-3
Ware, 1918
Warner, 1903
Warner Electric, 1895
Warren, 1905, 1911
Warren-Detroit, 1909-13
Warwick, 1901-4
Washington, 1907-12, 1921-23
Wasp, 1920
Waterloo, 1904-5
Waterman Arrowbile, 1937
Waterville, 1911
Watrous, 1905

Watson, 1907, 1916
Watt Steam, 1910
Waukesha, 1908
Waverly Electric, 1898-1917
Wayne, 1904-17
Webb, 1904
Webberville, 1920
Webb-Jay Steam, 1908
Weber, 1905
Weeks, 1908
Wege, 1917
Weier-Smith, 1917
Welch, 1904-9
Welch-Detroit, 1911
Welch & Lawson, 1895
Welch-Marquette, 1904
Welch-Pontiac, 1911
Westcott, 1910-24
Western, 1901-11
Westfield Steam, 1910
West Gasoline Vehicle, 1895
Westinghouse, 1901
Westman, 1912
Weston, 1896
West Steamer, 1897
Weyher, 1910
W.F.S., 1912
Whaley-Henriette, 1900
Wharton, 1921-23
Wheel, 1902
Wheeler, 1903
Whippet, 1926-31
Whitcomb, 1928
White, 1901-19
White Hall, 1911
White Hickory, 1906, 1917
Whiteside, 1911
White Star, 1910-12
Whiting, 1905-7
Whitman, 1908-9
Whitney, 1898-99
Wichita, 1912
Wick, 1902
Wilcox, 1907-12
Wildfire, 1953
Wildman, 1902
Willard, 1905
Willet, 1912
Williams, 1907
Willingham, 1916
Wills St. Clair, 1921-27
Willys, 1930-62
Willys-Knight, 1913-32

Willys-Overland, 1908-51
Wilson, 1903-5
Windsor, 1906-11, 1929-30
Wing, 1896, 1922
Winkler, 1911
Winner, 1899
Winther, 1920-23
Winton, 1896-1925
Wisco, 1910
Wisconsin, 1899, 1910-11
Witt Thompson, 1921-23
Witt Will, 1917
Wizard, 1914, 1921
Wolfe, 1907
Wolverine, 1896, 1905-6, 1913,
  1917-21, 1927
Wolverine-Detroit, 1912
Wonder, 1909, 1917
Woodburn, 1912
Woodruff, 1902-5
Woods, 1899-1919
Woods Magnetic, 1917
Woods-Mobilette, 1907
Worth, 1907-8
Worthington, 1904-6
Wright, 1925
Wyeth, 1913

X

Xenia, 1915

Y

Yale, 1903, 1917, 1921
Yankee, 1910
Yankee Cyclecar, 1914
Yellow Cab, 1921
Yellow Coach, 1921
Yellow Knight, 1928
York, 1904-10
York-Pullman, 1908-17
Young, 1921

Z

Zeitler & Lamson, 1917
Zent, 1906-7
Zentmobile, 1903
Zephyr, 1936-40
Zimmerman, 1907-16
Zip, 1913

Highlights

The story of highway transportation in America and its influence on the American people and their way of life can sometimes be most succinctly told in terms of pure facts and figures. These cold numbers in the following tables actually are the highlights of that story.

Historical Motor Vehicle Statistics
Motor Vehicle Registrations Privately & Publically Owned Vehicles*

Year	Pass. Cars (Thousands)	Buses[1] (Thousands)	Trucks[3] (Thousands)	Total[3] (Thousands)	Year	Pass. Cars (Thousands)	Buses[1] (Thousands)	Trucks[3] (Thousands)	Total[3] (Thousands)
1900	8	-	-	8	1966	78,123	322	15,517	93,962
1905	77	-	1	79	1967	80,414	338	16,179	96,931
1910	458	-	10	469	1968	83,693	352	16,995	101,039
1915	2,332	-	159	2,491	1969	86,560	—18,142—		104,702
1920	8,132	-	1,108	9,239	1970	89,244	378	18,797	108,419
1925	17,481	18	2,570	20,069	1975	106,706	462	25,781	132,949
1926	19,268	24	2,908	22,200	1980	121,601	529	33,667	155,797
1927	20,193	28	3,082	23,303	1984	128,158	583	37,507	166,248
1928	21,362	32	3,294	24,689	1985	131,864	593	39,196	171,654
1929	23,121	34	3,550	26,705	1986	135,431	594	40,166	176,191
1930	23,035	41	3,675	26,750	1987	137,324	602	41,119	179,045
1931	22,396	42	3,656	26,094	1988	141,252	616	42,529	184,397
1932	20,901	43	3,446	24,391	1989	143,081	625	43,554	187,260
1933	20,657	45	3,457	24,159	1990	143,550	627	44,479	188,656
1934	21,545	52	3,665	25,262	1991	142,956	631	44,785	188,372
1935	22,568	59	3,919	26,546	1992	144,213	645	45,504	190,362
1936	24,183	63	4,262	28,507	1993	146,314	654	47,095	194,063
1937	25,467	83	4,509	30,059	1994	133,930	670	63,445	198,045
1938	25,250	88	4,476	29,814	1995	134,981	700**	64,765**	200,446
1939	26,226	92	4,691	31,010					
1940	27,466	101	4,886	32,453					
1941	29,624	120	5,150	34,894					
1942	27,973	136	4,895	33,004					
1943	26,009	152	4,727	30,888					
1944	25,566	153	4,760	30,479					
1945	25,797	162	5,076	31,035					
1946	28,217	174	5,982	34,373					
1947	30,849	187	6,805	37,841					
1948	33,355	197	7,534	41,086					
1949	36,458	209	8,023	44,690					
1950	40,339	224	8,599	49,162					
1951	42,688	230	8,994	51,913					
1952	43,823	240	9,199	53,262					
1953	46,429	244	9,544	56,217					
1954	48,468	248	9,789	58,505					
1955	52,145	255	10,289	62,689					
1956	54,211	259	10,679	65,148					
1957	55,918	264	10,943	67,125					
1958	56,891	270	11,136	68,297					
1959[2]	59,454	265	11,635	71,354					
1960	61,671	272	11,914	73,858					
1961	63,417	280	12,261	75,958					
1962	66,108	285	12,780	79,173					
1963	69,055	298	13,360	82,714					
1964	71,983	305	14,013	86,301					
1965	75,258	314	14,786	90,358					

NOTE: Registrations shown here are not synonymous with vehicles in use since the latter implies a count of vehicles in operation on a specific date or an average for a period of time, while registrations are a count of transactions (with transfers eliminated) during a specified period.

Beginning in 1994, data not comparable to prior years.

(1) Incomplete. Buses are not segregated from passenger cars or trucks in earlier years. Also included are municipally owned buses engaged in public transit. Due to new method of counting buses in 1959, the bus data for earlier years are not strictly comparable.

(2) Alaska and Hawaii data included since 1959.

(3) Data excludes farm trucks registered at a nominal fee in certain states and restricted to use in the vicinity of the owner's farms. There were 58,260 such trucks in the 1994 count.

*There were no publically owned vehicles before 1925; also excludes military vehicles for all years.

**Estimates by the American Automobile Manufacturers Association.

SOURCE: U.S. Department of Transportation, Federal Highway Administration.

Annual U.S. Motor Vehicle Production

Year	Passenger Cars	Trucks & Buses	Total	Year	Passenger Cars	Trucks & Buses	Total
1900	4,192	N.A.	4,192	1949	5,083,266	1,160,568	6,243,834
1901	7,000	N.A.	7,000	1950	6,628,598	1,377,261	8,005,859
1902	9,000	N.A.	9,000	1951	5,306,418	1,450,596	6,757,014
1903	11,235	N.A.	11,235	1952	4,323,603	1,238,193	5,561,796
1904	22,130	700	22,830	1953	6,132,244	1,216,879	7,349,123
1905	24,250	750	25,000	1954	5,507,417	1,029,312	6,536,729
1906	33,200	800	34,000	1955	7,950,377	1,253,672	9,204,049
1907	43,000	1,000	44,000	1956	5,806,756	1,112,002	6,918,758
1908	63,500	1,500	65,000	1957	6,120,029	1,100,402	7,220,431
1909	123,990	3,297	127,287	1958	4,247,427	873,842	5,121,269
1910	181,000	6,000	187,000	1959	5,599,492	1,124,096	6,723,588
1911	199,319	10,681	210,000	1960	6,703,108	1,202,011	7,905,119
1912	356,000	22,000	378,000	1961	5,522,019	1,127,505	6,649,524
1913	461,500	23,500	485,000	1962	6,943,334	1,254,220	8,197,554
1914	548,139	24,900	573,039	1963	7,644,377	1,463,412	9,107,789
1915	895,930	74,000	969,930	1964	7,745,492	1,560,644	9,306,136
1916	1,525,578	92,130	1,617,708	1965	9,335,227	1,785,109	11,120,336
1917	1,745,792	128,157	1,873,949	1966	8,604,712	1,791,586	10,396,298
1918	943,436	227,250	1,170,686	1967	7,412,659	1,611,077	9,023,736
1919	1,651,625	224,731	1,876,356	1968	8,848,620	1,971,790	10,820,410
1920	1,905,560	321,789	2,227,349	1969	8,224,392	1,981,519	10,205,911
1921	1,468,067	148,052	1,616,119	1970	6,550,128	1,733,821	8,283,949
1922	2,274,185	269,991	2,544,176	1971	8,583,653	2,088,001	10,671,654
1923	3,624,717	409,295	4,034,012	1972	8,828,205	2,482,503	11,310,708
1924	3,185,881	416,659	3,602,540	1973	9,667,152	3,014,361	12,681,513
1925	3,735,171	530,659	4,265,830	1974	7,324,504	2,746,538	10,071,042
1926	3,692,317	608,617	4,300,934	1975	6,716,951	2,269,562	8,986,513
1927	2,936,533	464,793	3,401,326	1976	8,497,893	2,999,703	11,497,596
1928	3,775,417	583,342	4,358,759	1977	9,213,654	3,489,128	12,702,782
1929	4,587,400	771,020	5,358,420	1978	9,176,635	3,722,567	12,899,202
1930	2,784,745	571,241	3,355,986	1979	8,433,662	3,046,331	11,479,993
1931	1,973,089	416,649	2,389,738	1980	6,375,506	1,634,335	8,009,841
1932	1,135,491	235,187	1,370,678	1981	6,253,138	1,689,778	7,942,916
1933	1,573,512	346,545	1,920,057	1982	5,073,496	1,912,099	6,985,595
1934	2,177,919	575,192	2,753,111	1983	6,781,184	2,443,637	9,224,821
1935	3,252,244	694,690	3,946,934	1984	7,773,332	3,151,449	10,924,781
1936	3,604,913	784,587	4,389,500	1985	8,184,821	3,467,922	11,652,743
1937	3,881,589	893,085	4,774,674	1986	7,828,783	3,505,992	11,334,775
1938	2,004,403	488,100	2,492,503	1987	7,098,910	3,825,776	10,924,686
1939	2,895,625	710,496	3,606,121	1988	7,113,137	4,100,550	11,213,687
1940	3,728,491	784,404	4,512,895	1989	6,823,097	4,050,935	10,874,032
1941	3,759,108	1,092,868	4,851,976	1990	6,077,449	3,705,548	9,782,997
1942				1991	5,438,579	3,371,942	8,810,521
1943		WORLD WAR II		1992	5,664,203	4,064,587	9,728,790
1944				1993	5,981,046	4,916,620	10,897,666
1945	83,786	701,090	784,876	1994	6,613,970	5,648,767	12,262,737
1946	2,149,635	951,185	3,100,820	1995	6,350,367	5,634,724	11,985,091
1947	3,510,744	1,284,843	4,795,587				
1948	3,871,173	1,349,582	5,220,775				

Note: Data through 1928 represent factory sales.
SOURCE: AAMA and Ward's Automotive Reports.

U.S. Retail Sales of Cars and Trucks
Annual U.S. Motor Vehicle Retail Sales (in Thousands)

Year	Passenger Cars			Trucks			Motor Vehicles		
	Domestic	Import	Total	Domestic	Import	Total	Domestic	Import	Total
1995	7,129	1,506	8,635	6,064	417	6,481	13,193	1,923	15,116
1994	7,255	1,735	8,991	5,995	426	6,421	13,251	2,161	15,411
1993	6,742	1,776	8,518	5,287	394	5,681	12,029	2,170	14,199
1992	6,277	1,937	8,213	4,481	422	4,903	10,758	2,359	13,116
1991	6,137	2,038	8,175	3,813	551	4,365	9,950	2,589	12,539
1990	6,897	2,403	9,300	4,215	631	4,846	11,112	3,034	14,146
1989	7,073	2,699	9,772	4,403	538	4,941	11,476	3,237	14,713
1988	7,526	3,004	10,530	4,508	641	5,149	12,034	3,645	15,679
1987	7,081	3,196	10,277	4,055	858	4,912	11,136	4,053	15,189
1986	8,215	3,245	11,460	3,921	941	4,863	12,136	4,186	16,322
1985	8,205	2,838	11,042	3,902	779	4,682	12,107	3,617	15,724
1984	7,952	2,439	10,390	3,475	618	4,093	11,427	3,057	14,484
1983	6,795	2,387	9,182	2,658	471	3,129	9,454	2,858	12,312
1982	5,759	2,224	7,982	2,146	414	2,560	7,905	2,637	10,542
1981	6,209	2,327	8,536	1,809	451	2,260	8,018	2,778	10,796
1980	6,581	2,398	8,979	2,001	487	2,487	8,582	2,884	11,466
1979	8,341	2,332	10,673	3,010	470	3,480	11,351	2,802	14,153
1978	9,312	2,002	11,314	3,773	336	4,109	13,085	2,338	15,423
1977	9,109	2,074	11,183	3,352	323	3,675	12,461	2,398	14,859
1976	8,611	1,499	10,110	2,944	237	3,181	11,555	1,736	13,291
1975	7,053	1,571	8,624	2,249	229	2,478	9,302	1,801	11,103
1974	7,454	1,399	8,853	2,512	176	2,688	9,966	1,575	11,541
1973	9,676	1,748	11,424	2,916	233	3,148	12,591	1,981	14,572
1972	9,327	1,614	10,940	2,486	143	2,629	11,813	1,757	13,569
1971	8,681	1,561	10,242	2,011	85	2,096	10,693	1,646	12,338
1970	7,119	1,280	8,400	1,746	65	1,811	8,865	1,346	10,211
1969	8,464	1,118	9,582	1,936	34	1,970	10,400	1,152	11,552
1968	8,625	1,031	9,656	1,807	24	1,831	10,432	1,055	11,487
1967	7,568	769	8,337	1,524	21	1,545	9,092	790	9,882
1966	8,377	651	9,028	1,619	17	1,636	9,996	668	10,664
1965	8,763	569	9,332	1,539	14	1,553	10,302	583	10,885
1964	7,617	484	8,101	1,351	42	1,393	8,968	526	9,494
1963	7,334	386	7,720	1,230	40	1,270	8,564	426	8,990
1962	6,753	339	7,092	1,068	32	1,100	7,821	371	8,192
1961	5,556	379	5,935	908	29	937	6,464	408	6,872
1959	5,486	614	6,100	928	37	965	6,414	651	7,065
1957	5,826	207	6,033	878	16	894	6,704	223	6,927
1955	7,408	58	7,466	1,012	3	1,015	8,420	61	8,481
1953	5,775	33	5,808	965	N.A.	965	6,740	33	6,773
1951	5,143	21	5,164	1,111	N.A.	1,111	6,254	21	6,275
1942-1950	N.A.	N.A.	N.A.	N.A.	N.A.	N.A.	N.A.	N.A.	N.A.
1941	3,763	N.A.	3,763	902	N.A.	902	4,665	N.A.	4,665
1939	2,724	N.A.	2,724	521	N.A.	521	3,245	N.A.	3,245
1937	3,508	N.A.	3,508	645	N.A.	645	4,153	N.A.	4,153
1935	2,867	N.A.	2,867	552	N.A.	552	3,419	N.A.	3,419
1933	1,526	N.A.	1,526	261	N.A.	261	1,787	N.A.	1,787
1931	1,903	N.A.	1,903	328	N.A.	328	2,231	N.A.	2,231

N.A. - Not Available

SOURCE: American Automobile Manufacturers Association

Index

C

Cadillac auto.: first, 17; Dewar Trophy, 24, 29; electric starter, 28, 29; V-8 engine, 30; synchro- mesh transmission, 41; V-16 engines, 43; power brakes, 43; front wheel drive, 81, 105; Eldorado, 85, 86* 95*; Seville, 94, 94*, 114; Cimarron, 102; Fleetwood Brougham, 115; Allante, 115

Cadillac Auto. Co., 17, 21

Cadillac Div. of G.M., 26, 74, 77; 70th anniversary, 88; headquarters, 118; production highlights, 90; builds Allante body in Italy, 108

Cadillac Motor Car Co., 21, 26, 36

CAFE (Corporate Average Fuel Economy), 97, 98, 100, 111, 113, 116

Caldwell, Philip, 100

"California Top", 19

Canada-U.S. tariff agreement, 77, 81

"Captive Imports", 86, 87

car haulers strike, 107

carburetors, 9, 15; twin, 23; thermostatic control, 36; down-draft, 42; intake silencer, 43

catalytic converter, 91, 95

Centennial Celebration, 120

Chadwick, Lee S., 123, 123*

Chalmers, Hugh, 123, 123*

Chandler auto., 42

Chapin, Roy D., 16, 22, 123, 123*

chassis: "simplified", 28; gold, 31; rubber springs, 43; without X-member, 47

Checker auto., 68, 75, 82

Checker Motors Corp., 68

Chevrolet, Louis, 26, 124, 124*

Chevrolet auto.: first, 26; 4-cylinder engine, 30; V-8 engine, 32; 6-cylinder engine, 42, 101; diesel engine, 103; production highlights, 46, 59, 72, 75, 77, 90; steel station wagon, 46*; vacuum operated gearshift, 48; Impala, 68*; Camaro, 85, 85*; Corvette, 85, 97, 98, 101; Cosworth Vega, 94; Camaro Z-28, 96; Citation, 99*; Cavalier, 102*, 103, 118*; Chevette Scooter, 102; Monte Carlo SS, 104; Corsica, 110*; Beretta, 113*; Impala SS 117*

Chevrolet Div. of G.M., 33, 56, 62

Chevrolet Motor Co., 28, 29, 33

Chicago Times-Herald Race, 10

chokes, automatic, 45

Christie, John W., 124, 124*

chromium plating, 40

Chrysler, Walter P., 38, 124, 124*

Chrysler auto.: developed, 38; rubber-mounted engine, 40; Town & Country series, 56*, 104; ignition key starting, 58; turbine, 63, 65, 72, 75, 77; Imperial, 86; Cordoba, 91, 93*; Valiant, 95; Dart, 95; Volare, 95; Aspen, 95; Eagle Vision, 117*

Chrysler Corp.: formed, 40; dividends, 41; purchases Dodge Bros., 42; Plymouth, DeSoto introduced, 42; 8-cylinder engine, 44, 87; "Superfinish", 48; Silver anniversary, 59; proving grounds, 61, 63; purchases Briggs auto plants, 62; loan from Prudential Insurance, 63; buys Universal Products Co., 64; plant expansion, 57, 64, 70, 78; 25 millionth, 67; purchases stock in Simca, 67; divi-

sions realigned, 69; Chrysler-Plymouth Div., 73; purchases Lone Star Boat Co., 78; ends convertible production, 87; production highlights, 90; rebates, 93; financial crisis, 93, 99; sells Airtemp, 95; U.S. Army contract, 95; sells European holdings, 98; guarantee program, 100; profit sharing, 102; pays back loans, 103; reintroduces convertible, 103; cigar lighters, 40

circuses, 11

Clarke, Louis S.,13, 17

Clifton, Charles, 32, 124, 125*

clocks, 89

clutches: centrifugal, 20; multiple disc, 28; vacuum-operated, 45; automatic, semi-automatic transmission, 52; suspended pedal, 61; E-stick automatic transmission, 72; interlock, 72

Coffin, Howard E., 22

Cole, Edward N., 124

colors, see paints

Commercial Car Manufacturers Assoc., 25

compact cars: Mercury, 86, 97, 104, 105; Pontiac, 87; Chrysler, 94; luxury, 96; AMC, 97; Ford, 97, 101, 104, 105

computers, 103, 110, 112; trip, 97

Comuta auto., 80

concrete pavement, 26

Continental auto., 64*

Continental Motors Corp., 60, 74

convertible bodies, 19, 31, 35, 44, 49*, 85, 86*, 87*, 90, 94, 95*, 103

cooling, 17, 21, 72, 83; see also radiators

Cord auto., 43*, 48*, 74, 78, 80

Cosmopolitan Race, 11

Couzens, James, 18

Crocker, Sewall K., 17*

Crosley, Powel, Jr., 49*, 125, 125*

Crosley auto., 49*, 55*, 59, 61

Crosley Corp., 54, 58, 59, 61

cross licensing, 31

cruise control, 90

Cummins, Clessie L., 125

Curtiss-Wright Corp., 69, 73

cyclecars, 30

cylinder casting, 27

D

dashboards, see instrument panels

Day, George H., 18

dealers, dealerships, 13, 14

Dearborn Motors Corp., 61

defrosters, 47, 84

DeLorean, John Z., 90, 99, 108

design, see bodies

DeSoto auto.: introduced, 42; vacuum-operated clutch, 45; "Airflow", 46, 46*; 9-passenger station wagon, 58; V-8 engine, 61; discontinued, 71

Detroit, early auto industry, 16, 22

Detroit Diesel Engine Div., 72

Dewar Trophy, 24, 29

Diamond-T Motor Car Co., 21, 28

Dietz, R.E., Co., 15

disabled veterans, 55

Doble, Abner, 125

Dodge, Horace, John, 18, 30, 125, 125*

Dodge auto., 30, 38, 58, 62*; Charger, 91;

Aspen, 94*; Magnum XE, 97*; Mirada, 101, 101*; Aries, 101, 102*; Shelby Charger, 104; Caravan, 105, 107*; Stealth, 113, 114*; Viper, 115*; Stratus, 118; Avenger, 118

Dodge Bros., 42; Div., 76

doors, power sliding, 116

Dorris, George P., 126

Dort auto., 36*

Drake, J. Walter, 36

"drive-it-yourself", 40

driver education, 56, 57, 60, 64

drivers' licenses, 14, 15, 64, 73, 83

dual-control, 57

Dual Motors Corp., 64, 65

Duesenberg, Frederick S., 126, 126*

Duesenberg auto., 35, 44*, 76

duPont, Pierre S., 35

Durant, William C., 24, 35, 37, 126, 126*

Durant Motors, 37, 38*

Duryea, Charles E., 9, 10, 126, 126*

Duryea, J. Frank, 9, 10, 10*, 126, 126*

Duryea auto., 9*, 10*11, 12; 100th anniversary, 116

Duryea Motor Wagon Co., 10, 11

Dyke, A.L., 14, 127, 127*

E

Eaton, Robert, 115, 127

Eaton, William, 24

economy runs, contests, 23, 32, 83

Edgar, Graham, 41

EGR valve, 88

electrical systems, 61, 62, 71, 81

Electric Autolite Co., 73

electric autos., 12, 15, 28, 38, 69, 74, 80, 82, 84, 95

Electric Fuel Propulsion, Inc., 84

Electric Vehicle Co., 15, 17

electrochemical fuel conversion, 69

Electrovair auto., 79, 80

Electrovan, 79

Ellerbeck, B.B., 44

Elliott, Sterling, 17

emissions, 85, 91, 96, 98, 102, 112

"Enduraflex", 105

energy crisis, 90, 99

engine mountings, rubber, 40, 44

engines: air-cooled, 13, 21, 23*, 69; under hood, 15, 17; valve-in-head, 13, 18; 6-cylinder, 22, 23, 38, 62; rotary, 22, 69; 12-cylinder, 22, 31, 43; 8-cylinder, 23, 30, 35, 39, 42, 44, 62; sleeve-valve, 25, 27, 36*; L-head, 38; V-8, 23, 30, 31, 45*, 57, 60*, 61, 62, 64, 70, 85, 94, 101; V-16, 43, 111; 4-cylinder, 85; V-6, 101, 102, 110, 112; superchargers, 46; interchangeable 6- or 8-cylinder, 50; high-compression, 57; gas turbine, 60, 63, 65, 69, 72, 73, 74, 77, 88; free-piston, 65; V-4, 65; aluminum, 70, 103, 110; fluid injected turbo-charged, 73; positive crankcase ventilating, 74; pre-heaters, 79; diesel, 82, 97, 98, 100; mid-engine design, 82, 85, 105; slant six, 95, 105; turbo, 97, 100, 105, 110; Wankel rotary, 88, 90, 92; hemi, 87; 6-pack, 87; "lean-burn", 95; GMRE (GM rotary engine), 85, 88, 91, 92, 96; variable displacement, 101, 103

EPA (Environmental Protection Agency), 102

Erskine, Albert R., 127, 127*
Erskine auto., 41
Essex auto., 34*
Essex Motor Car Co., 32
Ethyl Corp., 39
Euclid Road Machinery Co., 62
exhaust emission control, 70, 80, 81
Exner, Virgil, 127, 127*

F

factories, reinforced concrete, 18
Fageol Motors Co., 40, 41
Federal Aid Road Act, 32
fenders: aluminum, 31; full-skirted, 45; covers for rear, 46; middle of front door, 52, "reinforced reaction-injection molding", 102
Ferguson, Harry, Inc., 61
filters, 39, 41
financing, see installment buying
firsts, auto., see subjects: magazines, purchase, roads, etc.
Fischer auto., 20
Fisher, Alfred J., 128, 128*
Fisher, Carl G., 20, 26, 29, 128, 128*
Fisher, Charles T., Frederic J., Edward F., 25, 128, 128*
Fisher, Howard A., Lawrence P., 128, 128*
Fisher Body Co., 25, 34, 40
Flanders, Walter E., 128, 128*
"flat-rate" repair system, 34
Fleet Owner, 42
Fleetwood Body Corp., 40
Flint Auto., 38*
fluidic controls, 83
flying autos., 48, 52, 68, 84
Ford, Edsel B., 34, 128, 129*
Ford, Henry, 11*, 18, 34, 83, 129, 129*
Ford, Henry, II, 54*, 100, 109, 129, 129*
Ford auto.: Quadricycle, 11*; "999", 18*, 19; Model T, 24*, 29*, 39*, 41, 67; Model A, 41*, 45; V-8, 45*, 57*, 66, 102; Thunderbird, 67*, 96*, 103, 104*; turbine car, 76; Maverick, 83, 83*; Pantera, 86; Mustang II, 89*, 90; Torino, 88*; Torino Elite, 90*; Granada, 91*; Cobra II, 94; Mustang, 99, 103, 112*; Escort, 103; Probe, 111*, 116*; Tempo, 106*; Taurus, 107*, 120*
Ford Motor Co.: incorporated, 18; first ranch, 20; Selden Patent Case, 18, 26, 28; Highland Park plant, 23, 27, 29*; production highlights, 29, 30, 34, 35, 38, 39, 51, 67, 73, 75, 81, 98; $5.00 daily wage, 30; rebate plan, 30, 31; Rouge plant, 31; financial crisis, 35; buys Lincoln Motor Co., 37; prices reduced, 37; weekly purchase plan, 38; manufactures accessories, 39; 5-day work week, 40; $7.00 daily wage, 42; in National Auto Show, 46, 50; plant expansion, 48, 62, 63, 64, 74, 76, 77, 78, 80; production resumed after WW II, 54, 54*; Ford Div., 58; proving grounds, 63; stock offered to public, 65; joins AMA, 65; purchases Sherman Products, 70; Philco, Electric Autolite plants, 73; Industrial & Chemical Products Div., 81; purchases, 106, 109, 111; downsizing autos, 95, 96*, 99, 100; closes Romeo tractor plant, 109; 90th anniversary, 116; Ford 2000, 117; profits, 109; 75th anniversary, 98; agree-

ment with Vietnam, 118; Jaguar Div., 119
Ford Motor Credit Co., 69
Ford of Europe; Ford, Philippines, 81
Fordson tractor, 31
foreign activities, U.S. automakers, 36
four-wheel drive, 25, 27, 100
Four Wheel Drive Auto Co., 27, 67
frame construction, pressed steel, 18
Franklin, Herbert H., 129, 129*
Franklin auto., 23*
Frazer, E.M., 41
Frazer, Joseph W., 53, 130, 130*
Free-wheeling, 44, 45
front-wheel drive, 78, 81, 99, 99*, 101
Fry, Vernon, 18
fuel economy, 45, 92, 93, 96
fuel injection, 65, 94, 105, 109
fuel system check valve, 94
Furber, Frederick, 32

G

garages, see service stations
gas turbines, see engines
gasoline: ethyl, 36, 38, 39; octane scale, 41; high-octane, 57; prices, 112; leaded/unleaded, 85, 95; consumption, 92
gasoline-electric autos., 25
gasoline gauges, 37
gasoline stations, see service stations
gasoline tanks: plastic, 84; rubber bladder, 91
Gear, Inc., 113
gears, 25, 29, 40
gearshifts: on dashboard, 46, 52, 63; finger-tip control, 46, 48; vacuum-operated, 48; on steering column, 48
General Motors Acceptance Corp., 34, 106
General Motors auto: Saturn, 106, 112, 115, 116, 118, 119; "Impact", 113
General Motors concept car, 114
General Motors Co., 24; Corp.: acquires Buick, Oldsmobile, Oakland, 25; Cadillac, 26; stock dividends, 26, 31, 41; Chevrolet, 33; buys interest in Fisher Body Co., 34; GM Building, 36; proving grounds, 39, 60, 61, 82; Yellow Truck and Coach Co., 40; Fisher Body Corp., 40; all-steel turret tops, 46; plant expansion, 57, 74, 76, 77, 78, 80; Transportation Unlimited Show, 58; Euclid Road Machinery stock, 62; transmission plant fire, 62; production highlights, 63, 73, 76, 81, 99; Progress of Power Show, 84; product lineup redesign, 91; downsizing autos, 95, 97; expands and upgrades facilities, 101; lawsuits, 103; agreement with Toyota, 103; sales, 103
General Motors Research Corp., 35
General Tire & Rubber Co., 61, 74
generators, 46, 70
glass, safety, 40
Glidden, Charles J., 20, 130, 130*
Glidden Tours, 20, 21*, 25, 26
Goodyear Tire & Rubber Co., 73, 74, 76
governors, 15
Graham, Ray A., 130, 130*
Graham-Paige Motors Corp., 41, 52, 53, 56
Gramm, B.A., 18
Gray, John S., 18

grilles, see radiators
guarantees, see warranties

H

Hall, E.J., 32
Hammond, E.T., 18
Harroun, Ray, 28
Haynes, Elwood G., 9, 9*, 37, 130, 130*
Haynes-Apperson auto., 14
Haynes auto., 9, 9*, 14
headlamps, 20, 40; kerosene, 15; acetylene, 20; standard equipment, 20; electric-acetylene, 27; tilt-beam, 31; prism lenses, 31; dimming, 39, 61, 81; two-filament bulb, 39; sealed-beam, 49, 63, 65; concealed in front fenders, 52, 76, 83; dual-headlighting, 63, 65, 66, 69; automatically turned on, 70, 76; warning buzzer, 81; washers, 83; delayed, 84; rectangular, 91, 94, 95; halogen, 99; plastic halogen, 102
heating, ventilation, 32, 35, 40, 48, 49, 63; see also air conditioning
Herrington, Arthur W., 45, 50
Hewitt Motor Car Co., 23
Highway Act, 65
Highway Emergency Locating Plan, 77
Highway Research Board, 35
highways, see roads, turnpikes
Highway Safety Act, 79
hill climbs, 14, 23
Hines, Edward N., 28
Hoglund, William, 106
Holcomb, Bert, 13*
Honda, 103
hoods, lock releases, 49
horns, 21, 25, 81
Horseless Age, 10
horse power formula, 23
horse power ratings, 87
Howie, Robert G., 50
Hudson auto., 26*, 28, 39, 47, 66
Hudson Motor Car Co., 26, 63
"Hummer", 104
Hupmobile auto., 34*, 44, 46, 47
Hupmobile Motor Car Corp., 42, 58
Hurst/Olds, 104*
Hyundai Motor America, 107

I

Iacocca, Lee, 90, 98, 99, 115, 131, 131*
ignition systems, 9, 26, 58, 59, 70, 74; electronic, 87, 89, 92; High Energy Ignition (HEI), 91
Imperial auto., 69*
Indianapolis 500-Mile Race, 28, 81, 103
Indianapolis pace car, 98, 101*, 101, 103, 108*, 113*, 116*
Indianapolis Speedway, 26
installment buying, 21, 29, 38, 50, 58, 59, 60, 108
instrument panels, 34, 63, 70, 76, 94, 104, 107
insurance, 13, 37

J

Jackson, H. Nelson, 17*, 18
"Jeep", 50, 51; see also Willys Overland
Jeffery, Thomas B., 15; Co., 17, 31, 131, 131*
Jeffery Auto., 30

jitneys, 31
Jordan, Edward, 40, 131, 131*
Jordan Motor Car Co., 40, 40*
Joy, Henry B., 131, 131*

K

"K" cars, 100, 101
Kahn, Albert, 18
Kaiser, Henry, 52, 132, 132*
Kaiser auto., 56*
Kaiser-Frazer Corp., 54, 55, 56, 57, 61
Kaiser Industries Corp., 64
Kaiser Jeep Corp., 75
Kaiser Motors Corp., 63, 64
Kelvinator Corp., 48
Kerkorian, Kirk, 119
kerosene, 33
Kettering, Charles F., 28, 35, 57, 132, 132*
King, Charles B., 10, 11*, 17, 132, 132*
Kissel auto., 29, 35*
Knight, Charles Y., 25
Knight sleeve-valve engine, 25, 27, 36*
Knudsen, Semon E., 132, 133*
Knudsen, William S., 50, 132, 132*
Kurtis-Kraft, Inc., 58

L

labor strikes, 34, 54, 85, 87, 88, 117, 120
Lafayette Motors Corp., 36
Lanchester vibration dampener, 35
latches, trunk, door, 64, 65, 68, 70, 84
laws, legislation, 12, 16, 17, 19, 21, 23, 28, 32, 33, 52, 65, 68, 80, 83, 90, 96, 112; see also specific laws: Federal Aid, Red Flag, etc.
leasing, 102
Lee, Gordon, 36
Leland, Henry M., 32, 133, 133*
Leland & Faulconer Mfg. Co., 21
Levacar, 72
Liberty aircraft engines, 32
licenses, vehicle, 16; see also drivers' lights, emergency flashing, 70; see also headlamps, tail lamps, side lamps
Lincoln auto., 47*; downsized, 101; Versailles, 96; Continental, 88, 102, 113*, 118; Mark IV Designer series, 94; Mark VII, 105; Mark VIII, 115
Lincoln Highway, 29
Lincoln-Mercury Div., 61, 106, 112; golden anniversary, 87
Lincoln Motor Co., 32, 37
Little Motor Car Co., 29
locks, see latches
Locomobile auto., 17
Loomis, Gilbert, 13
Loughead, Malcolm, 33, 35, 41
lubrication, 19, 29, 40, 63, 71

M

Macauley, Alvan, 133, 133*
Mackinac Bridge, 66
magazines, 10, 14, 18, 40
magnetos, 16, 26
Major Award Trophy, 39
Malcolm Baldridge Quality Award, 112
Malcolmson, Alex Y., 18
manifolds, 32, 43, 47

Markette auto., 80
Marmon, Howard C., 133, 133*
Marmon, Walter C., 45
Marmon auto., racer, 28, 31
Marmon-Herrington Co., 59, 75
Marquette auto., 42*
Marriott, Fred, 22, 22*
Maserati, 106
Mason, George W., 48, 134, 134*
Matheson, Charles W., Frank, 134, 134*
Matter, Louis, 63
Maxim, Hiram P., 10, 11, 13*
Maxwell, Jonathan D., 9, 17, 134, 134*
Maxwell auto., 23*
Maxwell-Chalmers Corp., 39, 40
Maxwell Motor Co., 35
Mazda, 107, 116
mechanics, schools, 20; see also servicemen
Mercedes Benz, 116, 119
Mercer auto., 83
Mercury auto., 48; Zephyr, 97*; Capri, 99, 113; Mystique, 118
Mercury-Edsel-Lincoln Div., 67
methanol, 101
metric system, 97
Metropolitan auto., 59
Metz, Charles, 134
Metzger, William E., 13
Meyers, Gerald C., 103
Michelin, 112
Michigan International Speedway, 83
Michigan State College, 60
Microprocessed Sensing and Automatic Regulation (MISAR), 95
Midgley, Thomas, Jr., 36
Miles, Samuel A., 134*, 135
minivan, 105, 107*, 116
mirrors, 28, 40, 41, 66, 68, 70, 82
mobile phone, 106
Mobile Steamer, 14*
Mobil Oil Economy Run, 83
model announcement dates, 44, 47, 58
Morgan, William, 13
Morill, George H., Jr., 11
Morris & Salom Electrobat, 12
Motocycle, 10
Motor, 18
Motor Age, 14
Motor Vehicle Manufacturers Association (MVMA), 89, 117
Mueller, Oscar, 10
Mueller-Benz auto., 10
mufflers, 71
Murdock, J.M., 24
Murphy, Edward M., 23
"muscle cars", 88, 91, 92*, 100

N

NAFTA (North American Free Trade Agreement), 116
Narragansett Park Race, 11, 12*
Nash, Charles W., 31, 48, 135, 135*
Nash auto., 33*, 42, 47, 51, 51*, 58, 66
Nash-Kelvinator Corp., 48, 58, 59, 63
Nash Motors Co.: formed, 31; interest in Seaman Body, 34; Lafayette Motors

Corp., 36; stock held by employees, 41; merges with Kelvinator, 48
National Association of Auto. Advertising Men, 29
National Assoc. of Auto. Manufacturers, 15, 29
National Assoc. of Retail Auto. Dealers, 20
National Auto. Chamber of Commerce, 29, 30, 31, 36, 43, 44, 46
National Auto. Dealers Assoc., 33
National Driver Register Service, 73
National Traffic & Motor Vehicle Safety Act, 79
navigation system, 118
New York & Ohio Co., 14
New York Stock Exchange, 28
New York-to-Buffalo endurance run, 16
New York-to-Paris Race, 24
New York-to-Portland Race, 21
New York-to-St. Louis tour, 19*, 20
NHTSA (National Highway Traffic Safety Admin.), 103
nickel plate trim, 23
Nic-L-Silver Battery Co., 69
Nissan, 115, 119
Nixon, Richard M., 65, 87, 88, 90
Northstar engine, 115
Northern auto., 17
NSU Werke, 69
NUMMI, 106

O

Oakland Motor Car Co., 23, 25, 44
odometers, 84
Ohio Auto. Co., 17
Oldfield, Berner Eli, 19*, 19
"Old Pacific", 18
Olds, Ransom E., 12, 14, 20, 135, 135*
Oldsmobile auto., 12, 13, 16*, 21*, 37, 44, 45, 50*, 58, 60*; Toronado, 85, 108; Delta 88, 96*; Cutlass series, 96; Omega, 102; Ciera, 102; Ninety-Eight, 106*
Oldsmobile Div., 25, 73, 111; production highlights, 87, 94, 96; 75th anniversary, 88; Cutlass plant opens, 98
Olds Motor Vehicle Co., 13
Olds Motor Works, 14, 20
Oliver Corp., 71
Olympic flame, 105
OPEC, 99: oil embargo, 90
Overland auto., 18*
Overland Auto. Co., 25
Owen, Percy, 14
Owen auto., 27*

P

Packard, J.W., W.D., 14, 135, 135*
Packard auto., 14, 25*, 31, 36, 44*, 65, 67
Packard Motor Car Co.: moves, 18; straight "8" engine, 38; hypoid gears, 40; test track, 41; millionth, 56; merges with Studebaker, 63
Paige, Fred O., 135, 135*
Paige-Detroit Motor Car Co., 41
paints, finishes: baked enamel, 25; pyroxolin, 39; color ranges, 49; with wax, 68; electrocoating process, 76; medium blue popular, 81; reflective